PORCELAIN ON STEEL

WOMEN OF WEST POINT'S LONG GRAY LINE

DONNA M. MCALEER

Published & Manufactured in the United States of America

FORTIS
PUBLISHING
www.Fortis-Publishing.com

Porcelain On Steel

Women of West Point's Long Gray Line

By Donna M. McAleer

ISBN 978-0-9845511-1-8 (hardcover)
ISBN 978-0-9845511-2-5 (trade paperback)
ISBN 978-0-9845511-6-3 (ebook)
Library of Congress Control Number: 2010927949

Published by Fortis Publishing
Jacksonville, Florida—Herndon, Virginia
www.Fortis-Publishing.com

Cover designed by Whitney Brazell, www.WhitneyBrazell.com

Manufactured in the United States of America

Accolades

"Donna McAleer's *Porcelain on Steel* is a powerful and inspirational portrait of the women who serve—not just our country, but their families, their communities, and their own commitment to a purposeful and meaningful life. These women—like the author herself, had the courage and strength to attend West Point—the toughest and most elite military school in the nation—and serve as role models for women everywhere."

— Andrea Jung, Chairman and CEO, Avon Products, Inc.

* * *

"In a world where change and challenge is certain, character matters. The women of West Point have proven that they have the right stuff in terms of character to handle both change and challenge with courage, resilience, and grace. They have reached the pinnacles of leadership and faced the depths of pain and loss, both in their journey through the hallowed halls of West Point and on the distant fields of battle. They have been forged into strong, inspiring and worthy leaders. Donna McAleer's *Porcelain on Steel* is an intimate, evocative and candid portrait of the women who serve—not just our country, but their families, and their communities. They have proven to a global audience, women can do anything."

— Coach Mike Krzyzewski, Duke Men's Basketball

* * *

"The history of women on the hallowed grounds of West Point for the past 30 years has largely been overlooked. *Porcelain on Steel* by Donna McAleer begins to change that, and brings alive the quality, character and contributions of women of courage, integrity and honor. These women are the type of inspiring models that our young people deserve and require. This is a great book about some of the women who helped make our West Point Military Academy, "Best College and Business School in the Country" (Forbes, August, 2009). If you are a teacher, a mentor, a parent or young adult looking for stories of ordinary people that have done extraordinary things with their life—then you must read this book!"

— Frances Hesselbein, President & CEO, Leader to Leader Institute, and former CEO of the Girl Scouts of the USA

* * *

"The admission of women to West Point in 1976 strengthened the Army and enabled the institution to better reflect the composition of the society it defends. *Porcelain on Steel* tells the compelling and inspiring stories of several of these brave women. The record of women who graduated from West Point is superb, and they have served with distinction on our nation's battlefields and across a myriad of milieus. Indeed, in every conflict over the past 30 years, the women of West Point have demonstrated the exceptional traits our nation expects of a West Pointer—selfless service, courage under fire, and commitment to country and duty. These admirable traits come to life in the riveting pages of *Porcelain on Steel*."

— General Barry R. McCaffrey

* * *

"For more than 200 years, West Point has provided America outstanding leaders of character for both peace and war. Since 1976, women have been included in the West Point experience, and yet their stories have not been told. In this book, Donna McAleer fires the first shot. She captures the lives of fourteen females who graduated from the Academy to become leaders and outstanding women—

women who fight America's battles and women who fight their own personal battles. It's about time their stories have been told."

— Lieutenant General William J. Lennox, Jr., Superintendent, West Point 2001-2006

* * *

"*Porcelain on Steel* is an important and compelling book whose value goes far beyond the author's stated purpose. Ms. McAleer gives us portraits of fourteen women West Point graduates: their accomplishments, ordeals and sacrifices. She offers these remarkable stories as role models for young women. In truth, they are far more than that. They are role models for all young people and fellow citizens who exemplify the virtues needed in the perilous age now upon us."

— Erin Solaro, author, *Women in the Line of Fire: What You Should Know About Women in the Military*

* * *

"If you have young daughters and are dismayed by the female role models put forward by today's media, Donna McAleer's *Porcelain on Steel* is the book for you. Subtitled *"Women of West Point's Long Gray Line,"* Ms. McAleer's crisply-written, loaded-with-details work narrates the career and life stories of fourteen West Point grads who have redefined what it means to be a woman in today's world. Ms. McAleer's tale follows its heroes from the initial shock and harassment of "Beast Barracks," through four years in the Corps of Cadets and beyond. From Maj. Lissa Young, who became a crack helicopter pilot and wound up commanding a company of 300 soldiers and 18 Chinook choppers, to Capt. Dawn Halfaker, who lost an arm to an insurgent RPG in Baqubah, Iraq but went on to found and run her own company in support of the war on terrorism, the women profiled in *Porcelain on Steel* have blazed the trail that will be followed by thousands in the years to come. Men have no monopoly on courage, honor and the passion to serve. Thank you, Donna McAleer, for shining a light on these women who have lived out and been true to, often in the face of bitter and small-minded opposition, their own highest selves."

— Steven Pressfield, author of *Gates of Fire: An Epic Novel of the Battle of Thermopylae* and *The Afghan Campaign: A Novel*

* * *

"Women are making absolutely essential contributions to our ongoing wars in Iraq and Afghanistan. *Porcelain on Steel* tells the story of how many of them made their way from West Point to the battlefield, and will inspire their sisters and brothers to make the same thoughtful choice to serve our nation."

— Dr. John A. Nagl, President, Center for a New American Security, and author of *Learning to Eat Soup with a Knife: Counterinsurgency Lessons from Malaya and Vietnam*

* * *

"*Porcelain on Steel*, so apt a title for this book, takes us into the hallowed halls of West Point and shows, through a series of personal narratives, the remarkable impact women cadets have had on this 'man's world' military institution in just three decades. Women cadets at West Point, from those who broke gender barriers as members of that first Class of '80 to those standing in the Long Gray Line today, have exceptional stories. The fine sampling of these stories contained in this highly recommended book carry the reader through their experiences in various classes. While each story is unique, common threads are present which link these women together as courageous pioneers and leaders. Their tolerance for adversity is profound, as is their whole-hearted dedication to the

West Point ethos of Duty, Honor and Country, and service to the Nation."

— Brigadier General Evelyn "Pat" Foote, President Emeritus, The Alliance for National Defense.

* * *

"Good steel comes from a hot fire. In *Porcelain on Steel*, Donna McAleer has gathered the stories of an impressive array of women who have graduated from West Point and served as leaders in our nation's Army. All of the women in this collection have combined West Point's creed of Duty, Honor, Country, with their personal attributes of courage, perseverance, and vision, to achieve great success in their service to our country in uniform and beyond. From the beginning, the West Point experience is one of accepting and discharging responsibility—personal responsibility as well as the overarching responsibility that is woven into leading soldiers. Women entered West Point thirty-four years ago, and their skills and experience are now reaching into the upper ranks of our nation's senior leadership. These women, who share the common bond of West Point and have been molded by their service in the Army, share their moments of challenge and achievement in a unique book that is written by one who has been there, done that. This is an important contribution to the history of women in our nation's military leadership and beyond."

— Major General Joseph P. Franklin, Commandant of Cadets, West Point 1979-1982 and author of *Building Leaders the West Point Way: Ten Principles from the Nation's Most Powerful Leadership Lab*

* * *

"I have not had the privilege of meeting all of the women profiled in Donna McAleer's remarkable book, *Porcelain on Steel*, but I know their kind well. From high-ranking commanders to competitive athletes, from business leaders to stay at home moms, I've seen these women in action. They are uniformly tough, smart, resilient, courageous, honorable, and effective. This skillfully crafted collection of biographies of female West Pointers eloquently describes the triumphs and trials of some of our nation's most extraordinary women. These women are genuine role models, and this book is an inspiring read for men and women of all ages."

— David H. McCormick, Undersecretary of the Treasury, 2007-2009

* * *

"Porcelain on Steel: Women of West Point's Long Gray Line is a compelling and inspiring book, featuring remarkable leaders who drew upon their West Point experience to triumph over formidable professional, medical, and personal challenges and make a real difference in the public, private, and philanthropic sectors. A great read for anyone motivated by leadership, loyalty, courage and public service."

— Celina B. Realuyo, Assistant Professor, National Defense University

* * *

"A fascinating look at fourteen women of the Long Gray Line— ordinary people with extraordinary stories that span the breadth of the American experience. Their life stories will inspire and captivate—highly recommended for all who want to understand the journey of American women at West Point and beyond."

— Colonel Peter Mansoor, author of *Baghdad at Sunrise: A Brigade Commander's War in Iraq* and the General Raymond E. Mason, Jr. Chair of Military History, The Ohio State University

* * *

"Donna McAleer's collection of stories of leadership and service is an important contribution to the history of West Point's Long Gray Line. What these women have accomplished—what these officers and soldiers have accomplished—makes for an inspiring reminder of the best that our nation has to offer. *Porcelain on Steel* is an uplifting and important book."

— Bill Murphy Jr., author of *The Intelligent Entrepreneur: How 3 Harvard Business School Graduates Learned the 10 Rules of Successful Entrepreneurship* and *In a Time of War: the Proud & Perilous Journey of West Point's Class of 2002.*

DEDICATION

To the strong women in my life: Anna Nagy Matturro, Felicia Matturro, Helen Nagy, Carlyn Ann McAleer, Jeanne Green, and the Women of West Point.

Contents

Contents (continued)

From The Plain looking toward Washington Hall and the Cadet Chapel, West Point, NY. *(Photo by Sylvia Graham)*

INTRODUCTION

My experience as a high school volleyball coach in 2004 inspired the creation of *Porcelain on Steel: Women of West Point's Long Gray Line*. Concerned with several of the celebrity role models my young athletes admired, I remembered with pride many of the women with whom I had served at West Point and in the Army. These women exhibited courage, strength, and character during numerous stressful and challenging situations and could serve as sterling role models. I felt that if my team could learn about some of these women, perhaps they would consider pursuing comparable paths of excellence.

This collection of contemporary biographies introduces a group of role models who are ordinary women, not celebrities, who have extraordinary stories to share of their journeys of perseverance and integrity. While the women portrayed in this book share a common education and developmental experience at West Point and as Army officers, they have chosen varied paths in and out of the Army.

Research by psychologist Dr. Penelope Lockwood concluded that women need role models more than men, and women also benefit more than men do from having same-gender examples of success.[1] Imagining one's own potential is more difficult for young women who lack role models. For many young people of both genders, the journey of developing one's potential often begins with an understanding of what is possible. Meaningful role models, both in and out of military uniform, reveal possibilities.

The title of this collection of portraits, *Porcelain on Steel: Women of West Point's Long Gray Line*, was inspired by meeting sculptor, artist and filmmaker Tara Krause, Class of 1982, and viewing her artwork honoring our fallen warrior sisters. Porcelain is a strong, vitreous, translucent, ceramic material often used in the making of fine china. Steel is a hard, strong, durable and adaptable alloy of iron and carbon, widely used as a structural material in

---

[1] Lockwood, Penelope. (2006). "Someone like me can be successful": Do college students need same-gender role models? Psychology of Women Quarterly, 30, 36-46.

buildings but also in swords. As an adjective, steel is suggestive of character qualities such as hard and unflinching. The two materials, porcelain and steel, honor the beauty and underlying strength of West Point women.

* * *

McSorley's Old Ale House, firmly cemented in the Bohemian section of Manhattan's East Village, claims to be the oldest pub in continuous operation in New York City. With his homeland devastated by the great potato famine, John McSorley, a 24-year-old immigrant, fled Ireland by sea on *The Colonist*. He opened the bar in 1854, just three years after arriving in New York City. Opened in what was then a poor, tenement-packed neighborhood home to newly arrived immigrants, McSorley's now sits in one of the city's most trendy districts. In the mid 1950s, the village began to undergo a gentrification process that transformed it from a working class neighborhood into an *avant-garde* district and one of the most historic and ethnically diverse neighborhoods in the United States. In the midst of the transformed neighborhood, McSorley's remains a place where time stands still.

More than a century and a half after its establishment, McSorley's Old Ale House remains true to its roots—"an Irish working man's saloon" offering just two kinds of beer—light and dark. No other alcohol is served. The bar has never had a cash register and "probably never will."[2] Sawdust and discarded peanut shells cover the floor. On a gas chandelier, now powered by electricity, hang chicken bones dating back to World War I. The bones, originally hung for good luck by men going to war in Europe in 1917, remain in place in deference to their ultimate sacrifice on the battlefield. Generations of dust cling to the bones.

A bastion of machismo, McSorley's remains the quintessential manly man's bar, the embodiment of a bygone era. History pours

---

[2] www.mcsorleysnewyork.com/history_01.html.

from the walls as freely as beer flows from the taps. The bar has been the inspiration for numerous paintings, poems, books, and plays. Among its most celebrated are two paintings by American artist John F. Sloan. Best known for his portrayals of daily life in New York City's poorer neighborhoods, Sloan is a leading figure in the Ashcan school of realism. His urban genre paintings, *McSorley's Bar* and *McSorley's Saturday Night,* along with e.e. cummings' poem "*Sitting in McSorley's,*"[3] helped push the bar on 15 East Seventh Street toward fame. Any public exhibition of Sloan paintings caused business to boom at the bar. It gained additional attention in the 1940s, when *Life* magazine ran a picture story about a day in the life of the alehouse. Joseph Mitchell began writing about the bar in *The New Yorker.* His essays were later compiled in the book, *McSorley's Wonderful Saloon.*

In 1969, McSorley's returned to the headlines when National Organization for Women (NOW) attorney Faith Seidenberg filed a public accommodations suit to end the bar's century-old policy against serving women. On May 26, 1970, the U.S. Supreme court ruled, in *Seidenberg v. McSorleys' Old Ale House,* that sex discrimination had no foundation in reason and violated the equal protection clause of the 14th Amendment.[4] The court limited the impact of the decision, however, by applying it "only to situations where women had been denied the right to enter a public accommodation under sufficient control of the state."[5] Although McSorley's briefly considered becoming a private club, it reluctantly, and under court order, opened its doors to women. It took an additional 16 years, however, before McSorley's added another bathroom to accommodate its newest patrons.

While women now number among the bar's patrons, a glance around the establishment shows that McSorley's clings in homage to its masculine past. Among the sepia-colored photographs hanging cock-eyed, the black and white political campaign posters with

---

[3] www.mcsorleysnewyork.com/history_01.html.

[4] Seidenberg v. McSorleys' Old Ale House, Inc., 1970, U.S. District Court, Southern District of New York.

[5] www.feminist.org/research/chronicles/fc1970.html.

frayed edges and an original invitation to the opening of the Brooklyn Bridge, is a vestige to its discriminatory past. Hanging behind the bar is the class crest of West Point's Class of 1979—the last all-male class to graduate from the United States Military Academy at West Point, New York. Many in West Point's Class of 1979 considered themselves as the "LCWB—Last Class With Balls." Members of the class in one Cadet Company posed in *The Howitzer*, West Point's yearbook, holding various sports balls—basketballs, footballs, baseballs, volleyballs, and tennis, golf, and billiard balls to immortalize their sentiments.[6] To many men, this crest is a nod to a proud and chauvinistic past. To women, it is a symbol of progress.

* * *

Leaders of the women's and civil rights movements are not likely to mention West Point as an archetype of advancement on their behalf, nor would they probably point to the U.S. Army as an institutional model of minority progress and opportunity. But West Point and the Army have been microcosms where small battles and victories have led to fundamental social change.

In 1873, eight years after the end of the Civil War, Henry O. Flipper of Georgia arrived on the banks of the Hudson River to become the fourth African-American to join the Corps of Cadets and the first to graduate. Two more African-American's embarked on the trail blazed by Flipper, John H. Alexander (Class of 1887) and Charles Young (Class of 1889).[7] Nearly five decades passed between Charles Young's graduation and the admittance of Benjamin O. Davis, Jr. to West Point in 1933.

All endured an internal exile imposed by their peers known as silencing. This intense form of social ostracism and psychological

---

[6] Howitzer, Class of 1979, U.S. Military Academy, 1979, p. 153.

[7] John Grant, James Lynch and Ronald Bailey, West Point: The First Two Hundred Years, (Gilford, Connecticut. They included offerings in: Mass Media and American Politics, Homeland Security, Information Warfare, Politics, Democratization, and Government in the Middle East, and Winning the Peace. Globe Pequot Press, 2002), 103-112.

harassment intended to force the silenced cadet to leave the Academy. Tom Carhart, a 1966 graduate of West Point and noted military historian, described the treatment of African-American cadets in his book *West Point Warriors: Profiles of Duty, Honor, and Country in Battle*:

> During the period from 1870 through 1887, twenty-seven African Americans were nominated for appointment to West Point, twenty-four showed up, and twelve passed the rigorous admissions test. Of these twelve, six lasted one semester, one lasted one year, two lasted three and one-half years and three graduated.
>
> The first set of African-American cadets who arrived at West Point were harshly treated. Given the widespread antipathy toward members of their race at the time, it is not surprising that white cadets resisted their admission to their ranks. While under the law they could not prevent their arrival, they could turn their backs on blacks socially. And that's just what they did. From their first arrival, black cadets were "silenced," meaning no other cadets would speak to them except on official business. The penalty of breaking this exclusion was the silencing of the perpetrator. It was a harsh time indeed, and this silencing of African-American cadets lasted until 1948.[8]

Despite the passage of time, Davis received the same silencing treatment as Flipper, Alexander, and Young. "I was silenced solely because cadets did not want blacks at West Point," Davis wrote. "Their only purpose was to freeze me out. They did not

---

[8] Tom Carhart, West Point Warriors: Profiles of Duty, Honor, and Country in Battle. (New York: Grand Central Publishing; Warner Books Ed edition, 2002), p. 49.

realize that I was stubborn enough to put up with their treatment to reach the goal I had come to attain."[9]

Following graduation, Davis earned a long list of firsts at nearly every level of military leadership. He would later become the Army's second African-American general officer (his father was the first). His determination and stoicism throughout four years of silencing helped pave the way for future officers, such as General Roscoe Robinson, Class of 1951, the first African-American four-star general in the Army, and Generals "Chappie" James and Colin Powell to rise to the senior most responsible leadership positions in the American military and beyond.

In July 1948, President Harry Truman issued executive order 9981 to desegregate the armed forces, calling on the military to provide equal treatment and opportunity for black servicemen.[10] There have been African-American cadets in every incoming class at West Point since. Brigadier General Vincent Brooks, Class of 1980, became West Point's first African-American Brigade First Captain. African-Americans now comprise about six percent of the cadet corps.[11]

While African-Americans were the first to break the race barriers, it was hardly their war alone.[12] Hispanic and Asian-American cadets also endured their shares of challenges, obstacles, and indignation. There remained one wall to be shattered on the high plains of West Point, that of gender.

---

[9] IBID., p. 143.

[10] In July 1948, President Harry Truman issued executive order 9981 to desegregate the armed forces calling on the military to provide equal treatment and opportunity for black serviceman. http://www.trumanlibrary.org/9981a.htm.

[11] USMA Department of Admissions.

[12] Luis Esteves, class of 1915, was the first Puerto Rican Graduate of West Point. He was the first graduate of his class to become a general officer, ahead of classmates Dwight D. Eisenhower and Omar Bradley. During World War I, he was commander of three Officers' Training Camps in Puerto Rico. He founded the Puerto Rican National Guard after resigning his active duty commission in 1919. In 1937, he was made Adjutant General, a position he held until his retirement in 1957. http://www.usma.edu/Bicentennial/HispanicHeritage.asp.

* * *

The demand for men in fighting roles during World War II initiated a gender climate change in the armed forces. As Tom Brokaw explained in *The Greatest Generation*:

> The face of war is almost always one of a man. The familiar images of World War II are not different: FDR as commander in chief; Eisenhower directing the D-Day invasions; MacArthur wading ashore in the Philippines; Patton astride a tank, [ivory]-handled sidearms prominently displayed; General Jimmy Doolittle, his smiling face poking out of a cockpit; Marines raising the flag at Iwo Jima; B-24 pilots, their caps at a jaunty angle; Navy chiefs at their battle stations; GIs in a foxhole. The male was in his historic role as warrior
>
> Early in America's war effort, however, it was clear there were not enough men to do all the fighting and to fill all the support jobs such a massive military undertaking required. There was a desperate need for military clerks, drivers, telephone operators, medical technicians, cooks, and couriers. The Women's Auxiliary Corps—the WACs—was created to help fill that need. It was the beginning of a radical change for Americana's military services that continues to this day.[13]

With the end of America's involvement in Vietnam and the impending elimination of the selective service draft in 1973, military and civilian leadership faced the challenge of determining the composition of armed forces needed for the next century of war

---

[13] Brokaw, Tom. The Greatest Generation. (New York: Random House) 1998, p. 139.

fighting. With the draft ending, women provided a new source of recruits for an all-volunteer force. Dr. Stephen Grove, West Point's Historian explained:

> The impetus for the admission of women to the Military Academy was related as much to the end of an unpopular war and the elimination of the draft as to efforts to provide equal opportunities for women. In place of an increasingly unpopular and frankly discriminatory draft would be a Volunteer Army. But, following the end of an unpopular war in Vietnam, who would sign up for the Army in sufficient numbers to take the place of the draft? In 1973, a Conference on the Future of the Army was held, and a captain in our social sciences department, a decorated and badly wounded Vietnam-veteran, Barry McCaffrey, made a presentation suggesting an expansion in the number and opportunities for women in the Army would be helpful. Senior Army officers told him that since the conference papers were going to be published it would not help his career if his paper were included, so it wasn't. But the military leadership soon found it had little choice but to expand opportunities for women, from the 2% ceiling that had been in force not so many years before. Today, one in seven soldiers in Iraq is a woman.
>
> Women gained entry into the ranks of ROTC in 1972. Then the question arose, why not open up the service academies to women as well? Some women went to Court to try to gain entrance. Although women were admitted to the Merchant Marine Academy in 1974, Senator Barry Goldwater reputedly assured Superintendent William Knowlton that it would never happen here [at West Point]. The military service

academies were united in their opposition to admitting women. They argued that their environments were intensely masculine; inhospitable to women; and that the mission of the academies was to produce officers for combat.[14]

The feminist movement in the 1960's and the passage of the Equal Rights Amendments by Congress in 1972 led to significant changes in opportunities for women. On the educational front, many prestigious universities, such as Yale, Princeton, Harvard, and the University of Virginia breached the gender barricade. In the workplace, "legal barriers to gender-based employment and pay discrimination were eliminated. By 1970, occupational segregation by gender began to fall substantially," according to Irene Padavic, Associate Professor of Sociology at Florida State University.[15]

The mid seventies were a tumultuous period for the military academy. Public controversy and the increasing unpopularity of the Vietnam War brought unwanted attention to West Point, along with the end of mandatory attendance at religious services, and the infamous cheating scandal of 1976. Two external reviews questioned the Academy's curriculum and fiscal efficiency. Some officers found the thought of amalgamating women and men into the venerable society of West Point so repugnant that they considered resigning their commissions rather than supporting what they believed to be an absurd social experiment. Women being explicitly precluded from leading combat units led some male officers to simplistically view the exercise as futile, since West Point trained leaders for combat.

On October 8, 1975, the President of the United States, Gerald Ford, signed into law a bill directing the admittance of women to America's service academies. Despite the law, numerous challenges

---

[14] Dr. Stephen Grove, USMA Historian at West Point, remarks delivered at historical overview panel, USMA Women's Conference. April 28, 2006.

[15] Irene Padavic, "Patterns of Labor Force Participation and Sex Segregation" (conference paper, 3rd Annual Invitational Journalism-Work/Family Conference, Boston University and Brandeis University, Community, Families & Work Program, May 20–21, 2004).

awaited the women who entered the stone and iron gates of this citadel to join the Corps of Cadets on a path to becoming an officer in the United States Army.

While forced by law to open its doors to women, West Point, the nation's oldest military school, remains true to its roots: "to educate, train, and inspire the Corps of Cadets so that each graduate is a commissioned leader of character committed to the values of Duty, Honor, and Country and prepared for a career of professional excellence and service to the Nation as an officer in the United States Army."[16]

Cadets develop intellectual, military, and physical skills in a moral and ethical environment guided by the Cadet Honor Code: "A cadet will not lie, cheat or steal, or tolerate those who do."[17] West Point challenges Cadets in every possible way with an intense academic, mental, physical, spiritual, and military odyssey. The Academy's holistic curriculum, grounded in the Cadet Honor Code, fosters a commitment to honorable living in which integrity is paramount. West Point also prepares graduates in their quest to become commissioned officers and leaders of character in the United States Army. The pedagogy and mission enable Cadets to meet the many challenges of leadership, the increasingly integrated global political and economic climate, and the ever-evolving complex technologies.

To walk the grounds of the Academy is to walk through the nation's history. With its gray military gothic buildings, and bronze and marble statues overlooking the Hudson River as it turns sharply, West Point seems both contemporary yet deeply rooted in its past. Recognizing control of the Hudson River paramount to the success of the Continental Army during the American Revolution, George Washington selected Thaddeus Kosciuszko, an accomplished Polish engineer, to supervise the construction of the fortifications at West Point. These defenses provided the Continental Army fields of fire to

---

[16] United States Military Academy Website, http://www.usma.edu/mission.asp.

[17] United States Corps of Cadets Honor Code.

destroy British ships attempting to navigate the river's narrow curve around West Point. Because of its location, West Point became the most important strategic position in America, though never challenged directly by the British. During the immediate post-war years, it served as a storage site for arms and ammunition, and as an ad hoc school for officers.

In 1794, Congress approved the formation of a Corps of Artillerists and Engineers at West Point. This legislation also created the grade of cadet—in effect a junior officer—and provided limited expenditures on military instruction of these cadets. Finally, in the spring of 1802, President Thomas Jefferson signed into law the Military Peace Establishment Act, passed by Congress, which placed a separate Corps of Engineers at West Point and directed that it constitute a military academy—the United States Military Academy—to train engineers and artillerists for the fledgling American Army.

For more than a century and a half, West Point's doors were only open to men willing to pursue the profession of arms. As Lance Janda observed in his book, *Stronger Than Custom: West Point and the Admission of Women*, "for 173 years, the United States Military Academy at West Point was *omnes viri—all male*—and no one knew what bringing women into the Corps of Cadets would do to morale, discipline or the Spartan environment advocates maintained so crucial to preparing cadets for battle."[18] The first women cadets arrived in 1976 and found themselves the vanguard of a new generation of leaders in America. Their willingness to enter the fortress of West Point, face the challenges of a military education, and persevere through an almost overwhelming array of difficulties, opened the gates for many to follow. Despite detailed integration plans, the first women not only faced significant challenges as pioneers but also received frequent harassment from many of the cadets and faculty who saw their entrance into West Point as an affront to one of the few remaining bastions of manhood. One of the

---

[18] Lance Janda, Stronger Than Custom: West Point and the Admission of Women (Westport: Praeger Publishers, 2002), p. 16.

most popular comments the women received was, "I am going to do everything in my power to run you out of here and to make sure that you and your classmates (referring only to the women) do not graduate."[19] Many of the upper class men loved to say "your classmates," segregating the women from their male classmates of the same year, something they were reminded of every day of their first semester of plebe year.[20] Other women had their doors flung open and their rooms bombed with shaving cream-filled condoms. Some recalled having cadet dress sabers thrust through their bed sheets and pillows or left impaled into the mattresses.

For most of the women, it was the constant barrage of insidious and snide comments rather than the more dramatic incidents that tended to wear upon them. A frequent response many women received would follow the mandatory greeting of older cadets by plebes. When a woman would say "Good Morning, Sir," to a passing upper class cadet, a typical retort was, "It was a good morning until you bitches got here,"[21] a reminder each day that they were not welcome.

Lance Janda also addressed the distinction in the harassment women received:

> This pattern of harassment grew increasingly distinctive because it targeted cadets on the basis of their sex alone. They were hazed primarily because they were women, rather than on the basis of a perceived weakness that might be addressed, like physical fitness or personality. In this sense, the first female cadets at West Point had much in common with the first African-Americans at the Academy, for both groups were persecuted on the basis of characteristics

---

[19] This is a statement I received verbatim from several members of the Class of 1980 who were interviewed for this book.

[20] Plebe, short for plebeian, is a member of the freshman class who has completed the first summer of cadet basic training. The noun has its roots in the ancient Roman term for a member of the common people.

[21] This is a statement I received verbatim from several members of the Class of 1980 who were interviewed for this book.

(race and sex) that could never be changed. Both thus faced harassment with no prospect of winning over the hard core of cadets who committed themselves to persecution. Overweight cadets might get in shape, those whose personalities rubbed their peers the wrong way might improve their people skills or attempt to blend in but for women and African Americans, there existed no hope of redemption save time. The first African-American to graduate West Point was Henry Ossian Flipper, Class of 1877, and between his nightmarish cadet years and the 1970's the most virulent forms of racism vanished. African-American cadets faced far fewer institutional or societal hurdles than in the nineteenth and early twentieth centuries; for women the battle had only just begun.

Unlike their male counterparts, those early women West Pointers were subjected to additional pressures based on both their gender and neophyte status. As Barbara Benton of the *Quarterly Journal of Military History* observed, "The whole world is not watching every male cadet going into West Point, but the whole world is watching every female. In addition to the very rigorous training they receive, they are in a very public role."[22]

These pioneering women were immediately labeled "female cadets." While seemingly an appropriate description based solely on gender, it is a label that to this day invokes disdain from those to whom it was applied. As one 1980 graduate remarked, "female cadets were a breed of its own that didn't warrant (in the eyes of many) common courtesy and respect."[23] The label seemed to refute the notion that all cadets were equal in the eyes of the authorities.

---

[22] Tuchman, G. (Correspondent). (1 Jul 1996). West Point Marks 20 years as a Co-Ed School. [Television]. Atlanta: CNN.

[23] Colonel (retired) Kathleen Gerard Snook (interview with author), USMA Class of 1980, 2004.

While many did acknowledge this truth, others set their sights on encouraging the women to quit.

During my own plebe year in 1983, this mentality still existed in pockets. Several of the first class cadets of Company B-1, known throughout the Corps of Cadets as *Boys One*, reminded us repeatedly that their cadet company's mission was to "run all of the women out of the Corps." Frequently called "bitch," "whore," and "slut" that year, along with other crass and pejorative monikers, the women were accused of attending West Point for the sole purpose of finding a husband.

Similar to African-American cadets and other minorities who persevered despite institutional stigma, the women of West Point's Class of 1980 faced unique challenges, but they not only survived; they succeeded.

Of the 119 women who entered on July 1, 1976, 62 graduated four years later—just barely half. Ironically, the only 1980 West Point graduate awarded a prestigious Rhodes scholarship was Cadet Andrea Hollen. By 1990, a mere decade later, Cadet Kristen Baker became Brigade First Captain, the highest-ranking cadet in the corps.[24] Twenty-five years later, the Class of 2005 graduated 76% of the women who entered in 2001. By comparison, the classes of 1980 and 2005 graduated 62.3% and 79.1%, respectively, of the men who entered four years prior.[25] While the graduation percentage for women lagged the male figure in both cases, the gap had narrowed significantly in 25 years.[26] In 2008, women constituted approximately 15% of the Corps of Cadets.[27]

During their four years at West Point, the world changed dramatically for the class of 2005. The devastating attacks of

---

[24] IBID., p. 182-183.

[25] Data provided by Office of Policy, Planning, and Analysis, Institutional Research & Analysis Branch, USMA.

[26] The largest differential, in percentage terms, between the graduation rates of men and women to date was 18.3% for the class of 1983. Between 1984 and 2007 the average differential of the graduation rates between men and women is 6.03%. Data provided by Office of Policy, Planning, and Analysis, Institutional Research & Analysis Branch, USMA.

[27] IBID.

September 11, 2001, occurred only a few months into their plebe year, and the United States has been engaged in combating global terrorism ever since. America entered combat on multiple fronts, most notably in Afghanistan, Iraq, and the Philippines. Many of the women who graduated with the class of 2005 and beyond are leading soldiers in combat situations in these locations. On August 18, 2005, in Kandahar, Afghanistan, First Lieutenant Laura M. Walker, Class of 2003, became the first woman graduate killed in combat in the global war on terror. Thirteen months later, Second Lieutenant Emily Perez, the first graduate of her West Point Class of 2005 to arrive in Iraq, was killed when an improvised explosive device (IED) detonated near her vehicle during combat operations.

Between 1980 and 2009, 3,397 women graduated from West Point and have served selflessly in our great nation's armed forces. Most of them, whether or not they still wear the uniform, are ordinary women with extraordinary stories of perseverance and integrity. They are soldiers and wives, mothers and daughters. They are doctors, lawyers, teachers, clergy, and entrepreneurs. They are athletes and artists, cancer survivors and coaches. And they are all volunteers. They have experienced emotional, physical, intellectual, and spiritual challenges throughout their lives that have provided them with the strength to lead others and to make difficult decisions. Some have lost soldiers in their command. Some have lost spouses. Some have buried children. And some have made the ultimate personal sacrifice, dying in service to their country.

For most of these women, West Point and their experiences in the Army have served as a launching pad that allowed them to make significant contributions to their communities. All regard leading soldiers as a privilege and defending our nation as an honor. Many remain in uniform. The conditions under which they serve, however, have changed radically. In Iraq and Afghanistan the Army is developing new doctrines as it fights an unconventional enemy. One of the recurring lessons learned is that the historic notions of a forward combat zone and a safer rear echelon support area are not as applicable to these theaters of operation. The two are often indistinguishable, and women soldiers are everywhere on the battlefield. The "front line" is now a 360-degree circle, and women are often combat leaders, leading soldiers in harm's way.

While this changing dynamic of the battlefield provides a growing opportunity for women in the Army, in certain ways they are still limited. For example, military culture contends that the Infantry is the "Queen of Battle" and that command of an Infantry battalion is the pinnacle of an Army career. This ultimate goal of command responsibility currently is beyond reach for women. They cannot realistically aspire to command an Infantry battalion since it's against the rules. Pulitzer Prize-winning journalist, best-selling novelist and former *Newsweek* contributing editor Anna Quindlen, wrote, "Since promotion to the highest ranks is determined by combat experience, that means the ceiling for women in the military is not glass, it's concrete."[28]

Conventional wisdom and current law prevent women, no matter how able, from serving in units with direct offensive combat missions—Infantry, Armor, Special Forces, and specific Field Artillery, Air Defense Artillery, and Engineer units. The justifications for this exclusion include that women are not fit for combat and battlefield stress because they lack the emotional stability and physical strength.[29] The media often has proffered that Americans would not stand to see their daughters coming home in body bags. The purported fear and outcry of a women's violent death from enemy fire has not materialized during the war on terror. At least no more than it has for a man—we all suffer a terrible loss when we lose a Soldier. In reality, the strained Armed Forces need women in the fight. Circumstances have eclipsed arguments, and few in the military and government are anxious to rekindle the debate. Dr. Stephen Grove pointed out:

---

[28] Anna Quindlen, "Not Semi-Soldiers,". Newsweek. (November 12, 2007): 90.

[29] Corbett, Arthur J. Women in Combat: The Case for Combat Exclusion. Newport, RI, Naval War College, 1993. 210.

Indeed, most graduates of the 19th and early 20th century never saw any combat anyway. Furthermore, the Army is, and always has been, more than the combat arms branches, although sometimes the Army might like to forget that. Even if women were excluded from combat branches, there were many other branches in which they could serve. Finally, women have been in combat in all of America's wars, whether they were in combat arms branches or not. Indeed, one of the first, Margaret Corbin, who took her deceased husband's place at an artillery piece and served in the American Revolution, is buried in the West Point Cemetery.

Joining Corbin in the historic cemetery are Lieutenants Laura Walker and Emily Perez.

* * *

President Theodore Roosevelt remarked at the centennial celebration of the founding of West Point that "no other educational institution in the land has contributed as many names as West Point has contributed to the honor roll of the nation's greatest citizens." Now, after more than 200 years, West Point continues to provide the nation with the names of men *and women* of character to add to that honor roll.

For all graduates, going to West Point began with a choice: the choice to be willing to serve one's country in a military environment. That is the commitment accepted upon graduation from the United States Military Academy. To a teenager contemplating attending the Academy, it does not appear to be a life and death choice, but for many throughout the last two hundred years, it has been. Given the current nature of conflict, the service obligation and commitment guarantee an extremely uncertain and dangerous future.

While the names of the women who are profiled in this book are not as well known as those of previous graduates, such as Thomas "Stonewall' Jackson, Robert E. Lee, Ulysses S. Grant, Douglas MacArthur, Dwight D. Eisenhower, George S. Patton, Alexander Haig, Buzz Aldrin, H. Norman Schwarzkopf, and David Petraeus, they stand equally tall in a long, gray line of graduates extending back to 1802.

This book is a reminder of the importance of patriotism, both past and present. In the face of a cynical culture, the subjects of this book remind us of what has made us great as a people and as a nation. The women who graduate from West Point have accepted the responsibility of preserving our way of life. They have embraced the ideals of duty, honor, and country.

Porcelain on Steel provides both young people and adults with outstanding role models after whom they may pattern their own lives as they consider the various opportunities open to them. Meant to inspire the young about what they want to be and do, it also shows how they can contribute to our country and society.

While numerous books about West Point, its history, and its graduates exist, no single book focuses exclusively on the stories of the Academy's women graduates. Only five books have been published solely about West Point women. Three are individual stories, each focused on one woman's perspective and personal experience; three are non-fiction, and the other is fiction. The fifth book, academic in nature and the basis of Lance Janda's dissertation for his doctor of philosophy degree, is *Stronger than Custom: West Point and the Admission of Women.*

West Point holds a unique position in American military culture and history. The fact that a relatively small number of women have graduated from the institution makes a compilation of those women inherently of interest to those who study women, war and women, and women in the military.

Generations of men have sought to enter West Point in part because a father, grandfather or other male role model was a West Point graduate. The 2002 Register of Graduates includes a genealogical succession table, which provides a sequential list of all the graduates of every West Point class from 1802-2002 who have a descendant(s)/ancestor(s) who are also graduates. This list runs for more than 113 pages, and the class of 2002 has 60 graduates on just one page of the list.[30] Extrapolating that data, one estimates more than 6,780 graduates[31] with ancestral ties to the Academy. Now women are beginning to have that same experience of following in the footsteps of a female family member who graduated from West Point beginning in 1980. Beginning with the class of 2005 and continuing through the class of 2012, there are 13 women whose mothers are West Point graduates.[32,33]

* * *

The group of women selected for this anthology spans a range of classes that graduated women, and contains a mother and her daughter. The inclusion of a wide variety of experiences, both inside and outside the armed forces, reflects a spectrum of post-West Point life history for all graduates. Their experiences are as diverse as the women themselves are. The women in this book willingly shared some very personal and intimate experiences.

This collection of portraits captures the broad array of voices that speak of and for women graduates of West Point. I attempted to secure their voices, unencumbered, with as little formality and pretense as possible. I made every effort to inspire each woman to tell her story openly and authentically. Each chapter of this book is a foreword to the pages of each graduate's own book, should she write one.

---

[30] Register of Graduates and Former Cadets of the United States Military Academy; Bicentennial Edition, p. 3-1 through 3-113. 2002.

[31] This extrapolation is based on the author's research and estimation of 60 graduates per page.

[32] Register of Graduates and Former Cadets of the United States Military Academy; 2005, p. 62.

[33] Data provided by Office of Policy, Planning, and Analysis, Institutional Research & Analysis Branch, USMA, 2009.

In writing this book, I wanted to remain true and honest to both the graduates and the institution. Therefore, in each story you will find themes that resonate with and reinforce the time-honored principles espoused by the West Point's core values—duty, honor, country. Found in the carefully guarded construction of professional identity, *Officership* is comprised of four prevailing components: *Warrior, Servant of the Nation, Member of a Profession, and Leader of Character*.[34] These constructs are touchstones to guide the development of the identity of every officer:

Warrior: The warrior is a fighter: one who places the mission first, never gives up, never accepts defeat, and never leaves a fallen comrade behind. A warrior understands that combat is intellectual and physical in nature and prepares oneself to lead effectively in complex and harsh environments. He or she is tactically and technically proficient in the threat or application of violent force. The warrior role distinguishes the military profession from all others.

Servant of the Nation: Service describes the fundamental nature of the relationship between the military and society. This characteristic also establishes the democratic principle of military subordination to civilian control. An officer is responsive to the needs of the nation, regardless of the personal sacrifices required—servanthood implies sacrifice as well as obedience and dedication.

Member of a Profession: This characteristic of officership describes the nature of the Army officer corps as a collective body unified in purpose, identity, and goals. Officership includes a unique competence or expertise, an authority delegated by society, a distinct culture, and an ethical basis. Officers have a moral obligation to be competent; they must continue to study and perfect their

---

[34] Cadet Leader Development System for Cadets. United States Military Academy (USMA) USMA Circular 1-101-1, February 2005, p.10-11.

professional knowledge and skill throughout their career. Professions are life-long callings, not simply occupations.

Leader of Character: One who seeks to discover truth, decide what is right, and has the courage and commitment to act accordingly…always. Leaders of character consistently pursue virtuous living and apply values and principles in their decisions and actions. Leaders of character have the courage and self-discipline to do what is right every time…even when no one is looking.

The guiding principles of the West Point leadership development experience are encapsulated in the United States Army's shared values—*The Seven Army Values*. These values act as both the individual's and the institution's guideposts for all actions and thought at West Point. These values are the foundation upon which the United States Army and the United States Military Academy operate. They constitute the bedrock of everything the Army does or fails to do. To understand these values is to understand much of what makes a West Point graduate a West Point graduate.

The Seven Army Values[35]

1. **Loyalty:** Bear true faith and allegiance to the U.S. Constitution, the Army, and other soldiers. Be loyal to the nation and its heritage.
2. **Duty:** Fulfill your obligations. Accept responsibility for your own actions and those entrusted to your care. Find opportunities to improve oneself for the good of the group.
3. **Respect:** Rely upon the golden rule. How we consider others reflects upon each of us, both personally and as a professional organization.

---

[35] IBID., p. 20.

4. **Selfless Service:** Put the welfare of the nation, the Army, and your subordinates before your own. Selfless service leads to organizational teamwork and encompasses discipline, self-control, and faith in the system.
5. **Honor:** Live up to all the Army values.
6. **Integrity:** Do what is right, legally, and morally. Be willing to do what is right even when no one is looking. It is our "moral compass" an inner voice.
7. **Personal Courage:** Our ability to face fear, danger, or adversity, both physical and moral courage.

The intent is to view each of these women graduate's stories through the lens created by these values. My belief is that they, and the West Point experience, are better understood if studied in this framework. These women's stories are diverse and broadly different, and yet there are clearly consistent themes that emerge. I hope you can study these values, read these stories, revisit these values and gain an insight into why West Point is a singular leader development institution and why the women who graduate possess a unique strain of those qualities.

The purpose of this book is to attempt to capture the essence of the female experience at the United States Military Academy at West Point, the nation's premier leadership school. What is evident is that the experience of women cadets and graduates of the United States Military Academy contains undeniable themes that are rooted in what we have come to understand as gender differences. In a variety of different domains of scholarship, it has been determined that women and men experience education, groups, institutions, leadership, and themselves differently, depending on the environment in which they find themselves. The expressed purpose is to be descriptive and not prescriptive, and therefore I ask the reader to engage actively to truly understand the implications of each and all of these women's experiences.

These stories demonstrate the one character trait West Point calls its *'raison d'être'*—the warrior ethos. Despite the centuries of painstaking effort expended in crafting the collective experiences that guarantee the genesis of the warrior ethic in each one of its graduates, West Point never has been able to truly contain, and therefore measure, exactly what "it" is that generates "character". One may argue that there is an interactive effect between the individual who arrives at the Academy prepared to begin the journey toward becoming an officer and the challenges encountered along that long road to graduation and commissioning. What West Point does believe is that it offers each one of its graduates the opportunity to develop into the very best officer he or she can be. It is almost entirely up to the individual to embrace that opportunity in order to optimize his or her own potential.

In addition to providing insight into the West Point experience from a woman graduate's perspective, it is also my intent to provide some thoughtful reflection on the institutional challenges created by such a fundamental paradigm shift as was introducing coeducation at West Point. This marked another momentous occasion in the hallowed institution's history, and it presents time-honored lessons for better understanding how it adjusted to this fundamental change. I have attempted to outline those lessons, from the organizational perspective, in the description of each woman's individual experience. In this manner, the hope is to broaden the lens through which the reader peers into the world of West Point.

These stories contain the DNA for a better understanding of education, professional development, institutional policymaking, and organizational leadership. Like one strand in a double helix, these insights are inseparable from the stories themselves, but certainly evident as distinctive blueprints for facilitating deeper understanding and clarity for the student of these disciplines.

These are stories about how to persevere in life. Each begins with an epigraph personally selected by the graduate from which she draws inspiration and provides focus to her own life. My hope is that these chronicles will light the fire of imagination within by igniting hearts, stimulating minds, and touching souls to affirm that anything is possible. Undoubtedly, there is more to each story—more challenges and more accomplishments—but that book is still unwritten.

West Point is a place that builds bridges to the future from a place where the past is always present.

The writing of this book has been a unique journey. I have laughed and cried with these women. I am unspeakably grateful to them for sharing their stories.

Members of the Class of 1979 from Company I-2 pose for their senior company picture in the *Howitzer*, the West Point yearbook. *(USMA Archives)*

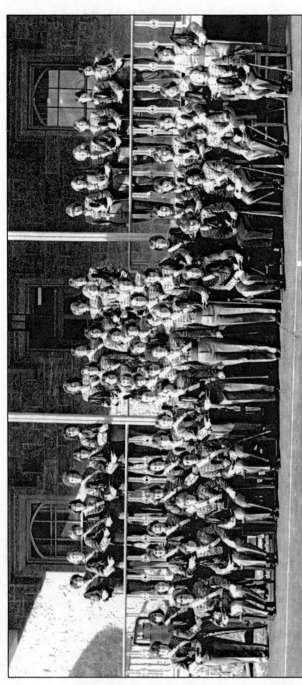

Sixty-one of the sixty-two women in the Class of 1980 posed for this photo just prior to graduation. *Left seated:* J. McEntee, K. Gerard, D. Dawson, J. Dallas. *Right seated:* A. Hollen, C. Young, P. Walker, C. Kirby, A. Muir. *Standing front:* B. Trehane, D. Wright, J. Harrington, S. Kellett, K. Wheless, J. Perkins, D. Maller, D. Johnson, R. Fennessy, D. Stoddard, J. Smith, S. Reichelt, D. Turner (*in front of the post*). R. Null, B. Benya, M. Flynn, D. Bracey, E. Griffin, C. Stevens. *Standing on the first step:* K. Wildey, K. Silvia, R. Todd. *Standing on the fourth step:* D. McCarthy, J. Calhoon, C. Barkalow. *Standing on the fifth step:* K. Kelly, A. Hughes, T. Kaseman. *Standing on the sixth step:* S. Nikituk, B. Fiedler, N. Gucwa, D. Alesch. *Left standing back:* M. Nyberg, K. Hinsey, S. Ashworth, D. Blyth, M. Rosinski, D. Lewis, B. Fulton. *Right standing back:* K. Kinzler, A. Fields, A. Colister, K. Zachgo, M. Gridley, V. Martin. *Not pictured:* T. Tepper. (*USMA Archives*)

First Class Cadet Kathy Wheless, USMA 1980.
(Photo courtesy of Kathy Wheless Gerstein)

MAKING HISTORY | KATHY WHELESS GERSTEIN, CLASS OF 1980

"We can do anything we want to do if we stick to it long enough."
— Helen Keller

The 70s were chaotic for the country and for West Point. The war in Vietnam reached its zenith, its nadir and eventually ended. "By the time the war finally ground to its agonized halt in 1975, the Army was demoralized and shaken to its roots by rampant drug use, racial tensions, and epidemic disciplinary problems."[36] Senior leaders in the Army had to re-build a force that had been demoralized and defeated in the rice paddies and hills of Southeast Asia. One of the major changes these leaders confronted was the elimination of the draft. The Armed Services would become an all-volunteer force with soldiers recruited instead of drafted.

In 1970, two years into his tenure as Superintendent of the United States Military Academy, Major General Samuel Koster was implicated in the cover-up of the My Lai massacre in Vietnam. As with all important announcements to the United States Corps of Cadets, General Koster delivered his resignation standing on the second-story stone balcony of cadet mess hall in front of more than 4,000 cadets.

In December 1972, federal courts ended obligatory cadet attendance at chapel services with its decision to show respect for a diversity of religious views. The justices ruled, "That compulsory attendance at church at the service academies violated the constitutional right to religious freedom under the First Amendment."[37] Mandatory chapel had been in place since the days of Sylvanus Thayer and was nearly as old as the Academy itself.

---

[36] John Grant, James Lynch and Ronald Bailey. West Point: The First Two Hundred Years (Gilford: The Globe Pequot Press, 2002), 264.

[37] IBID., p. 166.

General Andrew J. Goodpaster, who later served as superintendent, described the two-edge thrust of the Court's decision. He wrote:

> The decision preserved the principles of the Constitution, but its effect on the Corps of Cadets was to reduce the mandatory exposure of cadets to issues of ethics and moral standards. Voluntary chapel attendance continued, but there can be little doubt (at least in the minds of many old graduates) that change had a weakening effect in the moral-ethical sector of a cadets life, with nothing of equivalent strength provided to takes [sic] its place.[38]

It is interesting to note that the reason the military academy was established in 1802 by President Thomas Jefferson was to provide professional officers for the technical fields of artillery and engineering. Dr. Stephen Grove, West Point's historian noted that the role of officers in combat was rarely specified. He stated further:

> Indeed, most graduates of the 19th and early 20th century never saw combat anyway. Furthermore, the Army, is, and always has been, more than the combat arms branches, although sometimes the Army might like to forget that even if women were excluded from combat branches there were many other branches in which they could serve.

He also noted that despite no specific and direct assignment to a combat arms branch, women have served in combat in all of America's wars. Women played various roles in the American Revolution as nurses, cooks, and even as artillery combatants. Margaret Corbin, a Revolutionary heroine buried in the West Point

[38] IBID., p.162.

Cemetery, assumed her deceased husband's place behind an artillery piece.[39]

A dramatic change for the Academy occurred in 1975. In the spring of that year, both Congress and the Senate passed legislation admitting women to the nation's service academies. Many military officers voiced vociferous objections and criticism to this new law. One of the most vocal was then-Superintendent Major General Sidney Berry, West Point Class of 1948. Berry staunchly argued women had no place at the sacred institution whose mission, he believed, was to develop future combat leaders for the Army. Women were barred from direct combat duty and therefore should not be allowed to enter the Military Academy. Berry, along with other senior officers, reasoned, "[Women] are a threat to the cohesiveness, morale, and combat effectiveness of every unit in the army; and therefore women had no place at West Point."[40]

Other high-ranking officers were equally vocal. General William Westmoreland, a former Superintendent of West Point and then the Chief of Staff of the Army, stated, "Maybe you could find one woman in 10,000 who could lead in combat, but she would be a freak, and the Military Academy is not being run for freaks."[41]

In the spring of 1976, a massive cheating scandal erupted at West Point.[42] The scandal attracted droves of media to the majestic campus on the west bank of the Hudson River. One hundred and fifty-two cadets found guilty of collaboration on a take-home electrical engineering exam were dismissed but 98 were allowed to return later.

---

[39] Jane Green. Powder, Paper and Lace: An Anecdotal Herstory of Women at West Point. (Charlottesville: Priority Press), 1988.

[40] Lance Janda. Stronger Than Custom, West Point and the Integration of Women. (Westport: Praeger Publishers, 2002) p. 7.

[41] IBID., p. 5.

[42] This was not the first time a highly publicized cheating scandal had tarnished West Point's reputation for probity. In 1951 ninety cadets resigned, including thirty-seven members of the nationally ranked varsity football team, for cheating. Then in 1966 forty-nine cadets were ousted for honor code violations. But in scope and publicity the scandal of 1976 dwarfed all previous cases. John Grant, James Lynch and Ronald Bailey. West Point: The First Two Hundred Years (Gilford: The Globe Pequot Press, 2002), 163.

Three months after the honor scandal was first reported in the news and three days after the United States celebrated its bicentennial as an independent nation, West Point admitted 119 female new cadets into the class of 1980, ending the 175-year tradition of all-male exclusivity at the nation's service academies. The arrival of women at West Point signaled the beginning of a new era although it was not one the hallowed institution sought. Again, the media descended upon West Point from the nation's largest media market located just a mere 50 miles to the south. Media presence only heightened the nearly palpable tension on campus. Dr. Grove stated:

> The Military Academy saw the press as a way to say positive things about the Academy. The press was, not surprisingly, only interested in interviewing women— men had always been at the Academy. The resentment at being ignored compounded the resentments that many male cadets and some staff and faculty felt about the admission of women to THEIR Academy. The fact that some of the media were feminists interested in portraying this event as an example of women conquering a previously impregnable male bastion, led to some articles in which the writers manufactured comments that they attributed to women cadets. The fact that the women never made those statements did not help them as they received additional abuse from the males.

Despite detailed plans for seamless integration, the women who entered West Point that summer did so against tremendous odds. Not only did they confront the physical, intellectual, emotional, mental, and spiritual trials all cadets face, they were trailblazers and in nearly everyone's sights. Kathy Wheless Gerstein is one of these pioneering women.

While many of the women who entered West Point in the summer of 1976 understood the military as a profession and had some idea of the journey on which they were embarking, others did not. Some knowingly sought the challenge; some primarily wanted a free education at a world-renowned engineering school; still others were attracted by the idea of doing something new and audacious.

Like many of her high school classmates in Clearwater, Florida, Kathy thought she would attend either Florida State University or the University of Florida. Kathy's older brother Glen was a midshipman in the Class of 1978 at the United States Naval Academy in Annapolis, Maryland. As Kathy started her senior year in high school in the fall of 1975, Glen told her about the imminent admission of women to all of the service academies. Intrigued, Kathy thought it would be an exciting challenge and applied to the United States Military Academy. She recalled, "When I received my appointment, it seemed like a pretty cool thing for a 17 year-old to do. Deliberate, however, was not in my lexicon."

The morning of July 7, 1976, dawned gray and humid with sporadic rain showers that worsened an already dreary day. Kathy Wheless entered West Point along with approximately 1,500 other students. These recent high school graduates arrived both nervous and eager to cross the threshold between life as civilians and that of new cadets.

This first day of a cadet's journey is known officially as "Reception Day," though cadets and faculty call it simply "R-day." That gray morning the students and their loved ones arrived early at West Point's football stadium, the entrance and exit point of a cadet's four-year odyssey. They paused briefly to listen to various Academy officials describe what they could expect as cadets. After tearful and rushed good-byes, parents and friends departed for tours of the impressive grounds while the new cadets were directed onto buses for a short ride to the Central Gymnasium[43] for in-processing. This rite of passage, thoroughly planned and rehearsed by the upper class cadet cadre and staff, proved emotional for all involved. The

---

[43] Central Gymnasium is now known as Arvin Gymnasium.

incoming students said goodbye to a life they knew and entered the strange and mythical life of a West Point new cadet.

It was equally significant for the Academy, as the entrance of the Class of 1980 signaled the beginning of a new era at West Point, one that had been legislated by the federal government. As Rick Atkinson wrote in *The Long Gray Line*, "Had a company of Martians suddenly appeared on the Plain in dress gray and tar buckets, there would have been no greater sense of invasion and outrage than was provoked by the arrival of ten dozen American females."[44]

As soon as the buses were out of sight, the yelling began. It came from the cadet cadre of Cadet Basic Training (CBT), all upper class male cadets who were both the leaders of the Corps of Cadets and the enforcers of the Fourth Class System, the cornerstone of the cadet-regulated system for developing character, discipline, and military bearing. Commanded to sit still, keep their eyes forward, and not talk, the class of 1980 began swift transition from high school graduates to military officers-in-training during the six-week CBT period known as Beast Barracks. It is an intense program focusing on basic soldier skills and military courtesy, discipline, personal appearance, physical fitness, and drill and ceremonies.

Herded off the buses and moved through various stations inside the gym. They were stripped of their civilian clothes, fitted with, and issued new clothing. Their first uniform was gym alpha, consisting of white t-shirts, black gym shorts, black socks and low quarter shoes. The women received crew neck shirts, and the men retained the traditional white v-neck style. A green and yellow tag was pinned to each cadet's shorts, indicating what stations they had passed through, what equipment issued, and where they needed to go next.

The first day was a shock to everyone: learning how to become a cadet, how to march, how to salute, how to eat, and how to wear a uniform. The new recruits received proper military haircuts at the barbershop. For men, the "high and tight" was the standard—cut

---

[44] Rick Atkinson. The Long Gray Line (Boston: Houghton Mifflin Company, 1989) p. 408.

well above the ears and very short. For women, the definition of a proper military haircut was somewhat more ambiguous. Women's hair could not extend below the top of the collar of their shirt nor more than a limited distance in any direction away from their head. "USMA hair style standards stated that hair would be short and styled to facilitate femininity, conformity to the cadet uniform, and cleanliness during rigorous physical and field training."[45] In the few months prior to women arriving, cadet barbers attended seminars to provide instruction on the styling of women's hair. The cadet barbershop opened its doors to women living and working on post in order to give the barbers experience in cutting women's hair. That first day the cadet cadre ordered many women to the barbershop multiple times.

The new cadets also learned the legendary four responses that are the only acceptable answers to any question or order. The responses were "Yes, Sir," "No, Sir," "No excuse, Sir," and "Sir, I do not understand". They received a small book titled *Bugle Notes*. Known as the plebe bible, *Bugle Notes* contained the history of West Point and an array of miscellaneous trivia and information about the Academy and Army. Plebes were required to recite this knowledge on demand.

These tasks, along with many others, were overseen by intimidating male cadets barking orders and commands. The new cadets learned to walk at 120 steps per minute with eyes focused straight ahead. They squared corners and walked close to walls with their arms bent at a ninety-degree angle. They learned to eat while sitting straight with their back one fist distance from the chair. At five o'clock that same afternoon, a mere seven hours after they had arrived, the 1,500 students who had been wearing an array of civilian clothes marched through the Academy's famous sally ports, the above ground tunnels cut through the stone of Eisenhower and MacArthur barracks, in unison in starched identical uniforms with

---

[45] Alan G. Vitters and Nora Scott Kinzer, Report of the Admission of Women to the United States Military Academy, Project Athena I (West Point: BS&L, June 1978) p. 21.

cropped haircuts. They paraded onto The Plain, the sacred ceremonial ground in front of Washington Hall and the barracks, and stood in company columns in front of the granite buildings of the cadet area. Imposing statues of the great military generals for which these buildings were named gazed down on these new cadets.

The Superintendent welcomed the new cadets to West Point and the Army. Then, under the command of the highest-ranking cadet that summer, known colloquially as the King of Beast, the new cadets raised their right hands and repeated the Cadet Oath. These were no longer happy-go-lucky teenagers. They were young warriors-in-training charged with service to the nation and defense of their country. Lance Janda, author of *Stronger than Custom: West Point and the Admission of Women*, wrote, "They—the new cadets— were implicitly challenged with making the admission of the first women at West Point a success. This was history in action—one West Point replacing another."[46] They became members of the Long Gray Line, a metaphorical continuum of West Point's graduates and cadets.

In the heat and humidity of that New York summer, they spent time in the field learning how to navigate by compass and read a map, plan a patrol, disassemble, clean, assemble, and fire a rifle, use a bayonet, arm a grenade, clean a pistol, road march and bivouac. Although brief, the intensity of the basic training program and its sixteen-hour-plus days places extensive demands on new cadets. The indoctrination program tests their emotional stability and physical fitness, ability to organize and manage time, perform under extreme stress, and determination to succeed.

Each morning started before dawn with a run in formation around the Academy's gothic-like buildings and sprawling 16,000-acre reservation. During Beast Barracks, running was the primary gauge measuring success or failure. It determined the official and unofficial hierarchy among cadets. Kathy recalled, "Success in the morning runs was the only thing that got you accepted. It was the

---

[46] Lance Janda, Stronger Than Custom, West Point and the Integration of Women. (Westport: Praeger Publishers) 2002, p. 82.

sole measure of physical fitness, and that equaled leadership." One either completed the run in formation or fell out of the run.

The emphasis on physical fitness makes a certain amount of sense at West Point as Lance Janda articulated,

> Every group has its rites of passage, test which potential members must pass to be accepted...the more exclusive the group, the more challenging the rites. Earning a Ph.D. is more difficult than earning a bachelor's degree, being a neurosurgeon more prestigious than practicing family medicine, and joining an elite combat unit more physically challenging than doing paperwork in an administrative section. West Point made its test both physical and mental; but true to military tradition, physical prowess counted the most. Always. No vocation demanded more physically than the society of warriors as future Army officers charged with winning America's wars, West Pointers historically pride themselves on being especially tough and demanding. Women seemed to threaten this tradition, particularly when they did not have to meet the same physical standards as men.[47]

There were so many challenges that Kathy and her female contemporaries had little time to think about the impact of their presence. That first summer, running was Kathy's greatest test. She recounted,

> When we entered, Title IX was only four years old.[48] We were not exposed to the plethora of sports that

---

[47] IBID., p.84.

[48] Title IX of the Education Amendments was created to prohibit sex discrimination in education programs that receive federal financial assistance. It is widely credited for the growth of women's sports at all scholastic levels.

girls are today. For most of us, high school may have provided participation in swimming or track. I do not think anyone really knew what to expect. We did not come in with the idea that we were going to be so severely tested and rated by how well we could run.

We also ran in formation, with combat boots and fatigue pants. I really hated when we did a rifle run—boots and the M-14s. Women carried the lighter M-16, but it was still very difficult.

Kathy vividly remembers not being able to complete many of the runs the first three weeks of Beast Barracks. "Falling out of a run" effectively ruined one's entire day. Almost immediately, this discounted the individual's performance in any other area. Both the cadet and officer leadership treated the individual who fell out of the run with disdain. Feeling unworthy for not completing a run, Kathy remembered that it only got worse as the hazing from the cadre intensified. Kathy recalled,

I remember trying to memorize everything and 'pop off' without any hesitation. Regardless of one's proficiency in mundane tasks such as shining shoes, marksmanship, drill and plebe knowledge—the regurgitation of everything from the front page of The New York Times, to various figures about the number of certain lights in various buildings—nothing mattered if you fell out of a run. The ability to run equaled the ability to lead.

For Kathy and the others who were not able to complete the runs, any spare time they had focused on remedial running training. The training was successful. Halfway through the summer, Kathy was completing the runs. An increased fitness level and the desire to minimize the amount of hazing provided her motivation. Her outlook changed completely, and she then was able to focus on all the other daily tasks. The hazing, however, did not stop; it shifted to other activities. Pull-ups were another challenge for all new cadets. Few women who entered West Point were able to do more than two pull-ups at the outset.

As Beast Barracks concluded, the women gained a sense of accomplishment for persevering through the intensity and scrutiny. None were prepared for what they would endure at the start of the fall academic term, however, as the entire Corps of Cadets—numbering nearly 4,400—returned to the Academy from their summer assignments around the globe.

The first week of the academic semester, known as "Re-Orgy Week," short for reorganization week, commenced as Beast Barracks ended and dramatically changed the lives of the plebes. During Beast Barracks, new cadets outnumbered upper class cadets ten to one. The odds now reversed, and the upperclassmen outnumbered the plebes, three to one, significantly increasing the probability of being harassed. Although the school term brought some respite from the physical regimen and military training, there was little free time, as an intense scholastic program, intramural athletics, military drill, and strict maintenance of the barracks according to military regulations increased the demands of the daily regimen.

At a loss for words, Kathy's voice faltered as she described the fall of 1976. The vast majority of the returning upperclassmen, all men, eagerly awaited their first opportunity to haze the female cadets. They took it as their mission to test the mettle of each plebe, their hardiness, and their knowledge. The women became the objects of both ridicule and curiosity. Kathy remembers her squad leader telling her to keep a low profile. Kathy said,

> This was just not possible as a female cadet, especially
> during parades. The women's full dress uniform was
> made without the tails of the male full dress because it
> was believed the tails would protrude off the butts of

the women. The difference in uniforms just brought more attention and mockery.

The first Corps-wide parade was a nightmare. Beginning about 15 minutes before the parade, lining up in the area, marching out onto The Plain and through the pass and review, we were heckled nearly continuously by the rest of the cadets in the company. I was anxious for our classes to begin and not being [sic] on show all the time.

The curriculum at the time was based heavily in math, science and engineering. For Kathy, the first challenge was learning how to study efficiently and effectively.

It seems as if all my classes were some configuration or aberration of a math class. For a while, I was in the 'ejection section'—those with the lowest grades in math. If you failed, you would be ejected out of the Academy. Class grades were always recomputed every week or two and classes were shuffled so a class would basically be at the same level of understanding. I remember one time a math instructor, Major Pinzutti, called on me to prove some theorem. I stated 'Sir, I am required to prove...' followed by a very long pause. Finally I just turned to him and said, 'Sir, I do not even know what I am trying to prove.' He burst out laughing at my comment and then proceeded to explain most of the lesson in terms that even I was able to understand. I could think and write logically and eloquently, but mathematical problem solving was a different game entirely. Academics were a rude awakening for me.

The attitudes towards and about women that first year varied considerably, but hostility was prominent among them. Plebes are required to greet enthusiastically all upper classmen, "Good morning, Sir!" When that greeting came from a woman, the response often was "It was a good morning until you got here, bitch." As Rick Atkinson wrote in *The Long Gray Line*,

> Male cadets anonymously scrawled crude sexual slurs on the barracks walls, scattered condoms on the women's bunks, and sent vibrators to them through the mail. During a lecture in Mahan Hall one evening, when a psychologist made disparaging remarks about women in an effort to provoke a reaction from the cadets, the men stood and cheered...
>
> Some of the women cultivated a deliberate androgyny by artificially lowering their voices and refused to wear skirts or makeup. Those considered too feminine by the men were "fluffs"; those too masculine were "dykes." "Whore" was a favorite all-purpose epithet. The men ridiculed the women for lacking a man's upper body strength and endurance and for having longer hair. Some upperclassman prowled the barracks with rulers, measuring locks that extended below the collar. When some women began to gain weight from the daily four-thousand-calorie mess hall fare, they were badgered for contracting "Hudson hip disease." [49]

Kathy worked hard not to allow the antagonism to get to her.

> As much as I did not like it, I really tried just to shrug it off. I kept telling myself that my being at West Point

---

[49] Atkinson, p. 411.

was not my problem it was theirs. I was not there to diminish the experience. I was there to be challenged. This is where a good sense of humor is critical to survival.

Kathy also reasoned that some of the hostility was born out of ignorance and unfamiliarity with women in a professional setting. Most men had only known and interacted with women in familial roles, as mothers, sisters, and girlfriends. These women, now cadets and contemporaries, challenged their views and stereotypes. They did not know how to react and might have just been acting out of ignorance. Kathy recalled, "Any mention of cramps and the upperclassmen reacted almost the exact same way, 'Quick! Get the Midol.' It was like they could just give us a pill, and they wouldn't have to think about women and their periods."

Although everyone has a reason for attending West Point, it seemed male cadets loved to challenge the women with the question, "Why are you here?" The implication was that no women could have a valid reason for attending the Military Academy. When asked this question, Kathy's typical response was "for the education." Upon receiving this somewhat mundane answer, upper class cadets would continue on their way.

Most of the women heard more than once from some male cadet, "I am going to run you out of my Academy or rid the Corps of Cadets of women." Kathy and some of her classmates said that the irony is that the harassment and lack of respect motivated many to stay and graduate. In retrospect, enduring the challenges of plebe year and the attention and harassment related to being a female cadet only strengthened their resolve.

Many men resented the attention that the women received from both the press and the GAP, the Great American Public; the media's constant presence blamed on the women cadets. It also seemed that most visitors to West Point sought to identify and point out women in the Corps during any type of training. Often in loud and thunderous tones, someone would yell, "There's one. There's a woman cadet."

The media paid particular attention to the women at West Point, eager to the point of annoyance to interview them about their unique experiences. Kathy said they all learned quickly how to respond to media inquires after a significant *faux pas* by one woman. Asked during Plebe Parent Weekend how she thought her male classmates would feel about a woman obtaining a high leadership position, she was quoted as having said, "I have the bars." This meant she would wear a rank with many bars, signifying her leadership position. Most of the women knew her quote was taken out of context. Little did it matter as she suffered a rash of hazing by cadets who criticized her for assuming that rank eliminated the need to earn individual respect. Kathy said, "There was always a high probability you would be quoted and the statement taken out of context and misconstrued. Many of us just routinely replied, 'I do not have anything to say.'"

Kathy said the next three years were somewhat of a blur, with few specific recollections. Each of the subsequent years had continued physical, emotional, and intellectual challenges. The second summer at Camp Buckner was "the best summer of a cadet's life." Kathy recalled it being more relaxed than Beast Barracks but still a challenge.

As more women came to West Point in the classes of 1981, 1982, and 1983, attitudes began to change. That first year, women were placed in only twelve of the thirty-six cadet companies. As each of the remaining fourteen companies received women in the subsequent years, women became less of a novelty. Nevertheless, each company had its share of young men who did not like women at the Academy as demonstrated in a series of surveys.

Cadet hostility surfaced in the meetings and in surveys conducted by the Academy. It far exceeded the mere chauvinism shown by the 40 percent in a survey who agreed, "A woman's activities are best confined in the home." One cadet said flatly, "I think it is a disgrace for women to be here." Another wrote, "I feel it is my duty to the alumni and the entire Army to run out as many females as possible."[50]

Even in her final year at the Academy, Kathy recounted that the tension had not dissipated completely. It remained fueled by the increasing media presence as graduation and officer commissioning approached. In May 1980, nearly every major newspaper and magazine ran a lead or cover story about the service academies' impending graduation of women ready to take command of military units. Kathy recalled the anticipation of graduation and commissioning, "I could not wait to leave. We had been counting the days since R-Day four years earlier, and we were finally at the end."

The New York Times ran a cover story on January 25, 1980, titled "West Point Women Draw Duty in Combat Branches." The article pointed out that women entering the branches of field artillery, air defense artillery, engineers and aviation, all combat branches, did so by personal choice. Their selection of branches was an indication of what the graduating women hoped to do with their training. The article failed to acknowledge however that the women ranked near the bottom of the class, typically the lowest ten percent, did not get their first selection of branch, and received assignment to air defense artillery and field artillery. The men of similar class rank went to the infantry. Kathy elected the Signal Corps as her branch specialty as a matter of practicality more than anything else. She observed that being in an electronics field would be useful in or out of uniform.

On May 28, 1980, the West Point Class of 1980 comprised of 62 women and 858 men threw their white hats high into a glorious blue sky above the West Point Football Stadium ending their cadet odyssey in the same place where it began. It was a historical day for both the institution and the individuals. The graduating women represented half of the original number that had entered the

---

[50] John Grant, James Lynch and Ronald Bailey. West Point: The First Two Hundred Years (Gilford: The Globe Pequot Press, 2002), 167.

Academy four years earlier amid fierce male opposition, Army leadership scrutiny, and public curiosity. This was a day for celebration. "Every West Point commencement is an historic occasion. This one, with women graduates, takes on special significance. Every member of this class is to be congratulated for a job well done," said Secretary of Defense Harold Brown in his commencement address to the graduates, family, friends, and spectators gathered for the occasion.

Kathy remembered fondly the exhilaration of throwing her white hat high into the air.

> Like everyone else, when Vince Brooks issued his final command as Brigade First Captain, "Class Dismissed!" I launched my hat. During the four years, I experienced every emotion possible, from sheer terror to incredible exhilaration. I have often been asked if I would do it again. Fortunately, I do not have to do it again, so the question goes unanswered. Describing the impact of my experience at West Point would take years of therapy!

The following day, a picture of Kathy holding her diploma above her head ran in the *New York Times* along with an article, "Service Academies Hail First Female Graduates."[51]

The women of the West Point Class of 1980 are proven survivors and leaders. They triumphed after a four-year struggle that weeded out all but the strongest and most determined. While a nearly 50% attrition rate seems high, many West Point officials believed it would be far greater. "When you consider what they were up against—decades of ingrained prejudice and tradition—the real surprise is that this many made it. The survivors are remarkable young women, tough and resilient," a spokesman for USMA said.[52]

---

[51] By James Feron, May 29, 1980, p. A18.

[52] "Academy Women: Ready to Take Command," by William L. Chaze. U.S. News & World Report. May 26, 1980, p. 32-36.

Kathy's first assignment as a second lieutenant was as a student at the Signal Officer Basic Course at Fort Gordon, Georgia. There she lived in the Bachelor Officers Quarters (BOQ), on-post housing for single officers. The BOQ consisted of two-room apartments with shared kitchens. It was here that she and Dan Gerstein, a classmate, met. Kathy joked about their vastly differing experiences at the Academy.

> Dan was a corps squad (varsity) swimmer. Studying came much easier to him than it did for me. Rarely did he stay up past ten at night. He probably marched in a total of five parades. Meanwhile, I was up to all hours studying and highlighting my textbooks. There are times I think that we went to two different schools.

By the end of the course, the two were married. When fellow officers asked how they met, Dan replied laughing, "The Army issued her to me!"

The Gersteins were assigned jointly to Hoechst, Germany, the home station of the 22nd Signal Brigade but to different battalions within the brigade, Dan to the 17th Signal Battalion and Kathy to 32nd. The military couple quickly became a curiosity to their fellow soldiers. No one in their chain of command had ever known of two married officers who were both West Point graduates. They joined their respective units with many other young "butter bars."[53]

As signal officers, Dan and Kathy spent a significant amount of time in the field. Typically, signal units deploy prior to ground units to enable battlefield communications. They are among the last units to leave the field as communications structures and architectures are dismantled. The length of their field time varied with the scope of the exercise and the number of units involved. Some exercises lasted a few days; others lasted several weeks.

---

[53] Butter bars refer to the gold bars of a second lieutenant, the most junior rank for an Army officer.

As they entered their fifth year of service, the Gersteins decided they wanted to start a family. Raised by mothers who did not work, they determined one needed to be a full-time parent. Kathy said, "Being a platoon leader and executive officer were interesting and challenging, but I knew there were other things I wanted to do. Being a parent was first and foremost."

Kathy watched many servicewomen of all ranks have a child, take their 28 days of military maternity leave and go back out into the field. "I saw too many young female soldiers give their newborn to whoever would look after them and return to the field. This was not what Dan or I wanted to do to our child," recalled Kathy. In May 1985, nearly five years to the date she entered the Army, Kathy resigned her commission. She admitted that it was an easy decision since Dan liked the Army significantly more than she did.

Many of her West Point classmates also decided to leave active duty. Kathy remembered many invoking the unofficial class motto, "out and alive in '85," referring to the end of their five-year active duty service obligation. Few, however, made the decision to be a stay-at-home mom and Army wife. Making the choice was easy; living with it, initially, was not. Several senior officers in Kathy's unit questioned her choice, especially given that she had graduated in West Point's first class of women, the implication being that she was wasting her education and leadership experience. Kathy often responded that the Gersteins were still a military family. She recalled being pregnant and reading the West Point alumni publication, *ASSEMBLY* magazine, about her classmates who were achieving all kinds of professional accolades in their chosen careers. She remembered,

> It was tough. You sometimes have expectations of yourself, grounded in others' expectations of you. While it was a conscious and thought-out choice to raise our children, you cannot help but question your decision when you see the successes of others. When you leave something, there are often feelings of

anxiety. I have never regretted the decision. I think it would have been very difficult for both of us to be signal officers, remain in the military, and raise a family.

She continued, "When I got out, I was very thankful that we could afford for me to stay at home." Quickly, Kathy became involved as a volunteer in various support groups for soldiers' families. She found that her experience as an Army officer gave her instant credibility with the women as they acknowledged she understood the trials and tribulations of being in a military family in an overseas assignment.

As a volunteer, Kathy tried to eliminate the wearing of her husband's rank. She said, "In the military everyone is very rank conscious. Sometimes the volunteer chain of command in the family support groups tended to be the spousal mirror of the military unit. However, rank is not necessarily effective in a volunteer organization. What you really need are people willing to work together for the benefit of the group."

With Dan's acceptance into the graduate engineering school at Georgia Institute of Technology, the Gersteins returned stateside and moved to Atlanta. During the two years in Georgia, Kathy and Dan also became parents, bringing into the world two daughters, Sarah and Rachel, two years apart.

Assigned to the Pentagon following graduate school, the Gersteins moved to Gaithersburg, Maryland. Initially Dan served in the office of the Deputy Chief of Staff for Operations and Training and eventually became the aide-de-camp to the Vice Chief of Staff of the Army. As they were the only military family in their neighborhood, Kathy found this to be somewhat of a lonely time, especially during Dan's four-month deployment to Iraq and Saudi Arabia in support of Desert Storm. Attached to the 3rd Armored Division, then headquartered in Germany, the family support structure did not stretch to Maryland. It was assumed that living stateside, family members of deployed soldiers were near their own families and friends, and an organized group was unnecessary. Kathy turned her energy toward involvement with her daughters' school, volunteering as a class aide. She says that she also watched a lot of CNN.

> Since we weren't collocated with the unit Dan was attached to, I had no idea that groups had formed for a support system. After Dan came home and we moved to Fort Leavenworth, Kansas for his attendance at the Command and General Staff College (CGSC), I found out what other spouses had had in the way of support. I'm glad the Army has gone to this support system when service members are deployed.

After Operation Desert Storm, the Army adopted a more formalized family support structure. The rapid deployment of so many people demonstrated the need for a more structured group regardless of the military family's location. The military really relies on many women who are unpaid volunteers.

Five years later and back in Germany for a second tour of duty, Lieutenant Colonel Dan Gerstein assumed command of the 141st Signal Battalion, 1st Armored Division. During his two years of command, the unit deployed for a total of 18 months in support of military operations in the Balkans 1996-1998. Throughout this period Kathy realized the importance of family support groups. Most of the wives' groups tended to be grass roots organizations with women drawing on their experiences from church programs and school parent-teacher associations. Kathy admitted, "While this sounds trite, people in the military form close bonds. Typically, women are the spouses left behind and are the ones that come together to support and help each other." Kathy organized many activities for the families during these long deployments. They included sightseeing trips, hikes, coffees, lunches, and play dates for children. "My girls even helped out as babysitters, so the other women could have some personal time. Honestly, I really enjoyed making a small impact during the deployment." In Dan's absence, Kathy's relationship with her daughters strengthened as they often traveled throughout Germany, visiting various towns and sampling regional cuisine. Kathy recalled,

> I have always been conscious of how I allocate my time. I have never been one to spread myself too thin. I need to be able to focus. I was very involved with my girls. We do have a very close relationship. Even Dan has commented about the girls' bond with me.

In July 1998, the Gersteins returned to the States for Dan's next assignment at the National War College, in Washington D.C. Kathy remembered, "That was really a great year; Dan was home much more and had pretty regular hours. We were able to stay another two years in D.C. after he graduated and keep both the girls in a great school system." By 2003 and recently promoted to Colonel, Dan Gerstein became the Commander of the 93rd Signal Brigade at Fort Gordon, Georgia. The 93rd is a tactical signal brigade responsible for theater tactical communications support for the United States Army's Southern Command. At the time, the Army had only 13 signal brigades. While Dan Gerstein's focus as a commander was on preparing the unit's soldiers for war, Kathy's focus remained on her family.

As Sarah and Rachel began thinking about college choices, Kathy found herself very involved in the research. She laughed, "I did far more college search stuff with my daughters than I did myself. And while we often talked about West Point in our house, I was a little surprised when Sarah decided to seek admission to the Military Academy but I did support her."

Sarah received her appointment shortly after the United States invaded Iraq in March 2003. While both Dan and Kathy anticipated the Global War on Terror (GWOT) would be a long one, they, like many others, thought the United States would be out of Iraq in a few years.

Sarah's R-day was a little different than the one Dan and Kathy had experienced 23 years earlier. The Gerstein family drove to West Point with Sarah. They knew that once they said their 90-second goodbyes, they would not see her again unless they were able to pick her out of the 1300-plus new cadets and cadre in the parade later that afternoon that signified their daughter's rite of passage as a military officer-in-training. That day they gave their daughter to a demanding profession and to a country that she swore, as they had, to defend. Kathy remembered, "Being a nation at war, you try not to focus on the worrisome and frightening possibilities that may or may not exist. Besides, graduation for Sarah was four years in the future."

Like all the parents of the Class of 2007, Kathy and Dan were proud. Five classmates also had children entering the Class of 2007 and the couples met and looked for each other's new cadets in the parade. They reminisced while trying not to laugh when they realized how they must have looked their own first day of Beast Barracks. When asked about the comparison of her R-day with Sarah's, Kathy laughed, "No one was yelling at me!"

Kathy's most significant concern for Sarah was about all the physical demands, recalling her own challenges from running. As her cadet privileges increased and restrictions decreased, Sarah corresponded with her parents frequently. Sarah often asked both her parents for advice and counsel. Kathy has always tried to avoid getting into what she calls the "way back machine." Kathy said that, while there are similarities in their experiences, the environment is vastly different. Kathy remembered relying on postings on bulletin boards for plebe duty assignments, uniform notifications and meal announcements. Today, everything is via email and the Internet.

> Technology has had a huge impact. Cadets today are in constant communication with friends, family, and the outside world. Back in the mid-seventies, we prayed for letters once a week at best. Our knowledge of life outside West Point and what was occurring was based on what *The New York Times* thought we needed

to know and what we discussed in class. Now every cadet knows someone in Iraq and Afghanistan and can get real-time information on the global war on terror.

In many instances, Kathy provided Sarah more than a sympathetic ear regarding the hardships of being a cadet. Kathy recalled one conversation in which Sarah told her mother "she just didn't understand." Kathy thought briefly about listing examples from her own cadet days but realized how much has changed at West Point and that she probably did not understand the situation completely. Kathy said, "I didn't need to tell her to suck it up." When Sarah did complain about scheduled training events on Saturday, Kathy reminded her that when she was a cadet she had Saturday morning classes throughout the year and a thorough barracks room inspection that day.

Sarah's first year at West Point was also a year of transition for Kathy. The Gersteins bought a house in Virginia and a second income was needed to help pay for it. With Sarah in college and Rachel a high school junior, Kathy was ready to re-enter the workforce. She landed a position at the Office of the Chief Scientist of the Army. This particular agency is the Army's research and development office and its role is to research, design, develop, and commercialize the weapons systems and soldier support of the future. Initially, the position was for a year to replace temporarily an employee who decided to return to the active Army and Kathy was hired as contractor support. Two years later, she obtained a position as a Department of the Army civilian. One of the soldier support products that Kathy has been involved with is improved body armor for soldiers serving in combat zones.

During Sarah's final year at the Academy, the Army offered a new option intended to promote retention of officers after their five-year service obligation. Cadets willing to incur an additional three years of active duty service are guaranteed their choice of either branch, post, or graduate school, generally regardless of their class rank. Sarah discussed this option at great length with her parents. At the time, Dan was an active-duty colonel. The counsel the Gersteins provided was to leave oneself flexibility and options. Sarah heeded her parent's advice. She did receive both her first choice of branch and assignment, Military Intelligence and Fort Bragg, North Carolina.

The Army Sarah entered was a vastly different Army from the one Kathy served in during the early eighties. The United States was still in Iraq and still at war. Interestingly, one in seven U.S. soldiers in Iraq is a woman.[54] Kathy stated,

> The stakes just continue to increase. I am a mother. I feel it for Sarah and her classmates. I feel it for my classmates still on active duty. I know this is the best-trained military, but an IED shows no prejudice of training. It only takes one explosive or one sniper.

A year out from her own graduation, the Class of 1980 did not have people shooting at them. After tossing her own white cap into the air at Michie Stadium, Sarah and her family gathered at Sarah's sponsor's house for the bar-pinning ceremony. Kathy said,

> It was not a big party. It involved our family and Sarah's sponsor's family, a Colonel in the academic department—friends from many years prior whose sons swam with Sarah and Rachel on the Fort Myer summer swim team. Sarah, wearing the uniform of an Army officer for the first time, took her commissioning oath in a front yard overlooking the vast Hudson River. It was a simple, but profound, ceremony.

---

[54] Dr. Stephen Grove, USMA Historian. Remarks during the 2006 West Point Women's Conference, West Point, New York. April 2006.

Kathy admitted that Sarah's future in harm's way does scare her. She is, however, most impressed with Sarah's and her classmates commitment to the military.

> They did know what they were getting into, and they chose to stay. This is remarkable and very courageous. But now the cold, hard reality has set in. Within a few months of arriving at Ft. Bragg, Sarah deployed to Iraq.

Rachel's decision to attend the University of Mary Washington was a welcome one. While confident that Rachel physically and intellectually could handle West Point, Kathy believed that Rachel would not be happy with the regimentation of military life. She would be going for the wrong reasons—for her family and not for herself.

With her oldest daughter's graduation from her own alma mater, not a day goes by that Kathy does not think about the war on terror. Although Dan retired from active duty in 2006, he continues to be involved with national security, working for a training, simulation, and government services company. With three of four family members involved in the defense industry, the metaphorical elephant is always in the room. Kathy said, "My child is now in a profession in which they go to war. Soldiers march to the sound of guns. It is a clear and ever present danger, like that of firefighters and police officers."

It was a long, slow, and hard process in the beginning. Because of the challenges Kathy and her fellow classmates accepted and met graduates like Sarah, her daughter, no longer had to be concerned about being the first. The staff and faculty at the Academy, along with the Army, now have a generation of gender integration under their belts.

Much has changed in the 27 years separating Kathy's and Sarah's graduations from West Point. Technology is pervasive at the engineering institution. The cadet's reach to the world outside the

Spartan gates is instantaneous. They are in frequent communication with those they know serving in combat zones. Women are no longer a rare sight or a curiosity at the Academy.

Although graduates, regardless of gender, find themselves on the front line in a guerrilla war in the Middle East, the prohibition of women entering the combat branches of Infantry and Armor remains.

With ubiquitous and extensive media coverage, Kathy says that when she learns of an American soldier who has been killed, she learns about the family of that soldier—often in the person of the grieving mother. It is impossible not to be anxious and concerned for one's war-fighting child.

Cadet Kathy Wheless at U.S. Army Airborne School, Fort Benning, Georgia. *(Photo courtesy of Kathy Wheless Gerstein)*

The Gerstein family at Plebe Parent Weekend, West Point, NY, March 2004 (Dan, Rachel, Kathy, and Sarah). *(Photo courtesy of Kathy Wheless Gerstein)*

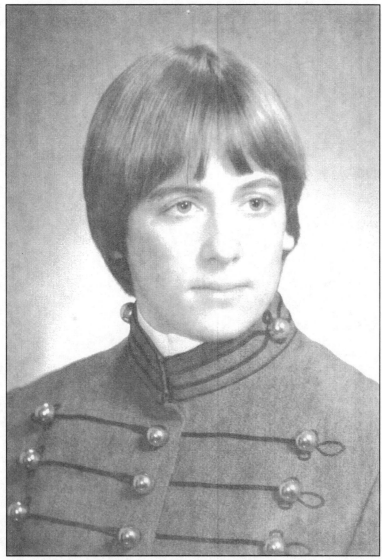

Cadet Lillian Pfluke, USMA 1980. *(Academy Photo)*

CLIMBING MOUNTAINS | MAJOR (RETIRED) LILLIAN A. PFLUKE, CLASS OF 1980

"Let me tell you what I think of bicycling. It has done more to emancipate women than anything else in the world. It gives a woman a feeling of freedom and self-reliance. I stand and rejoice every time I see a woman ride by on a wheel...the picture of free, untrammeled womanhood."

— Susan B. Anthony, 1896

Not familiar with Lil Pfluke as a cadet or officer, I came to learn about her through her interviews and commentaries on national television news programs such as *National Public Radio* and *The McNeil/Lehrer News Hour*. Candid and thoughtful, Lil regularly expressed her views on women in the military and their lack of opportunity. Being outspoken as an active duty officer has inherent risks, given a strong institutional culture pressuring one to be a team player and not to criticize doctrine or policy. Army officers are not supposed to sound like sociologists. Ironically, though, the United States Armed Forces have historically served as a microcosm for societal experiment and change. The military has been the great leveler of the playing field. One only has to look at the integration of black and women soldiers to see that it has served as the proving ground where people held back by discrimination could demonstrate their true skills and abilities.

The first few times I heard Lil interviewed, I did not understand why others might consider her views so controversial and significant. After all, women were in the military and performing well. Yes, there were and still are policies restricting women from combat units, specifically the Infantry, Armor, and Special Forces branches, but when one studies the advancement of women in the military since World War II, the progress has been significant. The Women's Army Corps[55] no longer exists, and women are serving in all branches of the Defense Department.

Lil's belief that women are "a separate and unequal class of soldier, able to endure all the risks and hardships of Army life but unable to reap the benefits,"[56] caused me pause for thought and reflection. Women, regardless of physical competence, mental toughness and leadership capabilities, remain excluded, by law and Army policy, from serving in combat arms units.[57] Technically and legally, ground infantry and armor combat operations are the purview of men only. This applies equally to specific positions and billets in the other combat arms branches of field artillery, air defense artillery, engineers, and aviation. At the same time, the jobs with the most influence and importance go to officers with extensive combat arms experience. Extremely limited access to combat arms positions, denies women the opportunity to compete for these jobs. Ground combat is paramount in the Army. The Army selects the vast majority of its senior leaders from branches with direct ground combat missions.

Although retired from the Army, Lil actively advocates for the expansion of the role of women in the Army. As the war on terrorism continues, women comprise nearly 15% of the active duty force, yet they remain barred from direct combat positions. Lil and others cite readiness as the driving reason for changing the policies on women in combat; the military needs the flexibility of using personnel more effectively. Servicewomen are in combat, are wounded (some severely), and are dying. Yet, the policy remains unchanged. She wrote:

---

[55] Major General Jeanne Holm, Women in the Military: An Unfinished Revolution. (Navato: Presidio Press) p. 285.

[56] Francine D'Amico and Laurie Weinstein, Gender Camouflage: Women and the U.S. Military. (New York: New York University Press, 1999) p.80-83.

[57] Army Regulation 600-13, Army Policy for the Assignment of Female Soldiers. March 27, 1992. www.army.mil/USAPA/epubs/pdf/r600_13.pdf.

I am confident that the current fusses involving military women (pregnancy rates, sexual harassment, fraternization, deployment issues, and so on) are all just growing pains and transitional problems that will get better as more and more women rise through the ranks. I am convinced however, that the issues will never go away until the Army adopts one simple policy: the best soldier for the job.[58]

Because of her love for sports and competition, especially football, many in her hometown of Palo Alto, California considered Lil a tomboy. She and her brothers loved running pass play options with their dad as the quarterback. Lil was the fastest, consistently out sprinting her brothers, diving and catching the long bomb passes. As the oldest of five children, she had an opportunity to lead at an early age. "There was always someone to lead around," she said. "So I learned early how to get others to do things they might not want to do otherwise."[59]

That she could not do something or play something just because she was a girl is something that Lil did not care to hear. She recalled, "When my brother John got a paper route, I wanted one, too. Unfortunately, the newspaper didn't want papergirls. So, I used my then four-year-old brother Paul's name to get the route. I was amused when, two years after I started my route, the newspaper finally changed its policy and allowed papergirls. They wrote an article about me as the first newspaper girl. I never told them I had had the route all along."[60]

Lil chalked up many other firsts. In high school, she was the first girl on the boys' swim team. She won the junior varsity city championship in both the butterfly and the freestyle sprint races her

[58] Francine D'Amico and Laurie Weinstein, Gender Camouflage: Women and the U.S. Military. (New York: New York University Press, 1999) p. 83.

[59] IBID., p. 80-83.

[60] IBID., p. 81.

first year. There were many articles about Lil in the local papers. She shakes her head at the memory, "I never understood what all the fuss was about. Of course, girls could compete with boys. Why not?"

Looking for smart, athletic, energetic girls to be in the first class of women, a West Point recruiter watching a high school swim competition found Lil. Living in California in a nonmilitary family, Lil had never heard of West Point, but the opportunity caught her attention because it offered all kinds of challenges. Lil said, "Shooting guns and jumping out of airplanes sounded like a lot more fun than just studying engineering at a civilian college."

Lil entered West Point on July 7, 1976, with 118 other women. Her family understood and nurtured her innate desire for challenge, and they drove across country in a van (two parents, five kids, and a dog) to see her enter the Corps of Cadets with the first class of women.

Everything at West Point was challenging—mentally, physically, academically, and emotionally. Lil said, "I loved every minute of it and pushed myself and others as hard as I could." Lil ranked first among the women of her class in physical aptitude throughout her four years. Although she anticipated some of the emotional challenges of breaking into a formerly all male club and the verbal hazing, she did not expect so much of it to be sexually degrading. Regardless of academic and physical performance and mental toughness, the hazing had a cumulative impact. Lil recalled:

> I never seemed to get a fair shake. Sure, everyone expects to get harassed as a plebe, but we women all seemed to get more than our share. It's no secret that we were regularly called bitch, whore, and worse; that we were accused of sexual promiscuity or lesbianism; that we were subjected to such inappropriate 'pranks' as shaving cream filled condoms in our bed or semen in our underwear drawer. What most people don't realize is the toll that juvenile and hateful treatments take on a person after a while. The constant barrage of

insults, harassment, and inequities made even the strongest among us harbor self-doubts. We all felt very isolated and defensive as a result of never being accepted as contributing members of the institution, and we became extraordinarily sensitive to all issues of prejudice.

Some male cadets vandalized various women's rooms. Others scribbled boorish sexual slurs on barracks and bathroom walls and mirrors. Upperclassman in one Cadet Company held a contest with the ultimate goal "to reduce every woman in the company to tears at least once."[61] Carol Barkalow, also a member of the class of 1980, wrote about the climate and similar instances in her book, *In the Men's House An Inside Account of Life in the Army by One of West Point's First Female Graduates.*

Lil sought refuge from the insults and comments in physical and military training. Continuing to challenge herself to her limits, Lil explained:

During my four years at West Point, I found that infantry training gave me the most personal satisfaction and seemed to be what I was best at. I relished the unique combination of mental and physical toughness required and sought out all of the infantry training experiences available to me, including the Jungle Operations Training Course in Panama and the Airborne School at Fort Benning. I was also selected as a cadet instructor for the challenging Recondo Course at West Point my firstie[62] year. I loved the intense physical demands, being outside, braving the elements, carrying everything I

[61] John Grant, James Lynch and Ronald Bailey. West Point: The First Two Hundred Years (Gilford: The Globe Pequot Press, 2002), 167.

[62] Firstie year is a cadet's senior year at West Point.

needed on my back, and finding my way in the woods. I especially enjoyed pushing myself to my personal limits. I enjoy risk, challenge, and adventure, and that is what the infantry offers.

At West Point, there were few gender-based limitations on participation. Women endure the same demands as the men—physically, academically, mentally, and militarily. However, there were two exceptions where gender dictated participation in different physical education classes. During plebe year, when the men fight through a semester of mandatory boxing, the women engage in a self-defense class. In the second year, when men grapple with wrestling, women practice advanced-level self-defense techniques. Even the opportunities for military schools during cadet summer assignments and the positions of leadership during various summer details are open to all.

Six months prior to graduation, Lil wrote a letter to then-Secretary of the Army John O. Marsh and requested an exception to the combat-exclusion policy and expressed her desire to become a commissioned officer in the Infantry. Even though denied, Lil was convinced that, once in the Army, she would be able to become an Infantry Airborne Ranger by consistently demonstrating physical, mental, and emotional competence and toughness. She never thought it presumptuous to aspire to become an Infantry battalion commander and an Airborne Ranger. Lil had internalized the West Point experience and Army socialization process that emphasized such goals and aspirations, and acknowledged them as important milestones in a career as an Army officer. She said,

> After all, for years every single role model I was exposed to in key senior leadership positions wore combat arms brass, airborne wings, and a Ranger tab.

Every Jody [63] cadence song started with *'I wanna be an Airborne Ranger.'* I didn't set out to be a maverick; I merely bought into the system and the institutional values as presented.

Prevented from entering a combat arms branch, Lil selected the Ordnance Corps for two reasons. She believed it to be a branch where she could best use her mechanical engineering degree, and she knew it was always close to the action. She spent six years running and leading maintenance facilities where everything necessary for a combat division—tanks, trucks, guns, and wheeled artillery—received repairs. "Army life was fun!" said Lil. "It's a real thrill to lead soldiers. To be part of a trained and smoothly functioning team is very fulfilling, especially when it is because of your efforts."

Determined to prove her ability and competence to be an Airborne Ranger Infantry battalion commander, Lil led by example. She had the airborne wings and nearly two hundred free fall parachute jumps. She recounted:

I was the National Military Triathlon Champion, the two-time National Military Cycling Champion, and the two–time inter-service European Ski Champion. I played rugby. I achieved a maximum score on every Army Physical Fitness Test taken in 15 years of service. I achieved a First Class score on the U.S. Marine Corps men's physical fitness test. I got a master's degree in mechanical engineering and years of perfect officer efficiency reports. I was physical, aggressive, and very competitive. I was a leader who could inspire people to their own personal bests by providing a powerful example and through my genuine infectious enthusiasm for adventure and challenge. Men

---

[63] A military cadence or cadence call is a traditional call-and-response work song sung by military personnel while running or marching. In the United States, these cadences are sometimes called jody calls or jodies, after Jody, a recurring character who figures in some traditional cadences.

followed me, bonded with me, respected me, and we fought as a team.

I was also absolutely consistent and outspoken about my views on women in the Army and their lack of opportunity. It was such a gnawing frustration for me to see wonderfully competent women not taken seriously because of the restrictions on our utilization. We were a separate class of soldier, able to endure all the risks and hardships of Army life but unable to reap the benefits. So, I wrote about these inequities, talked about them, and confronted my senior leaders about them. I quickly became an 'expert', but more important, an active-duty soldier willing to speak out on the record—a rarity in the Army because a strong part of the institutional culture is to be a team player and not 'rock the boat'. I wrote opinion pieces and did radio, television, and print interviews. Whenever the subject of Army women was in the news, so was my name.

Because of my notoriety, I was very close to the action as the Army leadership once again debated what to do about women in the years 1993-95. The actions and attitudes of the senior Army leadership in that time frame regarding the Army's women's assignment policies were extraordinarily disheartening and deeply personally disappointing to me. I had invested 19 years (four at West Point and 15 on active duty) proving my competence in the organization and suddenly realized that it was not a matter of competence. The Army was content to choose less qualified men over more qualified women for its key leadership positions because of politics and a deeply entrenched and dated attitude. In fact, it was fighting desperately for the ability to continue to do so.

As I approached consideration for lieutenant colonel, I realized that my personal ambitions of being an Airborne Ranger and Infantry battalion commander had slipped away. Since my hope for that institution was stalemated and my personal goals were unrealizable, I reluctantly concluded that with them went my reason for staying in the Army. I wanted to play on the varsity team and be a contributing member of the first string. I did not want to be tucked away in some support role. I retired on September 30, 1995.[64]

Not one to dwell in the past or on disappointments, Lil began focusing on other passions and goals of importance. Peter, Lil's husband, had recently accepted an assignment in France as the Defense Attaché. The family made the move overseas with two young boys, ages three and five. Lil accepted a part-time opportunity with the American Battle Monuments Commission to encourage the long-term support and maintenance for more than 1,000 neglected U.S. battle monuments privately built in Europe. She also helped Peter in the development and delivery of leadership training and motivation seminars for U.S. Army units in Europe. Many of these seminars held at various European battlefields, including Omaha Beach and Utah Beach in Normandy; focus on the impact of technology and terrain on military maneuvers and operations.

Not surprisingly, Lil continued her athletic pursuits. "I always wanted to be a competitive cyclist," she recalled. Lil competed with fierce determination in all kinds of cycling events—long distance road races, time trials, cyclocross, cross country mountain bike races, and track events. In the fall of 2002, at age 43

---

[64] Francine D'Amico and Laurie Weinstein, Gender Camouflage: Women and the U.S. Military. (New York: New York University Press, 1999) p. 80-83.

and in the best shape of her life, Lil Pfluke ranked 103rd among female cyclists in France, the "high-water" mark of her cycling career. This is especially impressive when you consider the average age of her competitors was 25. Competing in the World Masters Cycling Championships in Melbourne, Australia, Lil finished on the podium four times in various disciplines. She won a gold medal in the cross-country mountain bike, a silver medal in the road time trial, and two bronze medals in separate track events.

Returning home to Paris as a Masters World Cycling Champion, Lil scheduled a routine annual mammogram. Again, Lil recalled, "I needed to have my annual exam, so I scheduled it for the day I flew back to France, given that most of the day was shot to traveling." Immediately after the mammogram, she learned that further checks were needed and scheduled an ultrasound that same day. The doctor suspected breast cancer and informed her that surgery was required immediately. "What the hell are you talking about?" Lil asked. She had no symptoms and had never felt any lumps during regular self-exams. Two days later, Lil was lying on an operating table having two lumps removed from her left breast. The lumps were tested immediately and found to be cancerous. She described:

> I was in total shock. I also knew that I needed to get well. So there I was, recovering from the lumpectomy and facing chemotherapy, radiation, and an eventual mastectomy. Breast cancer can spread to the brain, bone and liver. I was spending a lot of time in waiting rooms anticipating the outcome of various tests. It was all very surreal and certainly my worst nightmare. I think it is easier for an athlete in the long run, because of the physical shape you are in. The athletic stuff centered me. I am not just a cancer patient; I am a mom, wife and athlete. I knew I had to keep living my life on my terms and marching down the paths, I wanted to take. So I kept cycling. The irony was that

working out made me feel better, even though I was puking my guts out. I had to get well. Naturally, my family was worried, but I didn't have time to worry. As the patient, you are fighting the fight. You do not have a lot to give to those caring for you. I never got off my bike. Each day I rode my bike 10 kilometers to and from the hospital for radiation treatments. Before that, I had ridden all through my chemotherapy treatments. I even did races. It was very important to continue to train, race and live my life as an athlete. Unfortunately, the cure makes you feel terrible. [65]

Between her third and fourth chemotherapy treatments, Lillian won a bronze medal at the World Masters Cyclocross Championship in Belgium. She also competed in triathlons, mountain bike races, and long-distance cycling races. Some triathlons she did with her two sons, each taking one leg of the competition.

While still receiving cancer treatments, Lillian applied for the Tour of Hope, a cross-country cycling journey sponsored by Bristol-Meyers Squibb Company. The tour covers 3,300 miles of varying landscape in nine days, starting in Los Angeles, California proceeding through the Mojave Desert, across the plains of Texas, through the hills of Arkansas and along the streets of towns in Indiana and Ohio, before finishing on the Ellipse on the National Mall in Washington, D.C. Passion propels this particular tour's members. "The riders—survivors, caretakers, healers, advocates and researchers—shared one mission, to help future generations move closer to the ultimate miracle—the cure."[66] Lillian was one of 26 people selected from an applicant pool of more than 1,000. The Tour required participation in an intense training regimen with 25 other cancer survivors. For Lil, it was the perfect challenge. To reach the physical goal of the ride the organization provided all the equipment

---

[65] Major (retired) Lillian Pfluke (interview with author), June 2005.

[66] www.tourofhope.org/team/2003_toh_team.htm.

and training regimens; the team members motivated each other. "The whole team was just awesome," Lil recalled fondly.

While Lil thoroughly enjoyed riding as part of the Tour of Hope team, she had some unfinished business with more bicycling to accomplish. The Tour of Hope completed as a relay with team members riding two three-hour shifts on each of the tour's nine days. Lil rode the noon to 3:00 P.M. and midnight to 3:00 A.M. shifts daily. Feeling she had missed seeing much of the United States because she was riding in the dark or someone else was riding, Lil vowed to cross the United States herself on a bicycle.

Cancer exhibits no prejudice. It invades men and women alike. A diagnosis of cancer is shocking and frightening to most. To a well-conditioned athlete like Lil, however, it was most surprising. Beating cancer taught her some life lessons. "It was a very powerful experience. It made me more humble. It made it easier to prioritize. Now I have a clear sense of direction — where I am going and what I am doing. I have much more empathy for other people. It is not as easy to blow by people when I am in a hurry, and they aren't. You never know what they are going through."

To celebrate the end of her cancer treatments on July 11, 2003, Lil and her two sons, Christopher and Raymond, climbed upon their triple bike and rode up L'Alpe d'Huez. For professional cyclists, this is one of the premier stages of the Tour de France. It is the start of the 9.6-mile, 3,800-foot climb to the mountaintop gateway to the Alps. The route has 21 switchbacks, or what the French call "bends." The average grade is 7.9 percent, with some sections as steep as 14 percent. The course ends in rarified air at 6,102 feet. The day after their climb, the three watched Lance Armstrong climb that mountain enroute to winning his fourth consecutive Tour de France title.

Lil continues to seek out challenges to meet with the same vigor and resolve she served with in the military and with which she fought cancer. In July 2005, Lil competed in the Grande Boucle Féminine Internationale, the Women's equivalent of the Tour de France, finishing in 58th place. "It was a wonderful experience, but hard as hell, "she said.

The following summer, Lillian fulfilled her personal pledge to cross the United States again. She and her two sons embarked on their triple bicycle in Astoria, Oregon and began pedaling across the country. Fifty-two days later, they finished their journey in Portsmouth, New Hampshire. Lil shared, "It was a fabulous experience to spend that much time and share in such a challenge with my two teen-aged boys. We had days that were so hard we just wanted to sit on the side of the road and cry. We had days where the sun shone and the wind blew us so well we hardly had to pedal. It was a wonderful way to see the country and an amazing summer."

Taking advantage of her fabulous physical shape, after cycling nearly 6,000 kilometers cross-country, Lil entered the 2006 Masters World Bicycle Track Championships. Her goal for the competition in Manchester, England was to break the Masters World Hour Record. The record for women 35 and older stood at 40.7556 kilometers ridden in one hour around the velodrome. For women 40 and older, the record stood at 40.7110 kilometers. Lil rode 41.2397 kilometers in one hour smashing the previous set world record.

Being a cancer champion is a new phenomenon for Lillian. She is still reflecting upon and processing the experience, but she knows that she wants to be influential in the fight against cancer. "I don't yet have a clear vision of exactly what my contribution is going to be in the long term," she said. "I do know I have a lot to offer." No doubt, Lil will continue riding over, around, through any limit perceived, or imposed.

Lillian Pfluke during chemotherapy treatment for breast cancer. (*Photo courtesy of Lillian Pfluke*)

Lillian Pfluke, post cancer, breaking the world hour record in Manchester, England at the 2006 Masters World Bicycle Track Championships, September 10, 2006. (*Photo courtesy of Lillian Pfluke*)

Cadet Becky Halstead, USMA
1981, dressed in full dress
uniform prior to a parade. *(Photo
courtesy of Becky Halstead)*

STEADFAST LEADERSHIP | BRIGADIER GENERAL REBECCA S. HALSTEAD, CLASS OF 1981

"Therefore, my beloved brethren, be steadfast, immovable, always abounding in the work of the Lord, knowing that your labor is not in vain in the Lord."

— I Corinthians 15:38

In August 2004, Rebecca Halstead made an indelible mark on history, becoming the first female West Point graduate to achieve the rank of Brigadier General. Two days later, Becky assumed her new post as commanding general of the 3rd Corps Support Command (COSCOM) based in Wiesbaden, Germany. Promoted "below the zone"[67] multiple times, it is not surprising that Becky was the first female Academy graduate to reach the general officer level—and by all accounts, those promotions were more than well deserved. In August 2006, she assumed command of the Army's Ordnance Center and Schools, the first female to be the Chief of Ordnance.

Becky Halstead is a woman of small stature, standing 5 feet 2 inches, and this is rounding up. In talking with Becky, however, she becomes a giant with an enormous commitment to her nation and to those with whom she serves. Becky is fond of saying that she is just a country girl from a town with no traffic lights. Hailing from Willseyville, New York, Becky grew up in a family filled with faith and patriotic values. Her father instilled a powerful, disciplined work ethic and the highest standard of morality and integrity. Truly, "do not lie, cheat, or steal, or tolerate those who do"[68] was imbued in Becky before she became a cadet at West Point in 1977 in the second class to accept women. Her father Dick served in the Air Force for four years, and as a youngster Becky loved dressing up in his uniform. A favorite childhood memory includes her grandfather's faithful raising of Old Glory to the top of their flagpole each

---

[67] "Below the Zone" indicates promotion in advance of one's military commissioning year cohort.

[68] The West Point Honor Code.

morning. She grew up in a Christian home, grounded in faith in God, and surrounded by women of strong character, especially her mother and grandmother—the latter a church missionary in Canada in the 1920s. Raised for the most part as a Baptist, Becky often listened to stories and Sunday sermons about serving God by serving others. The seed of selfless service planted at a very early age grew more meaningful throughout the years.

Becky credits her mother for pointing her in the direction of West Point. Her mother read an article in the local newspaper about the service academies opening their doors to women, and Becky recalled, "My mom read the article aloud to me and said, 'you are just what the academies are looking for, and this sounds just like you!" Betty Jeanne Halstead truly believed her daughter had all the right qualities that the academies sought: solid academics, athletic participation, and involvement in church and community. Most importantly, her mother and her entire family believed in Becky and her potential. She also received encouragement from many people in her small, tight-knit town. Although Candor High School had never had a student graduate from the Military Academy, the guidance counselor, various sports coaches, many teachers and long time friends, and members of her church encouraged Becky to seek an appointment to West Point. Her varsity sport coach, Carole LaVena, was especially influential. Becky said, "Before joining the Army, my dream was to be a gym teacher and be a coach for women's sports, like Coach LaVena. In the end, what she taught me most was to dream big, be very disciplined, and never ever quit." Carole died in a parachute accident at 28 during Becky's junior year in high school. Yet Becky and Carole's mother, Mrs. Liz LaVena, remain close to this day. "Mrs. LaVena always tells me Carole is watching over me and would be very proud," Becky said. The relationships Becky develops with people are enduring and deep. She cherishes those who have made a difference in her life along the way. From hometown friends to West Point and the Army, she remains steadfast in her friendships. When Becky returns to her hometown, she regularly gets "the girls" together for lunch, which includes some of the older women and widows as well as her grade school friends. They were there for Becky when she was growing up and now, whenever she can manage it, Becky is there for them.

When Becky entered West Point in 1977, she had strong patriotic feelings but gave little thought to a career in the military. "I applied, never dreaming I would be accepted," she said. "Surprised by my appointment, I could not turn down the unique opportunity, so I attended." That year, 104 women entered the Academy; 63 would graduate four years later.

Her reception into West Point was a challenge, and being short was certainly no advantage. With each new rigor, whether military, physical, or academic, Becky's small successes and triumphs slowly increased her confidence that West Point was the right choice. Playing on the volleyball, softball and team handball teams, as well as managing the women's basketball and swimming teams, gave her a refuge from the demands of cadet life. Becky's parents regularly made the three-and-a-half-hour drive south to cheer on their daughter and various Army sports teams. Becky said,

> They came to most home football games with their best friends, Janet and George Jeffrey, who provide the tailgate party boodle[69] for my teammates and company mates. My mom and dad were the "911" call if I ever wanted to quit. They were totally and unconditionally supportive.

When Becky began her junior year at West Point, she knew she had at least seven years remaining in the service—two more at West Point and five years as an officer to fulfill her service obligation. A long, but manageable, period. Looking back, Becky remembered, "I did not have any intentions of serving 20 years." Now, having served 27 years in the Army, Becky offers guidance to many soldiers, reflecting on her own experience:

---

[69] Boodle is cadet slang for food, from home and elsewhere, not served in the mess hall.

I often encourage soldiers not to burden themselves thinking about a 20-year career. I believe in focusing on small increments and honorably fulfilling the commitment you have signed up for, be it a West Point obligation or an enlistment contract. As a leader, though, it is my responsibility, and I believe the responsibility of others in senior positions, to inspire, encourage, and challenge subordinates to desire the long-term commitment to duty in the profession of arms by being a positive example for them.

Upon graduation from the Academy and commissioning in the Ordnance Corps, Becky knew she wanted to serve in at least two different assignments to experience varied people, commanders, and locations. She also knew she wanted to command a company. As it turned out, she had two company commands, back to back. During the second command, an extremely satisfying professional experience, she started thinking about a career that would extend beyond the required five years.

As a lieutenant in Italy, she married another Army officer and then had to consider the challenges of dual military careers and the possibility of raising a family. During her time in company command, Becky's marriage faced many challenges, and her health suffered. Her marriage ended in divorce, and she experienced her third major surgery in three years. She accepted the failure of her marriage with a deep desire to learn from the experiences, to avoid making the same mistakes twice, and to share with others the lessons learned.

Now single, Becky began looking at career decisions in a significantly different way not having to consider the impact on a spouse of assignments and moves. West Point's Department of Physics approached her with an option to attend graduate school and return to the Academy to teach. She found this ironic given her unremarkable undergraduate academic performance in the hard sciences. Nonetheless, the prospect was attractive. Becky sought the counsel of then-Colonel (now retired Major General) Dewitt "T" Irby, her commander, mentor, and occasional dispenser of "tough love." While he would not tell Becky what to do, he told her that her "strength was with and in leading people, not sitting behind a desk evaluating the trajectory of an ordnance round in flight." Part of Becky's decision-making process is her commitment to prayerfully consider her options. Each morning she tries to allocate time to quiet thought, prayer and devotion, a practice Becky learned from her family. Her grandmother often said, "We stand our tallest when we are on our knees in prayer."

In the end, Becky turned down graduate school and took a posting as a personnel officer for her branch instead. She assumed the responsibility for the assignment of junior officers to duty positions and military units around the globe.

As a captain, she served as the first female aide to a three-star general, then Lieutenant General Leon Salomon (who retired as a four-star General), and aide to Lieutenant General Sam Wakefield. As a Lieutenant Colonel, she commanded the 325th Forward Support Battalion, 25th Infantry Division (Light), based at Schofield Barracks, Hawaii.

During battalion command, Becky coined the phrase "Steadfast Leadership" as a way to convey to the 900-plus soldiers and leaders in her command her life, leadership and soldiering principles and priorities. As both a phrase and acronym, the words have powerful meaning. Steadfast in the *Random House College Dictionary* means "firm or unwavering in purpose, resolution, faith, and adherence." Halstead said,

> I like the simplicity and power. It defines my focus, priorities, and attitude. My soldiers know what is important. To me, steadfast means: Soldiers, Training, Excellence, Attitude, Discipline, Family and Friends, Accountability, Service, and Teamwork.

In 2002, as a colonel, she served as the executive assistant to four-star General Tom Hill, the Combatant Commander, United States Southern Command. This assignment followed her two-year brigade command as the Division Support Commander with the 10th Mountain Division at Fort Drum, New York. As she reflected on her career, Becky said, "I never got any assignment I asked for, but each assignment prepared me for increased responsibilities in subsequent ones."

Lieutenant Colonel Mark Migaleddi has served with General Halstead on two occasions; first as a major and staff officer in the 10th Mountain Division Support Command and at the Ordnance School as the Chief of Plans and Operations. Migaleddi said,

> General Halstead truly views each soldier in her command as a member of her family. She is a steadfast leader, unwavering in her commitment to others. She is also human and incredibly engaging. I remember, like it was yesterday, her in-brief when she became our commander at the 10th Mountain Division. In telling us who she is, she shared that she had experienced failure in a marriage that ended in divorce You could have heard a pin drop. Few, if any, leaders—let alone senior leaders—like to admit weakness or failure. Yet what Halstead conveyed was that she too is human.

Colonel Halstead deployed the Division Support Command to Uzbekistan and Afghanistan after the September 11 terrorist attacks.

Becky has kept meticulous notes throughout her Army career. "I have every steno pad from the rank of captain forward," she said. "They contain notes beneficial for the next potential leadership position; the memories and lessons learned along the way of the good, the bad and the ugly; and personal notes of reflection regarding the experiences and people who have come into my life during this military journey." She believes each day brings new opportunity to learn and to be better than the day before. Doing so has helped her prepare for the future and to help others do the same.

As Becky advanced through the officer ranks, people began telling her she could become a general officer. She says, "It would just flabbergast me. I never really allowed myself to look more than two jobs ahead. At some point, yes, I knew the reality of general officer existed, but I never let myself go there because of the potential let down, not so much for me but for all those who were pushing and pulling for me." It was only when Becky pinned on colonel's eagles in June 2000 and was in brigade command that she accepted the reality of attaining the rank of general officer.

Selected for Brigadier General in 2003, she took her first posting as the Deputy Commanding General for the 21st Theater Support Command in Europe. She served in this position as a promotable Colonel, pinning on her first star on August 31, 2004, just days before taking command of the 3rd Corps Support Command.

The long gray line, the metaphor used to describe the perpetual connection of West Point's graduates to those who came before them, was personified at Becky's promotion ceremony to general. In attendance were Colonel Susan Sowers, class of 1982 and Commander of the 37th Transportation Command in Germany at the time and later Becky's Chief of Staff for deployment to Iraq, and Susan's parents. Susan's father William, class of 1957 and Mary, her mother were also present. Mary's father was retired Major General Johnson, class of 1928. One set of stars used for Becky's promotion ceremony belonged to Susan's grandfather, Major General Johnson. In giving Halstead his general stars, he continued a tradition in the Long Gray Line of passing rank insignia from one graduate to another. Along with her family, many of Becky's Army friends, a West Point roommate, childhood friends, and half of her hometown from upstate New York attended the ceremony. "It was all very exciting," she said, "and one of the absolute best days. But this achievement was not something I did by myself." Retired Major General Dewitt Irby remarked, "Somebody had to be first and who better? No one could have been better in my mind." Irby, along with

Richard, Becky's father, pinned a single star on each of the lapels on her battle dress uniform. Betty Jeanne helped her daughter affix the ceremonial general officer pistol belt, and Joseph Barron, Becky's nephew, pinned a star on his aunt's Kevlar helmet.

A general's stars are heavy. With them, one carries an incredible responsibility to soldiers, their families and to the nation. Becky recognizes this and asserts, "I believe with the increase in rank comes the greater responsibility to serve than to be served, and the old adage of 'rank has its privileges' should really be 'rank has its responsibilities.'" Brigadier General Halstead clearly understood the reality that she had been entrusted with the lives of several thousand people. "These soldiers are America's sons, daughters, mothers, and fathers. They have families, they make personal sacrifices, and they selflessly serve our Nation," she often reminds herself.

With her promotion to general officer rank came a division-level command assignment, the 3rd Corps Support Command based in Wiesbaden, Germany. She would have less than a year to prepare the logistics command for a deployment to Iraq. As commander, her mission would be two-fold: to move and distribute all supplies needed by the Army in Iraq—be they bullets, fuel, food, ice, spare parts or boots, and to train Iraq Security Forces in logistical processes. Brigadier General Halstead said, "I know that, bar none, this mission may be the most important, most historic of any we, not just me but all the members of our team, have ever experienced in our lives. With God's strength, the support of friends, families and a grateful Nation, we will serve professionally and return with honor."

Becky often talks about the personal courage and achievements of women throughout history, ordinary women who have made extraordinary contributions. In her speech for Women's History Month at West Point in March 2005, Becky said,

> Women past and present have opened a new book on
> the shaping of the world through personal, social, and
> spiritual courage, which influence men and women in
> all walks of life. What I have discovered as I reflect on

my own life is, the more responsibility I am given, the more I depend on personal courage to lead and serve. Personal courage takes us out of our comfort zone. Ultimately, it is our gut, our values, our human instinct for right and wrong, which tells us when we should take a stand and take action. I often wonder if I would have possessed the personal and spiritual courage to act on my convictions as women like Rosa Parks[70] and Corrie Ten Boom.[71] If not, what is missing in my life that they possessed to do so? Perhaps these women 'up-armored'[72] themselves and their character with their conviction and faith. I know their actions encourage me to up-armor myself with my faith and with the Army values that are etched not only on my dog-tags which I drape over my head each day, but also etched in my heart...Loyalty, Duty, Respect, Selfless Service, Honor, Integrity, and Personal courage.

As the deployment date for Operation Iraqi Freedom neared, many eyes focused on the 3rd Corps Support Command (COSCOM). It was the first combat command group comprised solely of women–Brigadier General Becky Halstead, Commander, Colonel Sharon Duffy, the Deputy Commander, and Colonel Susan Sowers, Chief of Staff. At various times throughout their Army careers, these three

---

[70] One of Becky's particular heroes is Rosa Parks. Becky says, "I don't think she ever suspected that she would turn a page in history by refusing to give up her seat on the bus in 1955. She was simply tired from a long day's work and fed up with being pushed around. Think of the personal courage she needed to stand up for herself, and in doing so, sparked the fires of change that led to desegregation."

[71] Yet another hero of Becky's is Corrie Ten Boom who rescued Jewish people and members of the Dutch Resistance to the Nazi occupation during the holocaust until she was betrayed in 1944. Ten Boom lost her whole family except one brother in the concentration camps.

[72] The term "up-armored" is in reference to the Army's adding of additional armor to its High Mobility Multipurpose Wheeled Vehicle, or "HMMWV," beefing up protection for vehicles already in the field.

officers had worked together as part of a team. "Do we think it's neat? We think it's neat because we've known each other for years," said Halstead. "We all commanded companies together in the same battalion. We've grown up in the Army together. We never would have dreamed we'd all end up together in Iraq." Accomplished in their own right, none of the three chose the other for their respective positions. The stars and assignments just aligned, putting these three officers in the same command group. "We knew people were looking at us. Our focus, individually and collectively, was on the mission, not three women in the command group." Because there are so few women in high-ranking positions in the military, let alone in combat in Iraq, some thought the command's leadership was unique. "Gender does not differentiate how we accomplish our mission," affirmed Halstead. She however, does acknowledge the fact that who and where they are is significant. Halstead said, "It's encouraging for younger women as they see anything is possible." She was one of 14 female generals in an Army of more than 460,000 soldiers.

One year after assuming command, Brigadier General Halstead deployed the 3rd Support Command to Iraq. While in Iraq, Becky led a team of more than 20,000 soldiers and 5,000 civilians, dispersed among 50 bases throughout Iraq and Kuwait. Commanded by a major general (2-star) most combat divisions only number approximately 16,000 soldiers. The Support Command's mission was to orchestrate the theater logistics to sustain Coalition Forces serving in Operation Iraqi Freedom and provide support and training as part of the overall partnership effort with the Iraqi Security Forces. Simply stated, Halstead's position required her to determine how nearly all items the United States Army needs and uses in Iraq are transported. In addition to ensuring the logistics mission was successful, she also had the responsibility of implementing a new Army logistical support organization.

Prior to Operation Iraqi Freedom, combat division commanders operated with logistic support organic to their division with a colonel in command of what was known as a division support command, typically comprised of Ordnance, Transportation, and

Quartermaster battalions. The support commander reported directly to the division commander, as Becky had as a colonel and commander of the 10th Mountain Division Support Command. The transformation of logistics involved a cultural shift, as most division commanders initially felt they were losing an organic and large unit. It was Brigadier General Halstead's responsibility to prove that the division commanders did not lose a brigade and a full colonel but gained more battalions with supply chain expertise and a general to manage it all.

With a flattened organizational structure, all the logistics and sustainment capabilities were part of 3rd COSCOM and worked directly for Halstead. In actuality, Halstead described the new configuration as providing the combatant commander more flexibility on the battlefield. "The division commander gives me the mission of what needs to be accomplished, and we provide the solution, assuming all the risks," she said.

Task organized, her command included a combination of the Army's new Sustainment Brigades, traditional Corps Support Groups, Infantry Brigade Combat Teams, and Area Support Groups. With the Army transformation, the command and control of the logistics brigades moved from the Infantry and Armor Divisions to the Corps Support Command (now called the Expeditionary Sustainment Command). This was a significant change, and executing the transition and transformation while at war proved challenging, but Halstead and her team expertly implemented and pushed logistics transformation for the Army into the 21st century.

Complex and diverse, the 3rd COSCOM mission included force protection and base defense, theater security for the major supply routes across Iraq, logistical requirements of feeding, equipping, and transporting of forces, and providing soldiers with water, fuel, ammunition, repair parts, and all needed supplies. As Halstead put it, "If the soldiers in Iraq ate it, drank it, drove it, moved it, flew it, wore it, shot it, or fixed it, it was our responsibility to anticipate, plan, coordinate and synchronize the distribution to get it to them." The Command moved all classes of supply throughout the theater of operations, from Camp Arifjan in Kuwait to Mosul in Iraq, over a road network of more than 3,000 miles.[73] In the COSCOM's year of combat service, they provided food for 115 million meals and established water-bottling plants that produced more than 100 million liters of bottled water. Handled nearly eight million pieces of mail. Produced nine million gallons of water daily through reverse osmosis water purification systems. Transported 1.5 million gallons of fuel daily and maintained 28 million gallons of fuel at nine storage locations. Operated 15 ammunition locations. Completed over 73,000 maintenance work orders and processed over $7 million worth of repair parts just for vehicle air conditioners.[74] With more than 10,000 vehicles in the command, putting an average of 3,000 vehicles a night on the road, they conducted more than 37,000 convoys, accumulating over 108 million miles driven on IED-laden roads. More than 70% of their transportation operations were conducted at night, and they experienced more than 1,000 IED attacks, more than 350 small arms attacks, and more than 100 complex attacks (combination of small arms fire, IEDs, RPGs, etc). By all accounts and numbers, the Support Command performed superbly.

In the course of their year in a theater of war, the COSCOM suffered 291 military wounded in action, of which 243 were returned to duty within the theater; an incredible testament to the medical support and superior personal protective equipment and up-armored vehicles. The personnel losses were still too great and most certainly one of the hardest burdens a commander bears. It is a statistic that Halstead will not forget.

In her pocket, Brigadier General Halstead carries a second set of dog tags. Unlike the ones around her neck, these contain the names of the 25 soldiers, who did not come home from Iraq and the dates killed in action. Becky reflected,

---

[73] www.globalsecurity.org/military/agency/army/3coscom.htm.

[74] John D. Banusiewicz, Armed Forces Information Services "3rd Support Command Delivers Food for OIF Forces." 28 Jan 04, www.defense.gov/news/Jan2004/n01282004_200401281.html.

One might point to the size of our command of 20,000 and say 25 combat causalities is a statistically small number. However, for each one of those soldiers' families, it is not a small number; it is 100%. Each time I reach in my pocket, I can feel their presence. It keeps me cognizant of the sacrifices our soldiers and their families made and will continue to make.

Halstead bid farewell to each plane out of Balad Air Base in Iraq as her soldiers returned home, personally saying thank you to all the soldiers. On September 18, 2006, with the mission accomplished, the 3rd COSCOM returned with honor to its home station in Wiesbaden, Germany. In her final message to the 20,000 soldiers in her command, Brigadier General Halstead again said thank you. She wrote:

> Thank you! I believe these two words are the most important words I can say to capture my final message to all of you. Soldiers, leaders, civilians, family members, and friends.
>
> Thank you for:
> - making a difference in my life, personally and professionally.
> - making a difference in the lives of others...your own family, your unit, your battle buddy, the Iraqis, your community, your family readiness group, our military—present and future—and most importantly, our nation!
> - serving...selflessly serving and sacrificing personal pleasures and comfort for something much bigger than yourself.

- your positive attitude, endless energy, and focus until the mission's complete.
- And thank you for being an integral part of the team...part of the solution...critical to our mission success and completion.

Being your commander for the past year has been an extraordinary experience for me. There have been life-changing moments and events, new relationships and friendships, and a scrapbook of memories that will never be surpassed in my lifetime.

Thank you for being the ones who filled those pages of memories—the words, the photos, the emotions, the smiles, the touches, the tears, the ribbons, the awards, the honors, and the final ideal of duty, honor, and country that will be forever pressed on my heart and mind.

God bless, keep and strengthen each of you as you journey back home to new babies, new assignments, new adventures...my life is better for having had you in it...our TEAM and our world is better because of YOU.

Accomplishing the mission was not easy. Becky understood that fact going in and now reflects on her year in Iraq as one of the best in her life, yet one of the hardest. Although she fully accepted that, as the commander, she was responsible for all her unit did or failed to do, she also fully credits her team with the successes achieved. As she said, "Success is a team sport, and we should each define our success by how we make others successful." Her goal was to complete the mission, set the conditions for success for the next unit and depart Iraq with a respectable team reputation for service and support to others. Without doubt, the intensive training and preparation before deploying ensured that her soldiers, individually and as units, had the requisite skills and confidence first and foremost as soldiers and warriors. They left Iraq with a well-deserved reputation of competent logisticians who had ensured the sustainment of Coalition Forces across the spectrum of operations on the battlefield in Iraq.

While the debate in Congress continues about the role of women in combat, Becky Halstead was the only female commanding general in theater and the first female ever to lead this large a unit in combat. Her units served in a theater of war where, given the indiscriminate nature of the insurgency and a battlefield not distinguished by front and rear lines, every soldier and leader trained and prepared to engage in combat operations. There is no front line on an asymmetrical battlefield; the potential for combat exists at every location. She believes the truth is in the facts and the contributions made by women across all ranks and services. She does not categorize her soldiers as male or female. She leads soldiers, firmly believing that all soldiers, male and female, across all military occupational skills, are combat multipliers in today's military. It is their character and competence, not gender that counts most of all. Every soldier is proving his or her value and contributing to our Nation's freedom each day. Halstead said,

> As a military leader, I have always tried to remain focused on the soldier—the centerpiece of our formation—and forming successful teams. My simple desire has been to do what is right, and, at the end of the day and perhaps in some small measure, make a difference in somebody else's life. It truly is impossible to separate the personal from the professional. It is my faith in God that provides my anchor and balance in life.

When asked about gender, Brigadier General Halstead said, "You can make an issue of gender if you want to, or you can figure out other ways to skin the cat. I've always tried to figure out other ways to skin that cat."

Richard and Betty Jeanne Halstead are all smiles following Becky's graduation from West Point in May 1981. *(Photo courtesy of Becky Halstead)*

Brigadier General Becky Halstead with her parents Betty Jeanne and Richard after pinning on generals' stars. *(Photo courtesy of Becky Halstead)*

Brigadier General Becky Halstead in Iraq exiting a UH-60 Black Hawk Helicopter. *(Photo courtesy of Associated Press)*

Brigadier General Becky Halstead poses with soldiers from the 29th Brigade Combat Team (BCT), a brigade in Halstead's command, following a Naturalization Ceremony in Balad, Iraq. These soldiers, all Samoan, became US citizens during that ceremony. *(Photo courtesy of Becky Halstead)*

Cadet Cynthia Ramirez, USMA 1990. *(Academy Photo)*

Coming Home | Chaplain Cynthia R. Lindenmeyer, Class of 1990

"Each of our lives affects the other, and the other affects the next, and the world is full of stories, but the stories are all one."

—Mitch Albom

The road to West Point was a circuitous one for Cynthia Ramirez Lindenmeyer—she would travel it more than once.

As a young child, the story of a large gold ring worn by her Uncle Tom fascinated Cynthia. While serving in Vietnam, Tom was flying in a small plane over the jungles as a passenger on a mission. The sky suddenly turned gray with the smoke of missiles exploding around him. His aircraft hit, he immediately reached for the ejector handle. Words from a long-ago safety briefing echoed in his mind, reminding him to remove all jewelry before ejecting. Tom Coker pulled off his West Point Class of 1967 ring, dropped it on the floor, yanked the handle, and shot out of the plane, eventually landing in the dense jungle. Missing in action for a brief period, Tom eventually reunited with his unit, tired and weary, but unharmed. Eight years after leaving Vietnam, checking his mail one day, Tom opened an envelope without a return address and found his lost class ring inside. The theme of reunion in this family story strongly appealed to Cynthia. When she learned that women could attend West Point, she was drawn to the place where such stories of tradition, reunion, and honor originated.

Cynthia experienced a rough start in life with a traumatic childhood and a "home life" on the streets. Her parents divorced when she was just nine years old when her mother attempted suicide, and then was diagnosed with a mental illness. For six months, she and her mother lived on the streets of Austin, Texas. It was there, with little or nothing to her name, that Cynthia began to develop an understanding of community. "We all took care of one another. It was nice not to worry about possessions," she recalled.

With her mom institutionalized, Cynthia's father gained custody of her, but by this time, she had been in and out of several foster homes and juvenile detention centers. Arrested for shoplifting in 9th grade, petty criminal activity had become a part of her life. Released into the custody of her father, her parole officer told her how much she had screwed up her life. "He told me I would never amount to anything," Cynthia said. "I told him that I would go to college. He sarcastically questioned me, 'Oh yeah. Where will you go to college?' I told him I would go to West Point. After laughing, he looked me in the eye and said, 'No way could you make it in.' I have never liked someone telling me that I couldn't do something."

At that time, Dr. Albert Ramirez, Cynthia's father, was a professor at the University of Colorado in Boulder, teaching psychology and overseeing diversity issues for students, faculty, and staff. One of his graduate students was a devout Christian. Cynthia remembered,

> She began taking me to church on Wednesday nights in a renovated liquor store turned into a storefront church outside of Denver, Colorado. I quit stealing, lying, drinking, and swearing. I became a Christian, and it had a profound effect on me. After experiencing the powerful work of the Holy Spirit, my outlook on life totally changed. I went from dealing drugs, manipulating people for money, and hating life, to loving people and loving life. Though my current life was full of turmoil, inside I was becoming a very peaceful person. I underwent a complete transformation.

Despite many obstacles, and with the support and encouragement of some people in her church, she moved in with her aunt and uncle. She returned to school and excelled in academics, becoming a Hispanic National Merit Scholar. She also played several sports, earning varsity letters in softball, track, cross country, and basketball. In trying to fulfill the audacious dream she had announced to her parole officer, Cynthia applied to West Point, sought the proper congressional nominations, and underwent various physical and medical evaluations. Because of her juvenile police record, Cynthia could not directly enter the Academy, but instead received an opportunity to attend the USMA Preparatory School in Fort Monmouth, New Jersey. This one-year experience enabled her to mature and build a sense of discipline. She earned acceptance into the Military Academy the following year with the Class of 1990.

During that year at the Preparatory School, Cynthia visited West Point for the first time. She remembered:

> I had this feeling that I had finally found my home, although I had lived in more than 15 different homes up to that point. As the cadets stood in formation for lunch, the bells from the Cadet Chapel chimed out the melody of *The Church is One Foundation*. It was one of the few church hymns I knew. The cornerstone verse from that hymn comes from First Corinthians 3:10-11, 'By the grace God has given me, I laid a foundation as an expert builder, and someone else is building on it. But each one should be careful how he builds. For no one can lay any foundation other than the one already laid, which is Jesus Christ.'
>
> I knew I needed a solid foundation with a heavy dose of discipline, and a place where I could grow in my Christian faith. At that moment, hearing those bells, I knew that God called me to attend West Point. Little did I know that I would spend more time at West Point than any other place in my life!

West Point would become Cynthia's family, home, and community.

Although she felt that she was home, it was an environment of tough love with plenty of academic and physical obstacles along the way. Cynthia found that her most productive study time as a plebe came during the three hours after midnight. She and a few other night-owl classmates gathered after Taps (the military bugle call to signal lights out) sounded each night in Washington Hall to study, talk, and make snack runs to the Cadet Mess Hall. While the majority of the cadet corps slept, this "Breakfast Club" studied preparing for the next day's classes, engaged in provocative philosophical discussions and developed great relationships with the staff of the mess hall. Unfortunately, most of this group did not meet the academic standards at West Point and left the Academy. Cynthia's major challenges would emanate from the recovery and rehabilitation of an injury sustained while practicing for one of the annual physical fitness evaluations.

Early in the fall semester of her yearling[75] year, Cynthia prepared for the Indoor Obstacle Course Test, an annual graded physical test of muscular strength, endurance, agility, and military-relevant physical fitness. The course involves negotiating 11 obstacles in the shortest possible time. [76]

Cynthia's roommate asked her to demonstrate how to tackle 'the shelf,' the fourth obstacle in the course, following a tunnel crawl, tire run, and two-handed vault. Negotiating this nine-foot-high shelf requires one to jump up and grab while simultaneously swinging one's body to the side in order to hook one's heel on the shelf. From this dangling position, cadets are required to pull themselves onto the shelf to access the next obstacle.

Prior to meeting her roommate for the demonstration, Cynthia spent an hour in the pool learning the butterfly stroke from Ann Marie Wyckoff, a 19-time All American swimmer for Army. Not realizing the fatigue of her upper body from the swimming work out, as she attempted to pull up and swing her body onto the shelf, she

---

[75] A yearling at West Point is a sophomore.

[76] www.totten60.com/usma/IOCT_Tab.htm.

fell hard onto a thin mat. Attempting to break her fall, Cynthia extended her arm. "My entire body landed on this arm. The last thing I remember, as the ambulance rushed me to the Emergency Room at Keller Army Hospital, was seeing my left humerus bone sticking out of skin. For the next six months, I attended all formations, classes and everything else in a huge class shirt borrowed from one of the football players in my company. I had to get help from my roommates just to dress. Then, I spent the next year trying to do just one push-up."

Graduating from West Point in 1990, Cynthia was commissioned a second lieutenant in the Signal Corps. Her first call to ministry came early in her Army career. While learning how to jump out of airplanes at Airborne School in Fort Benning, Georgia, Cynthia encountered a woman chaplain. She said, "I was in shock. I didn't know women could be chaplains. I had been told women couldn't be chaplains. I was getting tired of being told who I could and could not be." Cynthia knew God was calling her into ordained ministry. Eventually she would resign her military commission to enroll in seminary, but not for another seven years. Following the introductory course for signal branch officers, Cynthia reported to her first Army unit at Fort Lewis, Washington. Assigned to the 199th Infantry Brigade (Motorized), there were few women in the unit (all assigned to the headquarters company). While some of the unit commanders were not thrilled to have a woman providing their tactical communications, she gradually gained credibility and acceptance by doing her job well.

Eighteen months later, the West Point Admissions Office asked her to become a minority outreach officer. Her job would be to introduce young people to the opportunities available to them at West Point and in the Army. Cynthia accepted the assignment, believing it an opportunity to influence high school students in a positive way. Instead of a posting to West Point, she went to Los Alamitos in Los Angeles, California, where she personally contacted approximately 13,200 students. Her aggressive efforts increased minority applicants by 22% in her region over the previous year.

That year, nominations for black applicants alone increased by a phenomenal 35% during a time when nationwide nominations and applications in total decreased.

Following the normal career progression of a first lieutenant, she returned to Fort Gordon, Georgia, and attended the advanced officer's course in the Signal Corps. With one year remaining on her active duty service obligation, she went to Korea. Her plan was to complete her fifth year of service there, resign from the Army, and enroll in a seminary. However, midway through her yearlong tour in Korea, she was offered a company command at Camp Long, near Wonju. There, at the end of her tour, in February 1996, she met another officer, Vincent Lindenmeyer. They married in September of that year and afterward moved to Fort Bragg, North Carolina, for their next assignment.

Cynthia felt God calling her into the ministry but she found ways to put this Divine calling on hold. "I kept saying let me just do this one thing and then I will enter seminary. This went on for three more years, before I finally answered God's call to attend seminary and serve as an Army Chaplain," she explained. Living in North Carolina with Vince working at Fort Bragg, Cynthia entered the Duke Divinity School, resigning her active duty commission to accept one in the Army Reserves. As a captain, she returned to the military classroom, attending the basic course again, this time as a chaplain candidate.

While West Point and the Army posed academic and physical struggles, Cynthia's most difficult challenges arose in the least expected place—the Army Chaplain Officer Basic Course at Fort Jackson, South Carolina. Greeted there with many degrading remarks and treated rudely by many of those training to provide religious support to soldiers worldwide. As she put it,

> Marginalization from other chaplains and Christians continues to be the most significant obstacle I encounter. It's difficult to overcome an overall attitude that God created half the population to be disbarred

from ordained ministry. This is the fundamental interpretation from Scriptures—that women are not to be ordained clergy. What I've come to realize is that people have their own prejudices and will always find a substantial and credible resource to support their claims in order to marginalize others. There's little I can do to change the attitude, but what I can do is not allow their little prejudiced understanding of the world to affect me and the life God has formed for me to live.

Fully committed in her desire to connect God, family and country, Cynthia earned a Master of Divinity degree from Duke in 2000 and graduated her basic course as Distinguished Honor Graduate. She then returned to a familiar place, one that would become home. Vince was accepted into the Tactical Officer Education Program at West Point, the first phase of a four-year assignment, and Cynthia returned there as a reserve officer.

As one of seven Protestant chaplains for the Corps of Cadets at West Point, Cynthia knows that a cadet's life journey will be significantly different depending on whether she or he graduates from West Point or resigns to pursue other opportunities. Her personal problems and the obstacles she overcame provided an excellent basis for helping others. Cynthia observed,

West Point structured my life at a time when there was no structure, as my family was not definable. My faith strengthened at West Point and developed deep roots. However, the strength of these roots was severely tested while I was a platoon leader. Two soldiers in my platoon were killed while supporting a classified mission. This was a very difficult time for me. Their deaths made me question many things. West Point gave me the strength to not only survive, but also to help others.

Ministry is a calling that brings some unique and special responsibilities. A minister, rabbi, or priest often plays a significant role in guiding people through life's triumphs and tragedies. He or she is involved in a person's circle of life from birth and baptism through confirmations and marriage, to illness and death. At West Point, Cynthia helped cadets struggle and manage competing claims of serving both God and country.

One of Cynthia's favorite places at West Point is the cemetery. It sits on a promontory once known as "German Flats," overlooking the Hudson River and Constitution Island. There are more than 7,000 men and women buried here (including those who died in virtually every armed conflict in which the United States has taken part). A beautiful yet solemn place, where the history of the Academy itself can be seen in the 24 graves of former superintendents and in the final resting places of many military, civilian, and sports legends in West Point and our Nation's history. In conducting many graveside ceremonies for deceased graduates, Cynthia reflected, "some of the greatest leaders of our time die alone, with nothing but a tombstone to mark their existence in the temporal world. Immortality is not achieved by a remnant in a cemetery, but in the lives of those who we come in contact with daily."

In the summer 2005, Cynthia shared her thoughts on the events of a particular day at West Point. She hopes they will not be lost to time.

On Thursday, August 25, 2005, West Point celebrated Women's Equality. A week ago, none here would realize the other two events that would eclipse the scheduled luncheon in honor of Women's Equality.

This morning was somber as the 10 o'clock hour neared, and a hearse pulled up to the Cadet Chapel, where we honored the first woman graduate to give her life in support of the war on terrorism. Listening to the eulogies for First Lieutenant Laura Walker, Class of 2003, I was proud to be a woman graduate of West Point. As Laura was interred in the cemetery, I reflected on her life and began to think about the three o'clock funeral at the Cadet Chapel for Command Sergeant Major (retired) Mary Sutherland, who was the first woman to serve as the Command Sergeant Major for the United States Corps of Cadets and West Point. When she retired from Active Duty in the Cadet Chapel last year, she earned the distinction of being the longest-serving woman on active duty in the history of the United States Army. For as long as West Point is here, they will rest about ten feet apart in the cemetery.

When Luke Lindenmeyer, Cynthia and Vincent's son, was born, Command Sergeant Major Sutherland gave them a blue baby blanket embroidered with his name. Sutherland did this for all the soldiers stationed at West Point as they welcomed children into their families. That day, following the burials of the two soldiers on August 25, Cynthia brought her two young children Carly, age 5, and Luke, age 2, to the West Point cemetery. She prayed that as the years go by, those who walk in the cemetery come to learn the significance of this day when two women who served our nation were laid to rest. These two soldiers exemplify the words of the West Point Alma Mater—'And when our work is done, our course on earth is run, may it be said 'Well done,' be thou at peace.'

Since the fatal attacks of September 11, West Point has lost 77 graduates[77], in the defense of freedom while fighting the global war on terrorism. The majority of these graduates, 49, were company grade officers, holding the rank of second lieutenant, first lieutenant or captain. At the time of their sacrifice, most were under the age of 30 years. First Lieutenant Walker, for example, graduated within the

---

[77] As of April 13, 2010. "In Memoriam," www.westpointaog.org/NetCommunity/Page.aspx?pid=734.

last five years. In spite of these sacrifices, the vast majority of West Point cadets are eager to graduate and lead soldiers in combat in defense of freedom. The war also has caused more cadets to reflect seriously about their religion particularly those who consider themselves Christian. Cynthia remains committed to helping cadets mature spiritually. She tells cadets, "Now is the time for you to discover who you are, so you can withstand the challenges you inevitably will face."

Most of the cadets who seek out Chaplain Lindenmeyer do not regularly attend church. She said,

> I relate best to the cadets who are seeking out faith, who don't want to be told what or how to believe. I understand that. How I understand God comes from the experiences of meeting God's people—whether they live in mansions or under a bridge, whether they endure four years of West Point or desire to leave during summer training, whether they are divorced or single…We all have our life scripts that we follow. Just be careful it is written by the One who created you, not by someone who has no idea of your life potential.

Each year, Cynthia mentors many cadets, but chooses one senior that she will meet with weekly. She remarked, "Usually, I learn from them!" Cynthia recalled a 2004 graduate, Dave Fraser, who had little free time since he was on the Varsity Track and Cross Country team, but devoted his spare time serving the West Point community by teaching Sunday school and building a bridge by the Youth Center. She described, "The hardest part of being a member of a family, of a community, is loss. After serving seven years as a chaplain at West Point, the most difficult moment came during the Thanksgiving Holiday in 2006. Dave was killed in Iraq during his final mission."

A fragile thread holds life together. The webs of relationships that surround us help us to be stronger, if we allow them. Cynthia knows the depths of disappointment, and the pinnacle of joy. And the path that weaves in between, for that is where she finds herself on most "ordinary" days. The legacy she hopes to leave with cadets is one of encouragement when things don't make sense. "Jesus taught in parables. That is how I see one's journey, like a parable. Some days things make sense, but most of time they don't. I have faith that when all is said and done, meaning to the parable of one's life emerges."

Captains Cynthia Ramirez and Vince Lindenmeyer, October 1996. *(Photo courtesy of Cynthia Lindenmeyer)*

Chaplain Cynthia Lindenmeyer with her children, Carly and Luke, at Command Sergeant Major Mary Sutherland's gravesite. Behind them is First Lieutenant Laura Walker's grave. Sutherland and Walker's funerals were on the same day. August 2005. *(Photo courtesy of Cynthia Lindenmeyer)*

Chaplain Cynthia Lindenmeyer standing with 2008 West Point graduates in December 2008 in Albuquerque, New Mexico before officiating at the wedding of Lieutenant Chris Goeke. *From left to right*: Nathan Bastian, Eric Justin Wong, Nicholas Privette, Mary Alice Pass, Cynthia Lindenmeyer, Daniel Newell, David Jeffrey, John Bockstanz, Adam C. Johnson. (As of March 2010, Mary Alice is in Medical School. Nick, Dan, Chris, and John are in Afghanistan, Adam is in Iraq and Eric is in Haiti). (*Photo courtesy of Cynthia Lindenmeyer*)

Cadets Heidi Brown and Alan Azzarita, USMA 1981, hug each other after receiving their diplomas from West Point. Chris Jackson, USMA 1981, is on the right. Heidi, Alan and Chris were all squad mates during Cadet Beast Barracks. This photo was in the Newburgh newspaper the day after graduation as well as in the West Point yearbook, the Howitzer. *(Photo courtesy of Heidi Brown)*

NOTHING IS IMPOSSIBLE | BRIGADIER GENERAL HEIDI BROWN, CLASS OF 1981

"Do what you feel in your heart to be right—for you'll be criticized anyway. You'll be damned if you do, and damned if you don't."
—Eleanor Roosevelt

Brigadier General Heidi V. Brown never set out to be a pioneer; it just happened that way. In fact, she looks forward to when she can say that being a female combat-arms officer is no longer a novelty. She said, "Someday, gender will be a non-issue in these positions."

Heidi's parents were the two most influential people in her decision to serve her country as a soldier. Orphaned as young children, Heidi's father, William Brown, and his sister grew up in foster homes and orphanages in Dover, New Hampshire. On the day William graduated from high school and returned to the orphanage, he was told he was old enough to be on his own. Shortly thereafter, he enlisted in the Army.

Virginia, Heidi's mom, grew up in a middle-class family, where her dad built the water works in and around Fort Leavenworth, Kansas. Virginia, attracted to public service by the influence of her own parents, volunteered to go to China with Special Services. Virginia took a second interesting job as a Red Cross volunteer in Germany, and there she and William met. After a brief courtship and at the conclusion of their overseas tours of duty they married. William a field artillery officer, served with distinction in World War II and the Korean War, receiving a silver star and several bronze stars. He retired as a major, and the Browns settled in El Paso, Texas, near Fort Bliss. Virginia left the Red Cross and focused on raising a family, while William pursued a second career as a teacher, continuing his service to the nation. Heidi said, "My parents imparted strong moral values and a desire to serve our country, in the military or another capacity, such as education."

Heidi is the second youngest of six children that, perhaps not surprisingly, all pursued service to their country. Five of the six decided to serve in the military. Heidi's oldest sister, Deborah, wanting to become a physician, joined the Army as a way to pay for medical school. She is still serving as a Colonel in the Army Reserves. Robert and Brian, twin brothers, enrolled in the junior reserve officer training course (JROTC) at their El Paso high school. Nearly three decades later, in 2000, Robert retired from Army Military Intelligence as a lieutenant colonel. Brian remains on active duty and is a Colonel in the Air Force. Micaela B. Newman, the fourth sibling, is a schoolteacher in Houston, Texas, instructing deaf students and adults. Anne, the youngest of the Brown's children, is an Army nurse and holds the rank of major.

As early as high school, Heidi thought of becoming an Army doctor, but did not enroll in JROTC because she wanted to blend in with her classmates. Shortly after the federal service academies opened to women the Air Force Academy in Colorado Springs, Colorado, recruited Heidi to join its swim team. While flattered, Heidi felt the Air Force Academy's short 23-year existence paled in comparison to the nearly two centuries of history at West Point. Ironically, the other aspect of the Military Academy that drew Heidi was the encouragement of her Uncle Dan Graham to apply for admission to the Air Force Academy. Dan had graduated from West Point in 1946, and did not like the prospect of it ending its 170 years of single sex education and training for the Army. "Uncle Dan was one of those graduates who were not eager to see West Point open its doors to women," recalled Heidi. At the same time, Colonel (retired) Buster Hayden, a 1945 graduate of the Military Academy, assisted Heidi in the West Point admissions process as a long-time field admissions representative in El Paso. Although Buster and Dan were at West Point at the same time, they did not know each other as cadets. Colonel Hayden remembered, "I just told her what to expect, the challenges and the opportunities. I told her we are in the leadership business. She liked what she heard."

In spite of the challenge and novelty of being in the second class of women to enter West Point, Heidi was determined to have a good time regardless of the Spartan environment, and the seemingly countless rules governing cadet life. During the second semester of plebe year, Heidi and her roommate established a bar serving alcoholic drinks in their room, a clear violation of cadet barracks regulations. During Saturday morning inspection, they would discreetly move their beverage bottles to a basement storage room to elude detection. Each week she and her roommates opened the bound cadet regulations manual to select randomly a rule to challenge and break without being caught. Jointly, the roommates defined how the rule had to be breeched and witnessed in order to receive peer recognition for a successful violation. Heidi recalled, "I challenged everything." While never caught violating cadet regulations in the barracks, her rebellious nature came with a dear consequence in athletics.

Heidi swam on an Army team that progressed from a club sport organization her first year to an intercollegiate varsity team by her third year. At the start of her fourth and final competitive collegiate season, Heidi began missing practices repeatedly in protest of not becoming the team captain and her aversion for the coach. Frustrated that this talented swimmer was not contributing to the team in either leadership or attitude, Dr. Sue Tendy, the team's coach, confronted Heidi, warning her that if she missed another practice she would be thrown off the team. Heidi did not show up for practice the following day.

Furious that this capable but immature cadet directly challenged her policies and put herself above the team, Coach Tendy sought guidance in addressing this situation from another physical education instructor, a Vietnam veteran. This officer gave her advice which Tendy continues to draw upon, that when you correct someone, do it with dignity, and provide the person an opportunity for change.

Two days before Christmas leave, Coach Tendy suspended Heidi from the team. The timing was painful as the team was within a few days of departing for a training camp in Puerto Rico the second week of the holiday break. Not invited to attend the camp, Heidi instead received an option. Coach Tendy wanted Heidi to think about her actions and their impact on her teammates. Heidi could continue to train at home during the vacation and rejoin the team in January. Heidi recalled,

> When I arrived home, my parents were livid with me for acting like an anarchist, thinking and saying that I knew more than the coach. I made a promise to my parents and my self to keep my mouth shut and just perform to my potential. Swimming was something I loved passionately. It had been taken away from me. It was my stress relief from the rigors of cadet life. But I had all the power to get it back. It was a real lesson in respecting authority. I realized that the team would only be a team if everyone was on board with expectations. I could not do my own thing. I learned that leadership and discipline are essential in working as part of a team. I also later learned that Coach Tendy really struggled with the decision, consulting many people. She gave me a way back on the team with dignity. To this day, this lesson is present in all I do and how I lead soldiers.

That year, Army's swim team finished third in the New York State Women's Intercollegiate Swimming and Diving Championships. Heidi wrote a poem entitled *"Nothing is Impossible"* for the team. Its theme resonates with Heidi in all she does.

Academics also left a lasting impression on Heidi. Most of the electives she took were in the Behavioral Sciences Department, studying psychology and counseling. Heidi felt regardless of her long-term profession, these courses would be applicable. One of the classes involved 'field work' at the Rockland County Children's Psychiatric Center, a group home providing in-patient mental health services for children and adults. Each week the cadets would visit and meet with young children at the hospital and there was one young girl with whom Heidi visited weekly for three years. Heidi said, "I began seeing an opportunity counseling people. It was a calling from which I have never deviated."

Although she had been an A student in high school, Heidi struggled at West Point with a passing grade point average just above the 2.0 minimum academic requirement. Nearing graduation, Heidi realized her choices for a military specialty were limited given her low class rank. While she wanted a commission in Military Intelligence, being ranked in the bottom 10 percent eliminated this option. Air Defense Artillery, a combat arms branch, became her second choice. At the earliest opportunity, Heidi intended to branch transfer to Military Intelligence, serve her five-year Army obligation, resign her commission, and pursue a civilian career in counseling.

Wanting to overcome her low class rank at West Point, Heidi decided to focus on studying and learning at the Officer Basic Class at Fort Bliss, Texas. She graduated first in her Hawk Missile Weapons class and enrolled in the Military Intelligence Officer Advanced Course by correspondence. While the Military Intelligence Advanced Course is typically a six-month resident program during which the officer attending has only the responsibilities of a student, Heidi would spend the next 12 months completing the course work on her own while leading a platoon. She anticipated that completion of this course would demonstrate her desire and competitiveness to transfer into the branch as a captain.

Her first assignment took her to Germany as a platoon leader and executive officer with the 6th Battalion, 52nd Air Defense Artillery Regiment of the 32nd Army Air Defense Command. Heidi applied herself to learning everything she could about the complex weapon systems for which she was responsible. She became the most junior soldier (and second woman) to earn the distinction of the Master Tactical Control Officer. Enjoying the Air Defense branch and intrigued by the complexity of the weapons technology, she decided against a transfer into Military Intelligence.

Heidi became the Electronics Counter-Countermeasures and Tactical Evaluation Officer, the principal trainer to run air battles for weapons crews across the brigade. Because of her performance, she was selected to command C Battery, 6th Battalion (HAWK), 52nd Air Defense Artillery Regiment as a first lieutenant. She was one of a very select few officers given a battery command during her first assignment in the Army, and prior to attending the Officer Advanced Course. Heidi remembered, "I loved what I was doing—leading soldiers and employing technologically sophisticated missile defense systems. I was challenged and having a blast. There was no need to pursue another career."

In 1986, she returned to Fort Bliss for the Officer Advanced Course, accepting a follow-on assignment as the Test Officer for the Pedestal Mounted Stinger (Avenger) missile system and later became a tactical doctrine writer for the Air Defense School. During her seventh year of active service, much to Heidi's astonishment, she was asked to return to the United States Military Academy. Heidi laughed, "When I was asked to return to West Point as a tactical officer,[78] I was both excited and shocked. I had a blast at West Point, and I always wanted to return as an instructor. Being selected to be a TAC was ironic, as I was not a stellar cadet, so I was quite surprised." When Heidi shared the news of this assignment with her parents, their thoughts were that they chose her intentionally because she knew a lot about getting in and out of trouble. In preparation for the assignment, she returned to graduate school, earning a Masters of Education from the University of South Carolina.

In 1989, Captains Heidi Brown and Mary Finch, a 1983 graduate, became the first women graduates to serve as tactical officers at the Military Academy. During this three-year assignment, there were several memorable incidents where the cadets in Heidi's company tried to outwit her. The cadets were operating an underground tanning salon in the company trunk room.[79] Heidi

---

[78] The Tactical Officers (TACs) and Tactical Non-Commissioned Officers (TACNCOs) form the Company TAC Teams and are the primary leader developers/integrators of the Academy's developmental programs. They oversee each cadet's individual development within the framework of the cadet company. The TAC is the legal commander of the cadet company, and as such is responsible for the establishment and maintenance of a command climate that fosters individual and unit excellence in all program areas. www.usma.edu/uscc/btd/btdindex.htm.

[79] The trunk room is the basement storage room.

discovered it when a cadet from another company was bumped from his scheduled appointment. The cadet came over to her company to reschedule his appointment and she overhead the conversation that brought the operation to light. When Captain Brown approached her cadets, they immediately referred to the cadet regulations manual to support their venture. Heidi recalled,

> The regulations manual clearly stated that cadets cannot have electrical appliances, but are authorized to have a lamp. They explained the tanning bed was just one huge lamp. As the cadets justified their operations, I realized this was a very well thought out attempt to beat the system. They implemented safety procedures with tanning goggles and time limits. They argued that this was providing cadets a foundation layer to prevent damaging sunburn during the upcoming spring break. They were really quite clever. I told them that I was prepared to go to the Brigade Tactical Officer to argue for their ability to keep the bed in operation. I also told them of the possible outcomes. One, although the least likely, was that nothing at all would happen. A second, and more likely outcome, was they could be awarded a significant number of demerits, resulting in hours of area walking tours. The choice was a gamble, but it was their choice. The cadets decided they wanted to remove the bed from the cadet area to mitigate any risk. I learned later they moved their operation to their sponsor's house on post but outside of the cadet area.

The frequency and audacity of antics typically increased during the two weeks leading up to the traditional service academy rivalry, the Army-Navy football game. These so-called spirit missions, carried out by both cadets and midshipmen, inspire and motivate each school's student body prior to its biggest football game of the season. The most revered of all spirit missions is the capture of the opposing team's mascot, the Army Mule and the Navy Goat. Capture of either by the opposing student body is a severe blow to a team's morale.

After nearly a semester of intense planning and reconnaissance, one of Heidi's cadets kidnapped Billy the Navy Goat and brought it to West Point. He was cheered and hailed as a hero by the Corps of Cadets. Another shut down the Naval Academy computer system by sending a blinking message across all the networked computers, "*Go Army, Beat Navy.*"

Following that first academic year, the Commandant of Cadets appointed Heidi to be the Deputy Commander of Cadet Field Training (CFT). This training takes place in the summer between a cadet's first and second year and introduces them to the field army, unit tactics, and major weapons systems. This very selective appointment was another first for a woman at West Point.

Before returning to the field Army herself, Heidi spent a year at Fort Leavenworth, Kansas, successfully completing the United States Army Command and General Staff College. Now a field grade officer, Major Heidi V. Brown reported to Fort Polk, Louisiana, as the brigade operations officer responsible for the tactical operations for the 108th Air Defense Artillery Brigade. After a year in this assignment she became a battalion executive officer, the second in command of an 800-person unit. This assignment presented Heidi with an entirely new challenge—a horrific command climate in the unit. Heidi described,

> The battalion commander managed by fear, intimidation, and aggravation. He disliked everyone— blacks, women, Hispanics, and any other minority. He was an equal opportunity bigot. He repeatedly embarrassed soldiers—yelling and humiliating them in front of others and in private. He regularly belittled his staff officers. I vividly remember him yelling and cursing at me, 'You fucking piece of shit. Who the fuck

do you think you are?' And ironically, he really respected me and the work I did for the battalion.

The commander expected all his staff to be in the office whenever he was. Typically, that meant six days a week from 6:00 A.M. to 11:00 P.M. Heidi remembered,

> We all had pagers and he would routinely page us to see if we would contact him within the required 30-minute timeline. It was absolute hell. He had little regard for soldiers' families. He threatened his staff that if they complained about the long hours he would end their careers. I seriously contemplated leaving the Army. I just did not want to continue in this environment. I hated getting up and going to work. I just dreaded each day. It was so vastly different from all of my previous assignments.

Not having experienced this type of environment previously, Heidi sought the counsel of her parents. She shared her frustrations with the attitude and actions of the battalion commander, and that no one should be subjected to this type of humiliation. Heidi confided that she was seriously considering resigning. Her parents told her they would support any decision she made. They reminded her that she had never before quit anything, a perspective Heidi had not previously considered.

The following day, she received a call from the brigade commander, her battalion commander's boss, asking Heidi to come to his office. When questioned about what was going on in the unit, Heidi shared that she was wrestling with the definition of loyalty. The brigade commander clarified for her that loyalty is to an organization, not an individual. With that, she confessed there was a horrible and unproductive climate in the organization, the morale in the unit was non-existent, and that she wanted to leave the Army. She told the Colonel that if the battalion went to war, the battalion commander would be the first one shot—by his own soldiers. This Colonel encouraged Heidi to stay, persuading her that if she left, the soldiers would have no one to turn to in confidence. Somehow, this became Heidi's motivation to stay, to be there for others, even if just in the near term. She also knew she might leave the unit altogether for a job in Washington as one of three finalists interviewing to be the military aide to then Vice President Al Gore. When she did not get this position, she believed it happened for a reason. She recalled, "I stayed to be there for the other soldiers. I got results in the battalion. When the battalion commander tore down the soldiers, I was there to build them up. Leading soldiers is what I love."

At 6:00 A.M. the next morning, the battalion commander called Heidi to his office and interrogated her about what she had said to the brigade commander. Heidi told him that his command climate was horrible. She remembered, "He proceeded to rip my face off, calling me everything and anything, including disloyal." Shocked that this commander was oblivious to the effect of his behavior on the unit, it affirmed for Heidi everything she did not want to be as a leader.

Although the brigade commander initiated an Inspector General[80] investigation, few in the battalion were willing to be as candid as Heidi, fearing both the wrath of the commander and the torpedoing of their careers. In the end, nothing happened to this obnoxious battalion commander. As her tour at Fort Polk concluded, Heidi told the brigade commander that his unwillingness to intervene in the battalion and his lack of action put the soldiers of the unit at great peril. She told him she would forgive him neither

---

[80] The Army inspector general's (IG) office routinely investigates allegations of misconduct by Army officials at the rank of colonel or below. Complaints can be filed by soldiers, their family members, retirees, former soldiers or civilians working for the Department of the Army. The position of Army inspector general was created by George Washington to improve the training, drills, discipline and organization of the ragtag Continental Army. Its self-described mission is "to inquire into, and periodically report on, the discipline, efficiency, economy, morale, training and readiness throughout the Army." The agency is not an independent watchdog. It does not report to Congress, but to the Secretary of the Army and the Army Chief of Staff. The IG's office has only limited subpoena authority; it cannot, for instance, subpoena civilian witnesses.

personally nor professionally for not relieving the battalion commander.

Now assigned to Army Headquarters at the Pentagon in Washington, D.C., Heidi served in the Air and Missile Defense Division as a systems integrator, executive officer, and division chief for the Deputy Chief of Staff for Operations and Plans. Soon after assuming her responsibilities at the Pentagon, Heidi received a phone call from her former brigade commander. He admitted to her that he should have relieved the battalion commander. The call came too late. The battalion commander completed his command and moved on to another assignment. The only satisfaction was that her old commander was not selected for the next higher-level brigade command. Sadly, however, he did retire from the Army with full pay and benefits as a Colonel

With her battalion level staff jobs completed and a promotion to Lieutenant Colonel, Heidi was now up for a battalion command. Three other women were also in consideration. While battalion command typically has a selection rate of 35-50%, all four of the women were chosen to command. This 100 percent selection rate earned the women the infamous label among their peers, as the "Fabulous 4" and the rumor that gender not performance, was the basis for selection. Two months prior to taking command, Fox News interviewed Heidi. Asked if she felt any pressure being the first woman to command a Patriot missile battalion, she responded, "Absolutely, I feel pressure because I have never led a battalion, and a lot of people will be watching how all of us do in command. I am going to do my job like every other battalion commander, not based on my gender but on my experiences. My intention is to leave the battalion I command better than I find it."

In September 1997, Lieutenant Colonel Heidi V. Brown assumed command of the 2nd Battalion (Patriot), 43rd Air Defense Artillery, 10 months ahead of the remaining three women selected for command at this level. The battalion had recently returned from a six-month rotation in Saudi Arabia as a forward deployed battalion providing air and missile defense in the region. The mission Heidi described is to provide 'no kidding coverage' for Saudi Arabia and Kuwait. The United States has maintained a defensive presence on Saudi soil since the conclusion of Operation Desert Storm in 1990.

As Heidi accepted the battalion's unit colors, William and Virginia Brown beamed with pride. At the conclusion of the change of command ceremony, William stood at attention and saluted his daughter with respect and admiration. Heidi recalled, "My parents are proud of all of us. Seeing as Dad retired as a major, he was so proud all of his children achieved a higher rank."

Six months into her command an evaluation conducted of all the stateside patriot battalions checked them for preparedness for the next rotation to Saudi Arabia. The only one of five active duty units fully trained and prepared for the mission, Heidi's battalion was selected to deploy again. Almost exactly one year from the date the 2-43rd relinquished the mission in Saudi, they returned to the region and assumed, for the second time, the job of providing air and missile defense protection. Immediately all three batteries in the battalion were converted from caretaker status to battle operational readiness posture in response to the repeated violations of the Iraqi no-fly zone by Saddam Hussein. Lieutenant Colonel Brown moved one of the three batteries from Kuwait to Saudi Arabia to protect a major oil refinery. Because the members of the unit had trained together for a year under Heidi's direction, she and the soldiers were confident in their capabilities and their equipment. Fortunately, they did not have to engage any of their systems and returned stateside six months later.

Following a successful 24 months in battalion command, Heidi received orders for a second assignment to the Pentagon. She relinquished the colors of the 2-43rd, thankful for the privilege to lead soldiers at this level. In her new capacity, Heidi served as the deputy chief of staff for operations and plans in the Air and Missile Defense Division. Wearing three hats—that of systems integrator, executive officer, and division chief—provided her an understanding of Air Defense Artillery operations from a theater-level perspective. After her time in the Pentagon, she attended the Army War College, the nation's premier strategic leadership development institution, at Carlisle Barracks, Pennsylvania. The yearlong course brings together senior military, civilian, and international leaders from all military services and government agencies to study and debate the strategic application of land power. She graduated with a Master's Degree in Strategic Studies and orders for brigade command.

Two days before taking command of the 31st Air Defense Artillery Brigade, one of only four active duty Air Defense brigades, Heidi's father entered the intensive care unit in an El Paso hospital. He had been ill the year before but kept telling her "I will live to see you take command." When Heidi was at West Point, William had been diagnosed with colon cancer. With a sizable portion of his intestines removed in the surgery following the diagnosis, he was now experiencing what is termed "short bowel syndrome." Not able to eat normally, William was fed through his stomach in an attempt to get his body to absorb the nutrients in the food. The morning of July 12, 2002, William's medical team gave him a day pass to attend his daughter's change of command ceremony. Heidi became the first woman to command an Air Defense brigade.

William arrived at the ceremony in an ambulance with two EMTs and with a doctor in tow. "My dad was beaming. We have a mutual admiration for each other." Extremely proud of Heidi, William again saluted his daughter and said, "I am riding on your coat tails." She quickly replied, "Dad, you aren't riding on mine, I've ridden on yours my whole life and am today." It was a tribute to her dad, a proud American veteran and Heidi's hero. After the reception, he returned to the intensive care unit of the hospital.

With the mission of providing decisive air and missile defense operations for the III Armored Corps, the 31st Air Defense Artillery (ADA) Brigade is the largest air defense brigade in the Army. The unit comprises two active Patriot Missile Battalions, 1-1st ADA and 3-2nd ADA, the 745th Forward Surgical Team, the 31st Combat Support Hospital, the 10th Medical Detachment, the 546th Personnel Service Detachment, and the 203rd Finance Detachment. In addition, there are two Army reserve units, the 4-200th ADA Battalion from the New Mexico Army National Guard, and the 3-265th ADA (Avenger) Battalion from the Florida Army National Guard. There were more than 2,000 soldiers under Colonel Brown's command.

Each evening after work, regardless of the time, Heidi went to the hospital to visit her dad, sharing memories, laughs, and tears. Each visit ended with a hug and "I love you." William's health was declining. Ten days later, Colonel Heidi Brown returned to Saudi Arabia to observe the air defense operations of one of the battalions in her brigade deployed in the region. The outgoing commander of that battalion told Colonel Brown that whispers of war plans permeated the air. Immediately, Colonel Brown and Command Sergeant Major Telles, the senior non-commissioned officer in the brigade, began work aimed at convincing others to allow them access to information on developing war plans and whether or not they included the 31st Air Defense Artillery Brigade. Having recently taken command, this information was critical to determining the time available to prepare the unit to go to war. While in Saudi Arabia, Heidi kept abreast of her father's medical condition by means of daily contact with his medical team. Immediately upon returning to the States, Heidi resumed her daily visits to the hospital, knowing in her heart that her father had precious little time left on earth.

With the exception of the deployed battalion in Saudi Arabia, Heidi quickly learned that most of the remaining units in her brigade were not prepared to go to war, having spent little time in the field during previous years under other commanders. She called in her leadership team—the brigade staff, all the battalion commanders and their staffs, and the battery commanders—and explained they were going to the field to train exclusively for their wartime mission. She wanted to ensure confidence in individual and unit tactics and the operability of all equipment. Heidi and her unit began intensive corps-level operational readiness training with deployments to Fort Hood and Korea. As the staff prepared to depart, William Brown died on Sunday morning, August 18, 2002. Heidi felt numb despite knowing and preparing herself for his death. "Nothing prepares you for the loss of a parent you love," Heidi said solemnly.

With her father's death, Heidi designated her deputy brigade commander to lead the exercise for the next week. She worked with an Army casualty assistance officer to take care of her father's affairs and personal arrangements. All of the Brown siblings got involved so that their mother did not have to worry about any of the details. The family decided to bury his ashes in Arlington National Cemetery in Washington, D.C., at a graveside service in September. A local memorial service and reception were held that Friday—the day after her mother's birthday. Heidi returned to her unit Monday to confirm that her brigade had some operational and equipment shortcomings. There was little time to grieve. Heidi recalled, "My father would want me to focus on getting my soldiers and unit ready to go to war."

As September approached, Colonel Brown once again gathered her staff and commanders, this time in New Mexico, for an offsite meeting to develop a vision and initial battle plan. They also devised family support plans as the potential for deployment into a combat theater increased. These plans articulated the procedures for casualty reporting and familial notification of the death of a service member. In retrospect, Heidi said, "The focus on casualty reporting was one of the best things we did in terms of preparing our military spouses and families. Little did I know that it would be invaluable for my soldiers' families."

The second aspect of the war planning involved initiating extensive coordination with the 32nd Army Air and Missile Defense Command (AAMDC) under the leadership of Brigadier General Howard Bromberg, the senior Air Defense Artillery Commander in the Army. This command is the sole theater level Army Air and Missile Defense organization with a worldwide, 72-hour deployment mission. The 32nd AAMDC consists of two brigades, the 11th and 35th Air Defense Artillery Brigades. While 32nd AAMDC was not technically in Heidi's chain of command, for the purposes of the war, she would coordinate with them.

As William Brown's funeral date approached, Heidi picked up his ashes and flew with her mother to Virginia and gathered with all of the Brown siblings to bury their father. The following day, Heidi flew to London to participate in an Allied Forces Joint Exercise. Virginia Brown returned to Fort Bliss alone.

In October 2002, Colonel Brown set up her Brigade Tactical Operations Center (TOC)[81] to review its layout and equipment configuration; it was the first set up of the 31st TOC in several years. She repeated this exercise several times before attempting to move and to jump[82] the TOC as anticipated in combat operations. Heidi said, "We practiced exactly what equipment, down to each map board, and who would go with the jump TOC, and what and who would go with the main element. This proved extremely valuable, because when the war started, I went with the jump TOC, as this is where the battle was taking place."

As media attention increased the speculation of an invasion of Iraq, the jockeying and negotiating in the political arena began. Israel asserted its political muscle, requesting the protection of a U.S. Army Patriot unit with a headquarters element from Germany. Simultaneously, various U.S. armor and infantry battalion commanders of III Armored Corps demanded Patriot battalions with Patriot Capability Three (PAC-3), the most advanced generation of Patriot Missile technologies, to provide air and missile defense of their ground movements. The two Patriot battalions of the 31st had only PAC 2 capabilities. Heidi's predecessor had seen little need to transition to PAC 3 technologies, given the peacetime nature of the Army. Weekly, higher command shifted the units in the two brigades as various commanders at all levels made adamant demands and engaged in various 'horse-trading' commitments to others.

Heidi worked with the 4th Infantry Division commander, Major General Ray Odierno, one of two divisions in III Armored Corps, to demonstrate the 31st's organic capability and missile

---

[81] Tactical Operations Center (TOC) is the physical field location from which wartime operations are conducted.

[82] Jump TOC operations involve moving a small element of the brigade's command and control forward of the unit to establish communications and to take control of the brigade prior to dismantling and moving the main element to later catch up with the forward TOC.

defense, and to develop a plan. The battle plan assumed the 4th Infantry Division would move from Turkey, then proceed south to enter Iraq enroute to Tikrit in the north. The 31st would provide protective coverage for a 300-mile cross-country movement with ground units spread along the entire route. After establishing a strong relationship with Major General Odierno built on confidence, demonstrated capability and open communication, Colonel Brown learned that her brigade's mission had changed completely from supporting III Armored Corps to supporting V Corps. Neither Colonel Brown nor Command Sergeant Major Telles knew anyone or any unit in V Corps. With no established relationships, the war planning for the 31st started again.

Immediately, she and her staff officers began intensive coordination to learn the operational plans of V Corps in order to develop a comprehensive air defense strategy. This involved not only movement routes, but logistical and communication plans, since there were no prior operational relationships with V Corps. As battle planning intensified and tactical operations were defined, Major John Noel, the brigade signal officer responsible for developing the essential technical architecture for battlefield communications between the 31st and all the ground units in V Corps, suffered a fatal heart attack and died suddenly on December 22. His death affected Heidi personally and professionally. The two shared a strong professional relationship built on respect and trust. Given his knowledge and experience, Heidi was uniquely confident in his abilities to enable battlefield communications for units that had not previously worked or trained together. With few Signal Officers in the brigade, Colonel Brown appointed a young signal captain to continue the building of the entire battlefield communications architecture.

The day after Christmas Brown received a phone call from a lieutenant in the Brigade Logistics Office who shared his own heart-breaking news. His ten year-old son, in the hospital for several months with cancer, had passed away. Heidi remembered the emotional drain of war planning and grieving,

It was an incredibly difficult period. There were three deaths of great importance to me in just a few short months, yet there was no time to grieve and reflect on any of them—my father, John Noel, and this lieutenant's young son. I had more than 2,000 soldiers in my direct command and thousands of others who would need the coverage and protection of our Air and Missile Defense systems.

Heidi put her feelings on hold and continued with her planning for the impending deployment.

In January 2003, several maneuver brigade commanders flew to Kuwait for a tactical planning meeting with Brigadier General Howard Bromberg, commander of the 32nd Air Army and Missile Defense Command (AAMDC). The purpose of this hastily ordered meeting was to develop air defense architecture independent of the ground maneuver units, given the constantly changing nature of the war planning effort. Interestingly, in the history of the air defense artillery, the foundation of missile defense was static and conducted from stationary sites. This operation was to be the first time an air defense brigade would maneuver on the ground with infantry and armor units.

At this meeting, the final decisions were made as to which battalions would be task organized to Colonel Brown. None of her organic battalions would be deploying with her to war. Two other battalions, one from Germany and the other from a different Brigade at Fort Bliss, would be the units she would take to war. She recalled,

We are less than two months from going to war, and I get a 'pick-up' team. I lost my two active Patriot battalions. I was given one Patriot battalion from Fort Bliss and another from V Corps. Once in the war theater, I was to receive a separate Patriot battalion. Assigned was a security force from a reserve unit in

Florida and some signal and communications assets from V Corps. None of these units had previously worked together. All the battalions now assigned to the 31st were short of both personnel and equipment. This was not a recipe for success. To this day, the reconstitution of my brigade remains the million-dollar question without an answer.

From this meeting, Colonel Brown flew to Germany for a Mission Rehearsal Exercise (MRE) where she met, for the first time, all of the division and corps level commanders who would be operating in the theater of operation, including Major General David Petreaus, commander of the 101st Airborne (Air Assault) Division, and Lieutenant General William Wallace, commander of V Corps. While they practiced several battle scenarios during the exercise, none compared to what they would eventually encounter. Outside the military base where the MRE unfolded, reported spy activity required the Army to change drastically its war plans again.

On February 7, Colonel Brown returned to Fort Bliss to complete final deployment preparations, learning that the Patriot batteries would move independent of any headquarters unit and would move in convoys with the units for which they were providing coverage. Brown was given one infantry company of approximately 130 soldiers to provide security during the 300 mile, 6,000-vehicle convoy movement from Kuwait into Iraq. Summoned to deploy immediately to Kuwait, she found out that same day the war plans had changed again.

As V Corps began to move their equipment into a staging area in Kuwait, Colonel Brown learned her brigade would be the last to load its equipment on a ship enroute to Kuwait. Furious, she recalled, "How do the other commanders think I am going to get these Patriot battalions into the fight if they are on the last ship headed to Southwest Asia?" The 31st Combat Support Hospital received their warning order to move immediately to accompany 3rd Infantry Division at the forward edge of the movement. They would be significantly forward of the remainder of their own brigade. The 745th Forward Surgical Team departed Fort Bliss for Kuwait even before Colonel Brown returned from Germany. The last unit attached, the second week of February, to the 31st Air Defense Artillery Brigade was the 507th Maintenance Company. The initial invasion of Iraq was less than a month away.

With war imminent, Heidi was well aware of the potential for casualties. She anticipated that they would occur near the Karbala Gap, given the new mission of providing air defense coverage for 3rd Infantry Division's long and ambitious convoy movement. Knowing that she needed to get one of her staff members in theater for last minute changes, she sent her brigade operations officer, Major Ron Mulkey, to Kuwait. He departed on Valentine's Day. Heidi also had a small cell of soldiers based in Germany fly to Kuwait to set up the brigade's initial tactical operations center at Camp Virginia.

On Thursday, February 20, 2003, Colonel Brown learned she needed to brief the V Corps commander on the air and missile defense support for the group movements of both the 3rd Infantry Division and 101st Division. The briefing was in Kuwait. The next day, with no military transport available to her, Colonel Heidi Brown left the United States on a commercial airline enroute to war. Upon her arrival at the Kuwait International Airport, she saw Major General David Petraeus, the commanding general of the 101st. Petraeus barely recognized her in blue jeans and loafers. He remarked, "Funny way to dress for war!"

For the next several weeks, Colonel Brown and her units, as they arrived piecemeal, began battle rehearsals. This was the first time any of these units had been together and there was little time to train. Many of the officers attended the multitude of strategic and tactical planning meetings, adjusting and modifying their battle plans continually. With two weeks remaining to the anticipated invasion, Brown asked her brigade supply officer to brief the combat service support plan, including how supplies, small arms ammunition, fuel, and repair parts were going to move to various brigade units once the maneuvering commenced. He was completely unprepared. Heidi recalled yet another challenge of inheriting soldiers about whom one had no knowledge and with whom one had not trained. She said,

> I immediately realized we were in trouble when he had only four note cards to brief the entire combat supply plan. He was totally clueless. I would have relieved him, but I had no one to replace him. I inherited him and now I was responsible. So I went to the division level supply officer and asked him to teach, coach, and mentor him fast—very fast. This is the staff I inherited from the previous commander. And that previous commander was also in theater with another unit.

As dusk fell on March 20, 2003, Saddam Hussein started firing SCUD missiles into the air. Colonel Brown immediately moved several batteries into attack positions. The brigade had rehearsed how it would move cross-country in specific convoy order and in pre-designated lanes. Later that night at 10:00 P.M. local time all the units assumed their convoy position and order and prepared to move. One aspect of the movement that Heidi had been adamant about in every planning meeting and rehearsal was the requirement for all the Patriot missile and support vehicles to remain on hard paved roads. Given the sheer weight of the vehicles, many of the vehicles would become stuck in the soft sand if they left paved roads. Not only would this significantly reduce the speed of movement, it would expose the soldiers unnecessarily to an even greater risk of enemy fire.

There were more than 6,000 vehicles positioned to cross several sand berms and spread out in 10 or 12 travel lanes. U.S. missiles were streaking across the sky, lighting up the night as they exploded. The *"shock and awe"* part of the liberation of Iraq was underway. Meanwhile, Brown waited for the long-haul communication cables needed to remain in contact with all her subordinate units, given the physical distance between her dispersed units in the northern and southern parts of the country. Unable to procure the needed cables from the corps that she was supporting, Heidi received the cables from III Armored Corps. Heidi spent most of that night on the radio guiding the transportation vehicles to her convoy location. The cables eventually arrived at four o'clock on the morning of March 21. Two hours later the 3rd Infantry Division convoy began its movement into Iraq.

The aggressive plan called for the last of the convoy's elements to arrive at the forward operation position in 36 hours, barring problems. As the convoy progressed slowly throughout the day, Colonel Brown's British Army Liaison Officer plotted the chosen route, determining the convoy was following the lines of a backwards "w." Moving on and off the hard road in movement order, the convoy came to a standstill in the soft sand. When Brown got out of her vehicle, she sank to her knees in the sand. She described it as an overwhelming mess as the number of vehicles mired in the sand increased by the minute. She and her soldiers spent the remainder of that day and night pulling trapped vehicles out of the sand. If they did not get the vehicle out far enough, it would immediately sink again, and the soldiers would have to find yet another tank retriever to pull them out.

As dawn broke the next day, the convoy resumed its slow, cross-country drive. Shortly thereafter, reports arrived of missile launchers stuck in the sand. While the air defense crews on each vehicle worked feverishly to get them out, the long line of vehicles continued its forward movement, passing and abandoning the stuck vehicles. In the distance, tank and mortar fire rang over the desert.

The movement instructions to Baghdad defined a travel strategy of avoiding urban areas. By daybreak on March 23, major U.S. ground combat units had advanced more than 200 miles into Iraq and were located approximately 130 miles north of the city of An Nasiriyah. This movement, unprecedented for speed of execution and depth of penetration, was meant to disable the Iraqi military's ability to mount a coherent defense.[83] That second night, Colonel Brown received a call from Colonel Anderson, the Chief of Staff of the 32nd AADMC, of the ambush of some of her soldiers from the 507th Maintenance Company near An Nasiriyah, Iraq.

In the 3rd Infantry Division's rapid advance towards Baghdad, the 507th Maintenance Company was the last unit in a convoy column of more than 600 vehicles. The company became isolated and detached from the main convoy as soldiers worked to recover several heavy wheeled vehicles trapped in the sand and repair broken down vehicles spread along the cross-country route through the Iraqi desert. Believing that this maintenance unit was slowing the progress of the entire convoy, the 3rd Forward Support Battalion Commander of 3rd Infantry Division and tactical commander of the convoy continued the forward movement of the convoy, abandoned the 507th Maintenance Company without leaving a security force for the unit's protection.

In the early morning hours of March 23, the 507th found itself strewn across miles of desert. Captain Troy King, the unit's company commander, decided to send part of the company onward with the main convoy to ensure some level of security while he waited for the company's remaining elements. He sent First Lieutenant Jeff Sharing, the company executive officer, forward with 32 soldiers in 17 vehicles with the main 3rd Forward Support Battalion convoy.

Captain King waited for the remaining 33 soldiers and 18 vehicles. The directions to Baghdad appeared simple enough: travel north to the Iraqi border; connect with Highway 8/Blue Route; travel west on Highway 1/Route Jackson until it intersected again with the Highway 8/Blue Route. The instructions adhered to the Coalition Forces strategy of bypassing urban areas while charging toward Baghdad. In the very early morning hours, King's segment of the convoy reached the Blue Route and looked for a manned traffic control point where they anticipated being directed west onto Route

[83] Department of Defense, Department of the Army, Special Report. "Attack on the 507th Maintenance Company." 23 March 2003. www.army.mil/features/507thMaintCmpy/AttackOnThe507MaintCmpy.pdf.

Jackson. Upon their arrival, they found the traffic control point abandoned. King found some Marines in the general vicinity and asked them if the Blue Route continued north. The Marines confirmed that it did. Although the movement instructions defined travel from Route Blue to Route Jackson to Route Blue, King highlighted on his personal map Route Blue all the way to Baghdad.

Now traveling north on Route Blue, King's segment of the vehicle convoy entered into An Nasiriyah, a moderate-sized, Shiite-dominated city of 300,000 along the Euphrates River. After verifying the direction on his map, King realized that they were off the designated convoy route. As he prepared to turn the convoy around, re-tracing the march route, he instructed his soldiers to "lock and load" their weapons and remain vigilant.

The convoy then made a series of turns on the Blue Route trying to get to the right route, at one spot driving past a checkpoint manned by uniformed Iraqi soldiers who cheered and waved at the U.S. soldiers. While turning around, a wrecker ran out of gas. The small convoy stopped as soldiers refueled the wrecker, by hand, using 5-gallon fuel cans. As the convoy resumed its hurried movement to get out of the city, they came under sporadic gunfire. The convoy missed another turn and attempted a second U-turn as the small arms fire increased.

Another truck broke down and a second truck towing a third became stuck in the sand. The soldiers quickly jumped into other vehicles. Now divided into three elements the convoy headed south back through the city. By this time, Iraqis had set up roadblocks and obstacles. Fedayeen militants, loyal to Saddam Hussein, occupied the checkpoint. Many of the soldiers returned fire, only to have their weapons jam. The soldiers carried standard issue M-16 assault rifles and ammunition magazines. Only one of the five-ton trucks had a .50 caliber machine gun mounted on its cab.

The last group of six vehicles, all towing disabled vehicles or trailers, had difficulty turning around due to their large sizes. The city of An Nasiriayh was awake, and the convoy came under fire from all directions from rifles and rocket-propelled grenades.

Colonel Anderson called Colonel Brown and informed her the soldiers of the 507th were ambushed in An Nasariyah some soldiers were dead or wounded, others were missing, and some were prisoners of war. Acting immediately, Brown contacted her Brigade Deputy Commander, Major Tom Harraghy, who was leading the rest of the Brigade Tactical Operations Center, still in Kuwait. Working with the Corps G-1 (personnel officer), Harraghy tried to determine the status of everyone in the 507th. Brown and Harraghy remained in nearly continual contact with the personnel officer. While still in a convoy moving toward her first location, Logistical Support Area (LSA) Bushmaster, Colonel Brown worked with Marine units of the 2nd Marine Expeditionary Force to reach the 507th. She had no communication with any of the elements in the 507th.

Although the original movement plan estimated travel time for the 31st Brigade to be 36 hours to the first location, it actually took 5 days to reach the destination. Upon arrival, the status of the 507th remained unknown. As the brigade's jump tactical operations center was erected with a security perimeter manned by one of the batteries, Al Jazeera, the Arabic News Channel, began broadcasting images of the captured and killed 507th soldiers. Colonel Brown learned shortly thereafter the names of the confirmed dead, Specialists Timothy Johnson and Jamal Addison. Still missing were Sergeant George Buggs, Specialist Edward Anguiano, Privates First Class Lori Piestewa and Jessica Lynch, and seven other soldiers.

Colonel Heidi Brown described the first battlefield memorial service the 31st Brigade conducted as simply gut-wrenching. Fortuitously, the unit had taken photographs of every soldier prior to leaving the United States for a unit history project. The photos of Specialists Howard Johnson and Jamal Addison were printed and displayed alongside empty combat boots, a helmet and rifle— symbols of the fallen soldiers. As Colonel Brown prayed, she also knew she had to stay focused on the mission. Lieutenant General William Wallace, V Corps Commander, attended the service, remaining solemn and quiet. These were the first of many casualties for this unit.

With various intelligence updates, Colonel Brown learned that Special Forces soldiers were working to locate and rescue the POWs. Although anxious to get the main element of her tactical operations center to their designated battlefield location, there was no security force available to move with remaining soldiers from Kuwait to LSA Bushmaster; this forced them to remain in Kuwait for 10 days. Meanwhile, 22 soldiers and Colonel Brown ran the 24-hour operations for those 10 days until the rest of the headquarters element arrived. The original plan was to move the second serial no more than two days after the lead serial. Anything more than that would be a drain on the few soldiers sent to man the jump TOC.

As the set-up of the operations center neared completion, a fierce sand storm blasted the area, followed by a heavy rain eliminating all visibility. Colonel Brown received a radio report that Captain Troy King and the 12 soldiers with him were alive and crossing the battlefield attempting to get to the tactical operations center. Their only communication was with the Marine unit. Meanwhile the 31st provided air defense coverage for the continued movement of both the 3rd Infantry and the 101st Airborne Divisions.

From start to finish, the attack on the 507th lasted between 60 to 90 minutes. Of the 33 United States soldiers in the convoy, 11 were killed in combat or died because of injuries, seven were captured by Iraqi forces and became prisoners of war, and the remaining 16 soldiers rejoined friendly forces. Nine of the 22 U.S. soldiers who survived the attacks against the convoy were wounded in action. Eight days later on March 31, 2003, the city of An Nasiriyah came under the control of the 1st Marine Expeditionary Force.[84] Seventeen Marines from the 2nd Marine Expeditionary Brigade out of Camp Lejeune, North Carolina, died trying to reach the 507th.

Poor weather delayed the advance toward Baghdad. No vehicle in the entire V Corps was to move. Needing to relocate her tactical operations center, Colonel Brown pleaded with the Corps Commander for an exception. With visibility less than 10 feet and the

---

[84] IBID.

exception granted, Colonel Brown began to move nearly 100 vehicles 30 kilometers. This drive toward Baghdad lasted 12 hours. In Heidi's pocket rested a guardian angel pin given to her by her mother. Her mother had it blessed by a priest before giving it to her, telling Heidi that it would keep her safe and that her father, who had died in August 2002, would be watching over her and her soldiers. Heidi felt the presence of her father helping to safely guide the convoy.

Colonel Brown set up the operations center at the Baghdad Airport. She received a call from the personnel officer of V Corps that the recovered remains of some of the missing soldiers were sent to Dover, Delaware for identification. The call was sad, numbing, and relieving as she would now be able to provide the soldiers' families with some closure. She held a second battlefield memorial service but still unknown were the whereabouts of Specialist Edward Anguiano.

Later that day, as United States Special Forces continued operating in An Nasiriyah, Colonel Brown learned that more remains had been located near a soccer field. Meanwhile, at the operations center, she watched the rescue of Private First Class Jessica Lynch from an Iraqi hospital on CNN International on a computer. Almost immediately, Brigadier General Bromberg came up on an Internet chat line asking for additional information about the POWs. Colonel Brown was also on an Internet chat line with Colonel John Seward, commander of 108th Air Defense Artillery Brigade. Seward confirmed the rescue of seven POWs. Brown said it was a high-five moment, "I remember yelling as loud as I could 'They're alive!' It was the best day as my prisoners of war were rescued alive. It also was the worst day in my Army career as my soldiers' remains were positively identified."

Several analyses concluded that the desperate and isolated situation that the 507th Maintenance Company found itself in was due to a navigational error caused by a number of factors. Among the factors were the rapid operational pace, acute fatigue from a continuous period of more than 65 hours with little rest, and the breakdown and recovery of so many heavy wheeled vehicles in the soft sand.

Brigadier General Howard Bromberg repeatedly asked Colonel Brown in retrospect if she would have included the 507th Maintenance Company in the maneuver. She recalled, "Why would I separate a maintenance company with all of our repair parts from the brigade they were supporting? Of course, I am going to keep them with the main forward support battalion. Yes, I would do it again." Explaining the situation, Colonel Brown said that had the unit remained on paved roads as planned and rehearsed, they would not have slowed down the pace of the convoy. The unanticipated vehicle breakdowns and recoveries would have been reduced considerably. Bromberg never seemed satisfied with her answer. Brown knows it was the right and appropriate decision to keep the company with the repair parts moving along with the unit they supported. While Heidi would not change the maneuver, she would change the outcome. Prior to assignment to Heidi's brigade and deploying for the war, the 507th Maintenance Company had been under Brigadier General Bromberg's command in garrison as the 32nd AAMDC was directly responsible for the 11th Air Defense Artillery Brigade.

Although violence, destruction, and loss of life are the realities of combat for soldiers, Colonel Brown said it changes your life and your perspective, and never leaves you. She said that you also learn from it, as soldiers expect commanders to make sound decisions and safeguard them. Upon the brigade's redeployment to the United States in June 2003, Colonel Brown revamped immediately the training in her brigade. Among the many tasks and rehearsals implemented were convoy live-fire exercises. Colonel Brown is confident that this training, now mandatory throughout the Air Defense Artillery branch, is saving lives of soldiers on the battlefield.

"We experienced the good, the bad, and the ugly of war. I do not know of any other unit that experienced this myriad of circumstances." Heidi said. There were no V Corps soldiers killed by SCUD missiles. Heidi pointed to the condition of the staff she inherited, "My only alternative was to get involved with all of my staff officers, teach, and mentor them during war." Additionally,

Heidi would realize fully the serious lack of training of the 507th when she redeployed through Kuwait. The 507th Battalion Commander was directed to brief Brigadier General Bromberg on his preparations for war for the last six months. Heidi said, "It was eye opening—I had no idea how unprepared they had been."

Assigned to the Pentagon after relinquishing command of the 31st Air Defense Artillery Brigade, Colonel Brown became the Executive Officer for the Assistant Secretary of the Army for Manpower and Reserve Affairs. Upon completion of that assignment, she returned to Fort Bliss and became the chief of staff of the Air Defense Center and Fort Bliss. Not being selected for promotion to Brigadier General was very disappointing. Heidi believes she performed very well in combat, and all the evidence suggests the same, given the extraordinary mission and the lack of talent and training in the unit she inherited, but as with other institutions, one's fate in the Army is not entirely performance-based.

Colonel Brown returned to Texas and served as the deputy commander of Fort Bliss and the assistant commandant of the Army Air and Missile Defense School (USAADASCH), a Brigadier General position. Heidi concluded, "I have done everything I could do. It is out of my hands. Maybe God's plan for me is to keep an eye on my mom. She lives just four miles away." Nothing is impossible, she reminded herself.

In July 2008, she found that belief well founded when nominated by President Bush for promotion to the rank of brigadier general. Six months later as general's stars were pinned on her shoulders she became the first woman in the Air Defense Artillery branch promoted to general and the first woman general on the I Corps Staff. Unfortunately her mother had passed in early June, never to learn of yet another in a long line of gender barriers her daughter, Heidi, broke in her career as the first woman to command a Patriot Missile Battalion and an Air Defense Brigade.

"I think female soldiers in air defense will see this as yet another tangible example of the fact that they too can attain this rank—that there is a possibility out there," said Brown. "Within the last month we had General Ann Dunwoody promoted—the first woman four-star. I think it is very positive because it's not just talk anymore."

Poolside at swimming practice. Two teammates display shirts with their team motto, "Nothing is Impossible". (*Photo courtesy of Dr. Sue Tendy*)

Mutual admiration. William Brown and his daughter Colonel Heidi Brown at the ceremony in which she assumed command of the 31st Air Defense Artillery Brigade on July 12, 2002. (*Photo courtesy of Heidi Brown*)

Brigadier General Heidi Brown addresses U.S. soldiers during the Transfer of Authority Ceremony from 555th Engineer Brigade to the 194th Engineer Brigade in Iraq. (*Photo courtesy of Heidi Brown*)

Brigadier General Heidi Brown exiting a U.S. Army UH-60 Black Hawk helicopter following an emergency landing after a bird strike broke the windshield in Iraq. (*Photo courtesy of Heidi Brown*)

Cadet Betsy Barron, USMA 1987. (*Academy Photo*)

ANGELS AMONG US | BETSY BARRON, CLASS OF 1987

"Be patient toward all that is unsolved within your heart, and try to love the questions themselves. Do not seek the answers, which cannot now be given you because you would not be able to live them, and the point is - to live everything. So, live the questions now. And perhaps you will gradually, without noticing it, live along some distant day, into the answer."

—Rainer Maria Rilke

Betsy Barron first learned about West Point at the impressionable age of 11. Although a favorite childhood babysitter declined admission to the Academy in 1976, as a member of the first class to include women, her decision piqued Betsy's curiosity. After asking her mother "what is West Point," Betsy announced that she would one day attend the United States Military Academy. She promptly went off and resumed tree climbing and fort building without giving it another thought. Years later, she discovered her high school guidance office and its piles of glossy books and catalogs about college life, none glossier than the one showing gray-clad cadets marching and living amidst stark castle-like buildings and acting in accord with the ethic of duty, honor, and country. One look and she was hooked.

Betsy and her younger brother Patrick had an unremarkable childhood in a middle-class family in Glenn Dale, Maryland. Guy Barron, their father, served a 30-year career in the Department of Defense, and JoAnne Riley, their mother, was a nurse. JoAnne raised the children with a nurse's practicality and strong devotion to her Catholic faith. Guy was a complex man whose Depression-era upbringing and early years as a U.S. Marine ingrained characteristics of efficiency, versatility, and frugality. In the winter, he would turn the heat down so low that Betsy and Patrick often wore coats while doing their homework. Recalling her father, Betsy describes him as a Renaissance man:

He could talk about anything. He knew all the birds by sight, the tree types by their leaves and bark, all the animals in the woods by their footprints. He was a gardener, sports fan, hunter, reader, and traveler. In his later years, he became an historian and amateur archeologist.

Betsy shared his love for learning, but he had an impatient side that led him to be critical of others. At times, he was condescending to Betsy and her mother. His comments often provoked altercations that ended with him telling Betsy that she was not good enough, or would never amount to anything. Betsy recalled,

Dad and I were at each other's throats a lot when I was a teen. Part of the problem was that I am just like him, hardheaded and impatient. My brother Pat was given the gift of patience and an easiness that allowed him to laugh and brush off my Dad's grumpiness. But I tended to take it personally. Almost everything he said to me caused me some level of resentment. Our relationship ultimately helped fuel my motivation to show the world and myself that I was o.k.

Her mom and dad were not the only strong adults in Betsy's life. Her parents traveled the world developing a close circle of global friends who took interest in both Betsy and Patrick. The wives in this group were well educated and well traveled. These women served as strong role models for Betsy, and their husbands as surrogate fathers of sorts. Betsy took her first international trip at the young age of eleven, when she made a solo trip to visit relatives in Australia. In her late teens, she toured Europe thanks to the generosity of her parents' close friends the Pfeiffer's, who lived in England at the time, and who remain Betsy's long time mentors.

A combination of genes, strong adult influences, and global exposure caused Betsy to possess an intense determination and love for life, and provided energy for her strong drive and sense of self-direction. But her father's criticism and strictness led Betsy to harbor a tendency towards self-doubt and eroded her confidence.

As she grew up, Betsy's appetite for literature helped develop a vibrant imagination and provided an escape from the strained father-daughter relationship. She read everything on which she could get her hands, from Plato, the Greek tragedies, Shakespeare, J.R.R. Tolkien, Herman Wouk, Jane Austen, and Charles Dickens to *National Geographic* magazine. Betsy found that literature opened a door into a world of limitless possibilities, causing her to think big and dream large. She said, "From these great and timeless stories, I learned that life could be amazing if one chose to experience it that way."

Betsy worked hard in high school, striving for perfection and achieving high marks each year. She was active in student government, school activities and sports, with soccer her favorite. Her years in competitive traveling soccer enabled her to develop a strong team ethic, a high level of fitness, an appreciation for strategy, and a tolerance for pain.

Although she achieved a high grade point average, she recalled a need for greater challenges: "I wanted to try something really hard." The idea of West Point and a subsequent commission as an officer in the United States Army presented a significant test. She enjoyed the feelings of being successful, strong, and athletic—all attributes central to success for cadets and Army officers. West Point was the perfect adventure on which to embark. Betsy added,

> I had a sense of destiny and direction at a young age. I wanted more than a normal college life. I was not interested in becoming a stockbroker, lawyer, or other normal occupation. I wanted to make a difference in my world and do something important, something bigger.

Initially, inclined to attend the Military Academy, Betsy also looked at the other service academies as entry points to her great adventure. The Air Force Academy seemed very far away and too technical in its curriculum. Not wanting to serve aboard a ship, she ruled out the Coast Guard and Naval Academies. That left West Point, which was also the only service academy with a women's soccer team at the time. It seemed the perfect fit.

At its deepest level, entrance into West Point would allow Betsy to experience the kinds of challenges she sought and to prove to all that she was indeed worthy. More than 20 years later, Betsy still believes, "West Point offered me the chance for significant personal growth while also entering a noble profession of service to the country."

Her work ethic paid off at West Point. Betsy excelled in and out of the classroom and achieved a high score each year on the annual Army Physical Fitness Test—consisting of a 2-mile run, push-ups, and sit-ups—and she performed well in all aspects of military training. The physical challenges of daily life aside, Betsy recalled that her most significant difficulties always involved academics and the high standards she set for herself. She said,

> I was not content with average grades and wanted to perform really well in the classroom. Plebe year, I really struggled in math and feared some horrible grade. But with a lot of sweat, concentration, and help from friends, I ended up with an A by the end of second semester.

Although an International Relations and Soviet Studies major, Betsy earned an A+ in Honors Physics and finished the course of instruction actually feeling as though she understood the opaque and troublesome-to-most topic of relativity. She wore academic stars on her dress uniform starting her junior year, signifying her ranking in the top 5% of her class of more than 1,000 cadets.

Despite their differences, her father became Betsy's biggest fan during her cadet years. While Guy couldn't always communicate how proud he was to his daughter, he told everyone else—friends, neighbors, co-workers, and anyone else who would listen. He spent hours preparing and mailing bags of air-popped corn and other edible treats for her late night study snacks, called regularly, sent money whenever his daughter needed it, and supported her through visits. He and JoAnne cheered for her on the soccer fields and went to several Army football tailgates and games. Yet, father and daughter struggled to talk to each other in meaningful ways. Their strong personalities and impatient natures prevented either from breaking through the barriers to communication they had established during her teen years.

Friendships were always important to Betsy. She developed many acquaintances during her teenage years, but only a few very close friends—friends with whom she remains close to this day. Paramount in her youth was the influence of her closest friend, Maureen, and Maureen's strong and devoutly Catholic parents and siblings. Betsy and Maureen were nearly inseparable, with each spending almost as many weekends with the other's family as they did their own. Also, one of the most important aspects of her experience at West Point was the relationships she developed with her Company F-1 roommates and other female classmates over the four years. Belonging to that group of talented, dynamic women was an incredibly meaningful experience for Betsy. She recalled, "We grew up together in those years. We got each other through." Although distance and circumstances prevent Betsy, her former roommates, and Maureen from spending much time together, she remains close to many of them to this day.

Daily attendance at Catholic mass provided Betsy a few moments of needed serenity. Betsy found it to be a perfect way to begin the often intense and difficult days that characterized cadet life. She recalled, "It was important to give thanks each day for allowing me this incredible opportunity, and to ask for strength, perseverance, and understanding during difficult times."

Drawing on her Catholic elementary school experiences and her mother's teachings at home, she often would reflect upon the lessons learned from her many academic and spiritual mentors. She recalled that her favorite grade school nun, Sister Jude, reminded her students, "When you don't get that prayer answered, you might consider that you asked for the wrong thing." Often during a challenging program like West Point, cadets find themselves asking for extra help through divine intervention. As Betsy negotiated the difficult road that the West Point experience entailed, she often found herself chuckling inwardly about Sister Jude's gentle reminder.

Given Betsy's high grade point average, achievements in athletics, and excellent performance in military development, in her senior year Betsy was selected as a battalion commander, the cadet leader for 360 other cadets. During her final semester at the Academy, Betsy chose the branch of Military Intelligence because it offered the best opportunity to apply the knowledge learned in her international relations course of study. Betsy graduated 20th in the class of 1987, the number-two woman in the class.

In early 1988, after her initial formal branch training, Betsy arrived in Munich, Germany, assigned to one of the Army's most desirable units for Military Intelligence Officers, given its location and strategic intelligence mission. She enjoyed life in Europe, the fast pace of her unit's mission, and the challenge of solving a range of problems involved with managing all types of resources and assets. Life abroad as a young lieutenant proved very lonely, however. With few social outlets available, Betsy found herself turning inward to a childhood interest, that of poetry, both reading and writing it. She said, "Poetry became an outlet for me in Germany because of the loneliness. It is a great way to occupy thought and develop a sense of reflection. I really enjoy the emotion and power that imagery and word combinations can evoke."

Betsy believes that poetry enabled her to develop an understanding of the role and importance of introspection, especially for those holding leadership positions. She explained,

Often as a leader in the Army, I found myself moving at hyper-speed. Part of that is the nature of the assignment, but the other part comes from personal drive and self-direction. Always traveling and operating at such speeds didn't allow me time to reflect on how I may have just interacted with someone or how something of seemingly little importance at the time influenced a person or outcome. To this day, poetry provides me a mirror of reflection. Leaders who fail to nurture a strong reflective side have a much greater chance of failing in their most important duty: serving those under them in a way that will enable that group to accomplish the mission most effectively.

During her four and a half years in Germany, Betsy served in a variety of positions of increasing responsibility for both people and equipment. As the assistant operations officer for her battalion, she helped direct her unit's intelligence support to the United States Army Central Command during Operations Desert Shield and Desert Storm—her first wartime experience. As a first lieutenant, Betsy successfully commanded a 120-person company, an assignment typically reserved for an Army captain. During the same period, she earned her first master's degree, completing Boston University's overseas program in international relations.

As she went through those first years of commissioned service, she could look back on her time at West Point and clearly see the many lessons learned. Perhaps most important, that she could achieve anything on which she set her mind, and for which she planned and prepared. Her Academy experience also taught her that she could handle more stress than she ever had imagined, and be satisfied with far less comfort.

However, there was another side to what Betsy learned. Her experience taught her that, at West Point and in the Army, chauvinism was accepted. "This is one thing I learned to hate," she said. "Over time I began to see the insidious side of hidden sexism—that oh-so-subtle undercurrent of suspicion and mistrust that so many military males hold for their female counterparts. In time, I began to learn to demand the same kind of respect from males as I was giving them."

She learned from her West Point experience that the military tended to focus on what one did wrong, instead of what one may have done right. Demerits, other ingenious forms of punishment, constant inspections, etc, built attention to detail and mental toughness, but did so from a point of view of scrutiny and criticism. She recalled working to unlearn this approach by spending subsequent years reminding herself that, "Despite the things I may have really screwed up, I also did these other marvelous or otherwise positive and productive things. The same went for those around me."

The Army reinforced many of West Point's lessons, but did so in an arena where actions carried greater consequences. Most prevalent was the lesson about the loneliness of the officer and leader. But she also learned that her people-first approach and human touch enabled her to become a leader who inspired loyalty. Betsy added,

> I had learned to be too hard on myself and have spent most of my time since the Army unlearning this habit. In addition, I learned never to underestimate the power of the human spirit—mine and others working for me. People know whether you have their backs covered or not, and you take your responsibility toward them lightly at your own peril. It's not about being nice. It's about being completely honest with them and yourself. People respond to integrity, fairness, consistency, flexibility, and, above all, humanity.

In 1991, competitively selected, Betsy attended the Post Graduate Intelligence Program (PGIP), a one-year Master of Science in Strategic Intelligence program at the Joint Military Intelligence College at Bolling Air Force Base in Washington, D.C. In July 1992, as the class salutatorian, she graduated with her second master's degree and traveled to Fort Huachuca, Arizona, to attend advanced Military Intelligence officer training. While in Arizona, Betsy met another Military Intelligence captain. For the purposes of this chapter, his name is "Jeff." Her intellectual strength and athletic interests attracted Jeff. Betsy was attracted to his charm, sensitivity, and awareness of the world around him. He loved music, athletics, singing, and writing poetry. "When he sang he sounded like Neil Young," recalled Betsy. But most of all, she was attracted by his serenity. She described him in the same way that she described her father, as a Renaissance man, with a love of sport, art, and music. In time, she would learn that his "renaissance" personality included a dark side.

In May 1994, after completing the Military Intelligence Advanced Course, they both received a follow-on assignment to Fort Meade, Maryland, in close proximity to Betsy's childhood home of Glenn Dale. Their relationship seemed to be progressing well, and now that they had a multi-year assignment ahead with which they could gain some stability, they decided to marry that fall. Their late October wedding day was magnificent. It seemed like the perfect beginning for a new life together.

On this same day, Betsy's rocky relationship with her father began to change. Guy liked her fiancé, but sensed his daughter struggling with some of the aspects of Jeff's strong personality and manner of coping with various demands. Just prior to walking her down the aisle, Guy leaned over to his daughter and said, "My car is right across the street. Just say the word and we can leave right now." Overwhelmed by his insight and loyalty to her, Betsy did not take her father up on his offer. That day Betsy began to see him more for the passionate and conscientious, if overly stern, father and friend that he truly was.

After a short honeymoon, Betsy and Jeff returned to their positions at Fort Meade. Offered a second company command marked Betsy as a fast-track officer. After his two company commands in various signal intelligence units, Jeff was selected to join a unique special operations unit that deployed frequently. It multiplied his work and life stress. The demands ultimately took their toll, and he began to experience severe mood swings. These concerned Betsy greatly, but she had faith in him and believed that he would find a way to work though his emotions.

Earlier in their marriage, as Betsy considered having children, she had difficulty reconciling the notion of nurturing a family while maintaining two professional military careers. She had come to believe that two command-track officers, like her and her husband, really had to be very careful about having children, since their careers often would take them away from those children. If she decided to try to have a child, she felt the need to reassess her career. With two successful company commands behind her, and given what she considered to be a disappointing environment in Army strategic military intelligence, Betsy resigned her commission after 8 ½ years as an active duty officer, and began her civilian life as an analyst at a think tank in Falls Church, Virginia. Jeff remained on active duty, assuming ever more demanding and challenging assignments in the intelligence community.

Disliking the corporate arena, Betsy returned to public service within a year joining the Department of Defense as an intelligence analyst. She hoped her move would help her gain a greater sense of purpose and the opportunity to contribute to the country from within the federal government.

With her situation thus stabilized, Betsy began to pay more attention to her deteriorating marriage. Although in love with Jeff, the couple struggled. Consumed with work and recreational sports pursuits, at home he continued to cope poorly. He tended to take his stress and emotions out on Betsy, often making outrageous accusations or claiming she had been coddled at West Point and in the Army because of her gender. Even though she believed Jeff did not mean these things, he began to undermine her self-confidence. A classic optimist, and a tad naive due to her somewhat sheltered upbringing, Betsy had spent her life up to this point searching for the best in people, and choosing to overlook their more questionable motives and actions. Her tendency for this had gotten her into hot water in the past; mainly because her positive outlook caused her to stumble into pitfalls, she would have been better off noticing. In the case of her marriage, her desire to make it work and to support her husband led her to accept behaviors from him that were unacceptable and wrong. She could no longer ignore the pattern of verbal abuse and physical aggression Jeff demonstrated. She recalled,

> Jeff was slowly undermining my sense of normalcy, chipping away at my sense of right and wrong. He knew how to play on my vulnerabilities, like self-doubt, and did so repeatedly. It seems crazy now as I describe it, but at the time, it was all very debilitating.

Jeff followed each violent outburst with some act of contrition—an apology, an explanation, an excuse, and a promise that it would not happen again. Betsy described it as a classic cycle but remained committed to their marriage. She believed that she understood him and wanted to support him. She said,

> I kept telling myself that Jeff is an educated, rounded man. He's a poet, for Pete's sake, just like me. He feels deeply and just has not developed the ability to channel his emotions positively. But the pattern became obvious over time. I was so torn because I was very committed to my marriage, and to him. I wanted to help him overcome some of his demons. I had also convinced myself that a successful, strong woman like me couldn't possibly get trapped into this kind of a relationship. I was again naive.

After almost three years of marriage, Betsy began to accept the fact that Jeff's unpredictability and temper were more than she could or should handle. In retrospect she said,

> I would eventually realize that the strength that attracted him to me also was very threatening to him. It seems that he must have felt he had to keep me under his thumb and on my toes all the time in order to feel safe in the relationship. Though I didn't quite realize it at the time, his unpredictability and anger frightened and intimidated me.

As she went through the difficulties of dealing with her thoughts of leaving her husband, she became pregnant. Betsy believed the pregnancy to be a sign that they were supposed to stay together, at least for the near-term. She recalled, "I was concerned but took a new look at how I could continue to work on our marriage. The pregnancy helped me recommit to the relationship."

During her last trimester, Betsy began to experience complications. After a sonogram confirmed a low amniotic fluid level and fetal heart rate, Betsy was immediately put on strict bed rest. Consumed in his work, Jeff seemed barely interested in the impending birth of their child or the effects the pregnancy had on his wife.

Her fears and concern grew as the baby's due date approached. At 37 ½ weeks, on February 3, 1998, baby Jacob was delivered through an emergency caesarean due to dangerously low levels of amniotic fluid. Immediately tested for potential kidney problems, these thankfully, proved negative. Although small, weighing only 5 pounds and 9 ounces, he seemed perfect. Although exhausted, Betsy was thrilled and grateful that all seemed well.

At 7:30 A.M. the next morning, Jacob underwent medical tests, though Betsy thought he was merely in the nursery. A new doctor entered her recovery room and introduced himself as Dr. Wulfsberg, her geneticist. He reported quietly, "I think your son has a genetic disorder, and I need more time to figure out what it is." Betsy realized this as the moment every mother feared most, hearing your doctor say that something is wrong with your baby. The struggles with and concerns about her marriage, her fears about the unknowns of having children, her concerns about career-motivated parents being there for their children, her life-long uncertainties and anxieties about her choices, judgment, and worth collided. The next few days passed in a blur.

The doctors detected a large heart murmur, a ventricular septal defect, in Jacob's heart and suspected additional problems. Mother and son were released from the hospital on day three. Despite Betsy's efforts to feed Jacob breast milk and formula, he was not able to eat sufficiently to keep up with the needs of his growing body. By day seven, his body temperature dropped to 95 degrees; a strong sign of infection, and Jacob was re-hospitalized as more tests were performed. The tests for infection came out negative four days later. Betsy reluctantly took Jacob home again.

Although the doctors could not diagnose Jacob's genetic condition immediately, they did confirm that he would most likely have to undergo life-saving open-heart surgery in the next four to six months.

Betsy immediately took a leave of absence from her job to be able to spend all of her time with Jacob. For the next few months, they visited numerous medical specialists and therapists, and Jake was put on a nasal-gastric feeding tube to help him obtain the calories he needed. Afraid of leaving her husband while having to care for a disabled child, Betsy continued to try to work through the problems in her marriage. She hoped Jacob's arrival would help turn things around; just the opposite happened. Jeff was incapable of handling the strain of a disabled and critically ill child. He grew increasingly distant and verbally violent, and repeatedly denied the health problems of his son. Betsy will never forget Jeff's stinging criticism: "You can't even have a baby right."

Jacob was soon diagnosed with Prader-Willi Syndrome, a complex genetic disorder arising from an irregularity in the 15th chromosome that affects approximately one baby in every 10,000 births. Betsy described PWS,

> A genetic fluke occurs at conception. It affects a child's facial and other physical features, growth, sexual development, ability to regulate body temperature and appetite, motor and cognitive development, and behavior. Obsessive Compulsive Disorder (ODC) characterizes the syndrome and other behavioral problems, especially in boys, as the children enter their teens and twenties. Some PWS young adults develop mental disorders requiring administration of psychotropic drugs during their adulthood.

At four months of therapy and treatment, Jacob still was not able to move his head on his own. Worse, by the summer of 1998, Betsy finally realized that though her marriage was in ruins, she would have to remain married long enough to get Jacob through heart surgery and recovery. Financially, she had no other choice— she was still on leave without pay and would have to remain so throughout Jacob's recovery. Afterwards, she decided, she would leave her husband. During the next six months, Betsy got her financial matters in order, paying all marital debts, ensuring all accounts settled, and assets distributed.

Then, during a planned cardiac catheterization designed to allow Jacob's cardiologist to map out exactly how he would conduct the planned open-heart survey, the surgeon instead discovered that one deformity in Jacob's thumb-sized heart actually compensated for, and ultimately corrected, the other deformities. After months of intensive cardiology visits, therapy, and mental preparation for open-heart surgery and recovery, Betsy was amazed when Jake's cardiologist informed her he would see them in a year.

After absorbing this incredible news and reality, Betsy began planning a more deliberate departure from her marriage. Her father also was there for her. To ease the financial strain, he offered to pay for the move. She put a down payment on an apartment in a nearby town and began packing. Upon Jeff's return from a short business trip, Betsy and the now 11-month-old Jacob left.

In retrospect, Betsy described the break-up of her marriage as one of the most wrenching experiences of her life. The negative lessons of her marriage haunt her to this day, but with time, she was able to realize that the experience enabled her to grow in some fundamental ways and gave her three gifts for which she remains eternally grateful. She said,

> The first and foremost is Jacob, my son and my angel. My life would not be the same without him. The second was my renewed relationship with my father. My troubled relationship with Jeff helped me see the importance of my relationship with my father and to see the qualities in Guy Barron that the younger, hardheaded Betsy couldn't have imagined. The third thing I gained was very much inside me. When you find yourself in a very difficult personal situation, you eventually realize you have to make some choices. Ultimately, I had to face the fact that, while my husband had serious anger management issues, I was part of the problem. I realized that many of my own negative patterns of thought and self-criticism had landed me in a situation where criticism from my partner seemed rather familiar and almost like home.

Despite the divorce, Betsy said she still has love for Jeff and certainly hopes for his happiness and success. For all the compromises that seemed right at the time but should have never occurred, she muses with chagrin—not regret—to this day. Experiencing all the emotional anguish of leaving a difficult marriage and beginning a life as a single mother facing career challenges and her child's medical difficulties was an incredibly humbling and frightening experience. But, without her relationship with Jeff, positives and negatives aside, she would not have the privilege of having young Jacob in her life. She said:

> Not a day goes by that I don't look at the golden little boy with whom I have been entrusted, and give thanks for the wonder that he is. He is unique, loving, tender, excited, and alive. He is a gift, and I wouldn't trade this child, beset with a genetic condition many would describe as a burden, for anything in the world.
>
> I drag him off to therapy sessions and specialist appointments, knowing his gains are incremental, his 'milestones' are more like…'inch-pebbles,' creeping forward along a twisting path bearing no resemblance to all the nice charts that come in the mommy books.
>
> I see the sunshine, energy, and life in his eyes, the delight in his laugh, and the trust and unrequited love he gives, effortlessly, to me, and to his world. He fearlessly charges forth every day, unhindered by his hindrances and, in the process, melts away for me the hazy 'what ifs' and the sheer weight of this responsibility. In his vulnerability, his fight to survive, he needed me to champion his cause. Unknowingly, he became my champion in the process. For all the hassles my son endures in his life, I continue to learn from him every day, how to love, how to give, how to live. This little angel, with his tiny hands and smaller heart, has saved me. Grateful can't come close to describing the thanks I feel.

In the years that have passed since her marriage, Jacob's birth and diagnosis, and her divorce and beginning of a new life for her and her son, Betsy has built her career in the Department of Defense and worked with countless teachers, therapists and specialists to provide Jacob with the most productive early intervention and therapy possible. Professionally, she is currently a senior manager at her Agency, and leads a fast-paced division of analysts and technicians providing direct support to the global war on terrorism and United States troops on the ground in Iraq and Afghanistan.

Jacob, now 12 years old, is beginning to develop verbal communications skills. Although intellectually developmentally delayed, he remains the joy of Betsy's heart and life. Ultimately, he remains her hope and life force, and he reminds all who know him of the value and importance of unqualified love and that essential life balance, so often forgotten in our fast-paced culture.

"Horizons bring to mind purple sky, first star and gentle moon.
And hazy but slightly discernable things for which to reach, and yearn, and wonder,
As twilight descends onto an accepting Earthen bosom.
Darkness brightens, in this moment, hopeful souls with the half-light of a million
Twirling stars,
Dancing and flickering in their endless void,
Each a tiny cell in an unknown being,
Each a tiny moment, a memory, of a life gone before,
And of a heart trying desperately to beat on."

— B. Barron, 1997

Major Jerry Tait, Barron's mentor, pins captains bars on Betsy in Munich, Germany. Lieutenant Colonel Bill Hotze, USMA 1971, Commander of 18th Military Intelligence Battalion, looks on with pride. (*Photo courtesy of Betsy Barron*)

Betsy and son Jacob, age 10 months in 1998. (*Photo courtesy of Betsy Barron*)

Betsy and son Jacob, age 9, December 2007. (*Photo courtesy of Betsy Barron*)

Cadet Dawn Halfaker compares class rings with friends during Ring Weekend August 24, 2000. *Left to right:* Cadets Dawn Halfaker, Therese Kelley, Melissa Barrett, and Charcy Schaefer. (*Photo courtesy of Connie Halfaker*)

No Front Lines | Captain (retired) Dawn Halfaker, Class of 2001

"You must do the thing you think you cannot do."
—Eleanor Roosevelt

Sport, particularly football, is a widely used metaphor for everything from running a business to fighting a war. The Long Gray Line of West Point has long produced linebackers who turn into leaders and halfbacks who turn into heroes. Although Dawn Halfaker was an Army basketball player, not a football player, she is both a leader and a hero.

A fiery, athletic, and competitive redheaded student from Ramona, California, Dawn played sports since childhood beginning with soccer and track and field at age 6. In high school, she excelled in running the hurdles and playing volleyball and basketball. She dreamt of playing basketball for a Division I college, an ambition shared by many high school players across the country. Dawn led the Rancho Bernardo Broncos to the state tournament twice. The Broncos captured the Palomar League Championship and the California Interscholastic Federation (CIF) San Diego Section Division I title in back-to-back seasons. In doing so, Dawn earned All-CIF San Diego Section honors twice, all-league first time selection, and San Diego and North County all-star honors. Recruited by several Division I schools, including West Point, she had the satisfaction of finding that her basketball ambitions were within reach.

After speaking with one of the coaches from West Point, Dawn realized that West Point was not just a school but also a future and she liked the future she saw. Firm in her decision to attend one of the nation's preeminent leadership schools, Dawn proudly, but hesitantly, told people where she was going to attend college and that she was going to serve in the Army. "They all seemed to be so impressed, or stunned, that I was confident in my decision. Many who knew me as hard-headed and immature found my decision very surprising given the regimentation of the military," recalled Dawn.

Mrs. Mann, Dawn's first grade teacher, described her as follows, "Dawn walked to the beat of her own drum. That drum took her to West Point and beyond."[85] A few thought Dawn would not succeed, and told her so. This made the challenge of West Point that much more appealing for Dawn. In the spring of her senior year at Rancho Bernardo, she quietly made the decision not to run the hurdles that last season, despite having the fastest time in the county. She knew she would be leaving for West Point shortly after graduation and wanted to spend time with Connie and Stephen, her parents, Dale, her brother, and her high school friends.

The most trying time for Dawn was the first summer at West Point, infamously known as Beast Barracks, the six-week initial transition and training period. "The adjustment from teenager to soldier in a very short time was intense. I grew up fast," she said. High school had come easily for Dawn and never presented a challenge or struggle, but West Point was very different. "The military aspect was somewhat of a shock to me. Others seemed to have more experience or a better understanding of what was going on. It just took me a little longer to figure out the rules and understand the concept of learning to follow instead of leading."

Once Beast Barracks concluded and the academic year began, Dawn focused on athletics and studies. Even for those recruited to play basketball, actually making and playing on the team was an honor to earn; achieved only through the right mix of talent, skill, hard work, sweat, and "teach-ability." Dawn made the Lady Knights basketball team but quickly learned that being a good player was not enough. There were some other lessons in leadership that she had to master. Dawn recalled,

> I had not earned the respect of other players, particularly the upperclassmen. Basketball helped me, because, again, I learned that I needed to earn that

---

[85] Captain (retired) Dawn Halfaker (interview with author), April 2005.

respect through my actions, attitudes, and words on
and off the court.

Once Dawn figured this out, she became both a starter and a
standout, making the Patriot League All-Rookie Team, even as the
Army team struggled that season. During her plebe year, they
endured one of the worst seasons in the short history of women's
basketball at the Academy, finishing the season in last place in the
Patriot League with a 1-19 record.[86] The athletic director gathered the
team and asked about the coach and her style. Not wanting to say
anything negative about the coach, Dawn merely said that the
coach's style did not seem to mesh with the teams. While
disappointed to see the coach leave, Dawn knew her departure
would benefit the team.

At the start of Dawn's yearling year, Sherri Abbey-Nowatzki
became the coach and introduced a new team concept and a style of
play that emphasized fundamentals, strength, and power. She also
brought a new style of discipline. Some of the players did not readily
accept this new approach, despite their previous four consecutive
losing seasons. Dawn was one of the team members that did not
initially appreciate the new leadership. Coach Nowatzki recalled,
"Dawn was one of the most difficult player challenges. She is very
headstrong and very strong willed, along with being a fierce
competitor. She was also rebellious and immature."

In the early part of preseason play that second year, Dawn
injured her posterior cruciate ligament (PCL) and spent the first half
of the season in rehabilitation. About the same time, Coach Nowatzki
kicked off the team two of the sophomores for poor attitudes that
were infecting other players. One was a close friend of Dawn's.
Although angry at the coach's decision and frustrated that her injury
had cost her a starting spot, Dawn continued to practice. Sitting on
the bench also allowed her to watch and better understand the coach

[86] In 1978, the women's basketball team, known as the "Sugar Smacks," was the first women's team to gain varsity status. The
team finished its initial varsity year with an 18-5 record.

before actually playing for her. She quickly realized that Coach Nowatzki was the spark that ignited the team. With this, Dawn's personal and the team transformation began. By mid season, Dawn's observation and rehabilitation paid off, earning her a starting position. While the team's record improved to 7-21, it included several losses that Coach Nowatzki considered "blowouts." The following year, the team better understood what it meant to work and play together. They added two more wins and kept most games within eight points. These seasons at Army were the first time Dawn had been on a consistently losing team, and she vowed to turn that around during her firstie year.

A description of Dawn that appeared on the Army Sports Information Website as she entered her final year on the team captures the quality of her talent:

> *Three-year letter winner ... fiery competitor who will play a key role in Army's success as the spark that ignites the team ... exceptional athlete and extremely competitive player ready for breakout season ... looking to showcase all-around versatility and expand scoring role ... talented off-guard who has improved outside shooting range ... explosive first step and scores well off the dribble ... slashing penetrator ... aggressive player with confidence, discipline and maturity who will be counted on in clutch situations ... nationally ranked in steals freshman year after setting USMA single-season record with 85 ... led Army in steals last year with 60 to head into final campaign ranked in the top 10 on the career charts with 165 ... just ten off fifth place and could move as high as second.* [87]

In the last regular season game of her college career, the Army women's team defeated Holy Cross for the first time in four years. In one of her most triumphant performances against inter-

---

[87] www.goarmysports.com.

league rival Bucknell, Dawn scored 21 points and made seven steals. The team finished the season at 19-10. But while Dawn aspired to play basketball professionally one day in the Women's National Basketball Association (WNBA), she focused on her career as a soldier first.

Like many, her desire to serve her country strengthened during her four years at West Point. In her final year, she elected to serve in the Military Police Branch. "Dawn went to Korea right away in her first year as an officer," Dawn's father said. "She became a military police officer because it was the most active branch a female could become involved with. She chose the action branch because she always likes to be close to the action."[88]

With less than three years service in the Army, Lieutenant Halfaker arrived in Iraq in early February 2004 as a platoon leader with the 293rd Military Police Company, a support asset of the 3rd Brigade, 2nd Infantry Division, based in Fort Lewis, Washington and then operating in Mosul. Sent to Diyala Province Police Station in Baghdad, her platoon relieved another unit that had only been in this particular area of operations for two weeks. Prior to the 293rd's arrival, the station was manned by an Army National Guard Field Artillery platoon, whose training for this alien role consisted of a one-week crash course in the basic missions of a Military Police company. Simply stated, the mission of Dawn's platoon was to train the Iraqi police assigned to the station so that eventually there could be a complete handover of operations to them.

In reality, the mission was more complex. Dawn explained,

> Now attached to the 1st Infantry Division, we were operating at an Iraqi police station in which we had a military police desk, a 300-person prison, an intelligence section with Iraqis and coalition forces working jointly providing force protection of the police station. We had people collecting, analyzing and

---

[88] Erika Ayn Finch, "RB alum recovering from injuries suffered in Iraq," North County Times. 22 July 2004.

disseminating intelligence, conducting raids, performing reconnaissance, and providing patrols and VIP escorts. As if that weren't enough, we also had a police academy with an academic curriculum, training events, and pistol ranges. So we had a little bit going on.

In Iraq, everyone operated at a level way above one's current pay grade. We learned by just doing. We gained confidence in our abilities at first by positive response from the Iraqis as to how much they were learning and their desire to become good police officers. Everyday was overwhelming. Everyday there were multiple 'holy cows.' However, not having a direct commander watching everything I did was beneficial. You have to make decisions and take action. You lead. You get into a groove. You adapt and overcome to execute and complete the mission.

Dawn organized her 33 soldiers into three squads and rotated them among the big three divisions of labor: administration and oversight of the police operations desk, management of the police station jail and Police Academy, and security and force protection of the station as a quick reaction force.

Dawn gives her alma mater credit for preparing her to accomplish this difficult mission. She said,

Upon deployment to Iraq, no one gives you a handy guidebook. What I did have were the intangibles. I had a set of values and the competence, knowledge, and leadership training that allows you to perform and react in and out of combat. I think West Point totally prepares you for that.

On June 18, 2004, Dawn lost a truck to an improvised explosive device. While the driver of the truck took shrapnel in his face, he returned to duty quickly. This, in the end, was a good day. The next day was not.

At about 1:00 A.M. that morning, Lieutenant Halfaker received the mission of helping a Field Artillery battalion sweep a slum-like neighborhood near the police station. "I informed Staff Sergeant Norberto Lara, one of my squad leaders, that I was going to accompany him on this mission, but he had control of the squad," said Dawn. When they rolled out as the lead humvee in a 4-vehicle patrol, Sergeant Lara occupied the front passenger seat of the armored humvee.[89] Also manning the vehicle were a driver and a gunner in the turret. Along with an Iraqi translator, Dawn sat in the back. As the patrol began, all the occupants quickly and routinely scanned near and far, for suspicious activity or even changes in the road surface, which could indicate the presence of IEDs.

Early in the patrol, one of the units in the area received small arms fire. Sergeant Lara's humvee responded, but the firing subsided and they returned to their area of operations, resumed driving and observation through the moonlit night.

At 3:30 A.M., the humvee came under small arms fire and a rocket-propelled grenade (RPG) attack in the town of Baqubah. The RPG pierced the front of the humvee, tore through the air filter, entered the passenger space, severed Sergeant Lara's arm, continued through the vehicle cabin, through Dawn's right upper arm and exploded next to the right side of her head. Sergeant Lara moaned and slumped over the radio, unconscious. Dazed and covered in blood, Lieutenant Halfaker yelled to the driver, "Get out of the kill zone." They were 35 miles northeast of Baghdad.[90]

Dawn remembered,

---

[89] HMMWV, High Mobility Multipurpose Wheeled Vehicle (M998 Truck). This vehicle replaced the jeep in the mid'80's as the Army's standard workhorse utility vehicle.

[90] John Doherty, "Women at War," The Times Herald Record. 8 March 2005.

You are thrown into frenzy for a split second. It is chaos with the sounds and smells of being blasted and rocked, being blinded from the flash, deafened from the sounds, and gasping for air. I thought I couldn't breathe because of the smoke; what I didn't know was that my lung was punctured from several ribs breaking. You go outside your body for a minute and then you come back in, and then, suddenly, you feel immense amounts of pain. The explosion forced my body forward and left. I fell forward and down. I remember leaning back up slowly, not yet knowing what had happened. I made eye contact with my driver, affirming he was OK. I yelled for him to keep driving, get out of the kill zone, and back to the station.

At this point, Dawn's arm was connected loosely to her shoulder by skin; the humerus bone above her elbow was gone.

As the driver maneuvered the humvee out of the ambush zone, the gunner, who was not seriously injured, dropped down from the turret and called the military police station on the radio, telling them to prepare for incoming wounded and a medical evacuation. The return drive probably took no more than a few minutes. When the humvee arrived and the right passenger door opened, everyone could see the extent of the injuries to Sergeant Lara and Lieutenant Halfaker.

Fortunately, there were both a physician's assistant and a medic at the station that immediately began dispensing morphine to lessen the pain. While Lara remained unconscious, Dawn floated in and out of consciousness. Each time she regained awareness, she yelled in severe pain. As they tended to her arm, she yelled, "You bastards better not cut my arm off." Dawn said,

We were put in a tracked vehicle to transport us to the spot from which we would be evacuated out of the area. I remember the ride being very bumpy. When we arrived at the forward operating base, the helicopters that were to fly us to a combat support hospital at Balad Air Base were ready to go, but we weren't. It was probably another 30 to 45 minutes before we could fly because our lungs needed to be stabilized. I remember an intense amount of physical pain, as if someone were hacking my arm bone with an axe. The last thing I remember is ascending in a Blackhawk. That is, until I woke up in Walter Reed on the 30th of June.

Dawn had spent 10 days in a coma.

The original call to her father provided little information about the extent and severity of Dawn's injury. A follow-up call was promised in 24 hours. In addition to the shattered arm and five broken ribs, Dawn had burns on her face and a severe infection brewing in her lungs and spreading throughout her body. A bacteria in the dirt deeply ingrained in her wounds most likely caused the infection in Dawn's body. The bacteria, know as Acinetobacter[91], is found in the soil in Iraq. A common pathogen in Vietnam, it starts to quickly invade the body where other bacteria have been killed off. Because Acinetobacter is resistant to drugs, often the only effective treatment is amputation of the limb. In Balad, Dawn repeatedly had screamed at the doctors not to cut off her arm. Some thought there was a slim chance it could be saved. Once stabilized, Dawn was evacuated to Landstuhl Regional Medical Center, Germany.

Connie Halfaker, Dawn's mother, began making phone calls to two of her daughter's best friends from West Point who had returned from 14-month tours of combat duty in Iraq. One stationed in Texas as a rear detachment commander, while her family was living in Virginia; the other classmate in Germany, but currently with her family in Minnesota. Connie asked for their prayers as well as

---

[91] Matthew Harper, "The Iraq Infection," Forbes Magazine. 02 August 2005. Available from www.forbes.com.

any means of getting additional information about her daughter's condition.

"It took about 12 hours to make sense of what happened and why we were not getting the information. We learned that she was stable enough to be evacuated out of Iraq to Germany," recalled Connie. The next call the Halfakers received told her that Dawn had landed in Germany at one o'clock Sunday morning. Four and a half hours later and nearly 24 hours after the original phone call, her parents were able to speak to a surgeon and discover the extent of Dawn's injuries. "We learned that her arm was still attached by the nerves and brachial artery which lie under the no longer existing humerus." The medical team administered medication to paralyze her in an attempt to save her and save her arm. Better understanding of the delicate balance in which Dawn's life was hanging, Connie asked the nurses to pray over her. The nurses went to Dawn's bedside immediately. "There are no words appropriate to describe the professionalism and personal touch of the entire medical trauma team at Landstuhl. They gave me the feeling that Dawn was the only person in the hospital and the most important person in the world," shared Connie.

At the same time, Dawn's teammate in Germany called Deanie Dempsey, who immediately drove 90 minutes from Frankfurt to the Landstuhl hospital to sit, talk, and be with Dawn. Deanie's husband, Major General Martin Dempsey, was the 1st Armored Division's commander in Iraq. Just three years earlier, Brigadier General Dempsey had issued the oath of office to his daughter Megan, Dawn, and three other basketball teammates following West Point's graduation exercises. The five new officers had recited the oath and pinned their gold second lieutenant bars on outside the Hollender Center, the place where they played as a team for four years. They stood next to a plaque, which bears General Douglas MacArthur's opinion on athletics:

> Upon the fields of friendly strife are sown the seed that upon other fields; on other days, will bear the fruits of victory.

Another of Dawn's teammates in Germany heard about her situation and raced to the hospital to see her. "My heart needed this," confided Connie. "Dawn said that if she ever got hurt, she did not want to be alone. She was not alone. This is when I understood what I had heard at Dawn's graduation. 'Being from West Point, you would never be without family.'"

What her parents did not know was that although Dawn had come out of her most recent surgery with stronger vital signs, she developed acute respiratory distress, a sudden, life-threatening lung failure. This syndrome occurs when the alveoli, the final branches of the respiratory tree, become inflamed, causing them to fill with liquid and collapse. Once the alveoli collapse, the lungs cannot perform normal gas exchanges and the body starves for oxygen.[92] To reduce the risk of death and to help prevent additional damage to the lungs and other vital organs, Dawn was placed on a mechanical ventilator.

In preparation for medical evacuation to the United States, the doctor had bolted her forearm to her hipbone and left the little skin holding her upper arm in place. Dawn and her parents arrived at Walter Reed at nearly the same time. The medical staff got Dawn situated and then invited her parents into the room.

"I would not have recognized Dawn if it were not for her red hair," said her mother. She continued:

The area of the injury was not as big as I expected. However, I was not prepared for all the swelling and all the medical machinery. Dawn's body had nearly shut down, and she was bloated from the respiratory distress. The only thing that looked like her was that right arm and hand. What we quickly learned was that the insurgents made dirty bombs so if the blast doesn't kill you, the germs will. Her body was fighting intensely to save her arm, consuming all of its

[92] U.S. Department of Health and Human Services. National Institutes of Health. National Heart, Lung, and Blood Institute. Diseases and conditions Index. Acute Respiratory Distress Syndrome (ARDS).

resources, yet the respiratory distress and accompanying infection were rapidly spreading through her body, slowly killing her.

The doctors explained to the Halfakers that they had tested the arm and identified significant problems with the blood supply. With the very remote possibility of saving the arm, her recovery would be long and tedious. There were no future guarantees that the arm might not be amputated. Dawn's parents made the decision to amputate her arm to provide blood to life sustaining organs and systems. Up to this point, the medical teams had been using artificial means chemicals, ventilators, and other medical equipment, to keep these organs performing. After the amputation, with Dawn in a medically induced coma, her family sat with her. Connie said, "We talked to her and played her favorite music. We also played a song that Dale, her brother, had recorded for her." Following the amputation, the doctors told the Halfakers that Dawn might have had only twelve hours to live. Forty-eight hours later, however, there came a major turning point with physical evidence that her body was regaining control of her internal systems.

"When I first woke up at Walter Reed, I was very confused," recalled Dawn.

The last thing I remembered was taking off in a helicopter. When I saw my parents, I was even more confused. When I found out I was at Walter Reed, I kept thinking, 'that is where people with injuries go.' I was lying there with all these tubes. Everything was blurry from the pain medication and lack of my glasses. When I was told that I no longer had an arm, I did not understand the implication. Actually, I refused to acknowledge it. The hours seemed like days, and time became irrelevant. Once I woke up from the coma, I didn't sleep for three days. I was afraid to go back to sleep, knowing that last time that I went to sleep I almost died. Now I see that I was already beginning the rehabilitation process and resuming my life. It starts with a nurse removing the feeding tube. The next day, the neck brace was removed. Each day the medical staff removed more stuff.

The yearlong rehabilitation process involved physical and occupational therapy—walking, getting dressed, tying shoes, writing, and driving—daily activities most people take for granted. "No one prepares you for losing a limb," said Dawn. "You just make the decision to live with it, or in my case, without it, and you drive on. Otherwise, it will kill you mentally, physically, and spiritually. My mantra became what Eleanor Roosevelt said, 'You must do the things you think you cannot do.'"

Connie spent that summer with Dawn at Walter Reed. She described the months together as the opportunity to reconnect. "This was a great time. Dawn left home for West Point when she was 17. It was our first opportunity since then to spend quality time together. She did not behave like someone with a severe injury. Losing a limb made her a stronger, more complete person."

Dawn is very matter-of-fact about her injury and her future. She has experienced more things in her short 25 years than most will ever see and experience in a lifetime. Yet she has met these challenges with determination, strength, grace, and a can-do attitude. She runs daily and often plays tennis. She also enjoys snowboarding, although she admits she is a little more cautious on the slopes than she used to be. "I mean, I'm still Dawn Halfaker. I still do the same things that I did before. The fact that I only have one arm; I don't want that to be the focus of my life," she said.

The American public has long been accustomed to men with missing arms and legs, or with other severely debilitating wounds, returning home from war. Many thought the images of severely wounded women would be a different issue. While shocking to some, the American public is becoming more accustomed to the sight because of Dawn and many other injured servicewomen.

When you lose an arm or leg, there is the challenge of finding a prosthetic device that is comfortable, effective, and relatively easy to use. Dawn tried several different devices. The first was a mechanical device designed to be a tool to assist her. It allowed her only to bend at the elbow. Weighing 15 pounds and strapped across her chest, it was heavy and uncomfortable. Dawn said, "I could barely breathe with the straps across my chest." Concerned with comfort and the aesthetic appeal of her "new arm," she now has a lightweight prosthetic that looks natural and is adaptive to her body. Dawn explained, "This new one is only 3 pounds. Many people want to see me wearing and using a prosthetic arm because it makes me look like my wound is healed. It actually hides the true extent of the injury." She laughed. Dawn's willingness to talk openly about her experiences increases the awareness of servicewomen in combat and the sacrifices that many make.

After putting her combat experience to work for two years as a consultant to the Defense Advance Research Project Agency, working on new technologies to change the battlefield, Dawn started a defense consultancy. Halfaker and Associates provides national security services to the U.S. Government. Dawn explained,

> We are focused on mission support for the War on Terrorism in the areas of Homeland Security, Emergency Management, Physical Security, Force Protection/Anti-Terrorism, Intelligence, and Border Security. We help businesses and government protect their workers and vital facilities. Security planning and operations are a challenge of monumental scale and complexity and we have the capabilities and professional competence to help customers defeat threats in today's world. We draw upon methods, tools, and personal experience in a variety of disciplines building practical and affordable solutions.

In addition to starting and running this company, Dawn earned a Master of Arts degree in Security Studies from Georgetown University.

Anyone who meets this incredible woman knows she is a hero, not just because of her service to our nation and her combat wounds, but because of her courage, strength, focus, and integrity. In his remarks to an audience of West Point plebes and their parents in October 2004, Brigadier General Curtis Scaparrotti, West Point's then Commandant of Cadets, cited Dawn as an example of soldierly values:

> *Our country deserves leaders like First Lieutenant Dawn Halfaker, Class of 2001. Dawn was a women's basketball player who chose to serve in the Military Police upon graduation. Military Police have some of the most dangerous duties in Iraq. Aside from conducting security patrols, they also provide training and assistance to the Iraqi Police Force, and therefore, serve in hundreds of Iraqi police stations in neighborhoods throughout Iraq. As you know from the news, these stations are frequent targets of insurgents. First Lieutenant Halfaker led her platoon bravely, until she was wounded during an attack and lost an arm. Lieutenant General Lennox, the Superintendent, visited her when she was in Walter Reed Army Medical Center in Washington, D.C., recovering from her wounds. When asked if, knowing then what she knew now, would she still do it all again, she looked the Superintendent straight in the eye and said she wouldn't change a thing. You see, Dawn Halfaker knows the meaning of our values of 'duty' and 'selfless service,' and she lives them.*[93]

---

[93] Brigadier General Curtis M. Scaparrotti, USMA Commandant, remarks at Plebe Parent weekend, 16 October 2004.

Colonel Martin Dempsey, USMA 1974, administers the oath of officer to Second Lieutenant Dawn Halfaker on June 1, 2001. Dawn, Dempsey's daughter Megan, and three other teammates received their gold lieutenant bars together outside the Hollender Center where they played basketball together during their four years at West Point. (*Photo courtesy of Connie Halfaker*)

Lieutenant Dawn Halfaker on a foot patrol in Baqubah, Iraq in April 2004. (*Photo courtesy of Connie Halfaker*)

Wounded in action by a rocket propelled grenade (RPG). Captain Dawn Halfaker poses with her prosthetic right arm at Walter Reed Army Medical Center. *(Photo courtesy of Dawn Halfaker)*

Army Women's Soccer Team pioneers in the fall of 1984. Lissa Young is in the front row with sunglasses. Holly Hagan is sitting directly behind Lissa. *From left to right and back to front*: Anne Drislane '85, Marie Stagg '87, Macaire Balzano '85, Annaliese Steele '87, Jill Spangler '86, Lynn "Kitty" Sprague '87, Lisa Studebaker '86, Martha Bowman '87, Frances Strebeck '88, Andrea Ford '88, Vanessa Jennings '85. *Middle row:* unidentified, Jeanne Bouchard '85, Maureen Callahan '85, Betsy Barron '87. *Seated:* unidentified, Holly Hagan '87, Lissa Young '86 and Kristen Knapp '86. (*Photo courtesy of Jeanne Bouchard LaVake*)

LIVING OUT LOUD | LISSA YOUNG, CLASS OF 1986

"If you asked me what I came into the world to do, I would tell you, 'I came to live out loud.' "

—Emile Zola

Inspiration to attend West Point often comes from the important people in our lives. For Lissa Young, that person was Marion Dent, her godmother and the wife of Fred Dent, Lissa's father's West Point roommate. Romain Young and Fred Dent were not only roommates at the Academy; they were best friends, Air Force F-100 wingmen, and best men in each other's weddings.

After watching her husband Fred and his classmates march onto the field for the Alumni Parade during the 25th Reunion of the Class of 1956, Marion wrote a letter to Lissa. Drawing inspiration from West Point's historic and majestic setting, Marion described what it meant to be a soldier and a person. Marion was intimately familiar with the demands of a military life and a soldier's commitment to service as the spouse of a career Air Force officer.[94]

Fred Dent served two tours in Vietnam. While supportive of her husband, Marion actively protested the war, marching in Washington, D.C. for the withdrawal of troops from Southeast Asia. Yet she wrote that a walk on the grounds of West Point was like a

---

[94] West Point served as the Air Force Academy through World War II. The Air Force became a separate service in 1947. Nevertheless, until the Air Force Academy was operating fully, up to 25% of USMA graduates were permitted to "branch" Air Force. The Air Force Academy produced its first graduating class in 1959 (207). 1960 had 227; 1961 (217); 1962 (298); 1963 (499); 1964 (499); 1965 (517). USMA's class of 1964 graduated 565 and 1965 had 596, so USAFA was approaching parity by then. During the height of wartime pilot training at West Point, the Class of January 1943 commissioned 162 directly into the Air Corps and another eight were transferred into the Air Corps within a year after graduation. Of 409 grads (several of whom were not commissioned due to disability), fully 170 were in the Air Corps almost immediately. The Class of 1956, however, commissioned 119 Air Force and 356 Army; '57 had 137 AF and 404 Army; '58 had 142 AF and 427 Army. Another point to note: When the Air Force was formed in 1947, all of the pilots went Air Force, but there also were Engineer, Signal and logistics officers who were transferred from the Army Air Corps to the Air Force Ground forces. Information provided by Lieutenant Colonel Jay Olejniczak, West Point Association of Graduates.

walk through American history. Marion encouraged Lissa to take the path less traveled for women in America and seek a commission in the Army through West Point. She encouraged Lissa to be part of our country's history. Lissa said:

> Marion presented me with an entirely new option, one that was truly unique and challenging. She described being part of history and part of the future by doing something utterly different. She wrote that if I really wanted to grasp the meaning of service to the nation, feel the burden of that responsibility, and make a difference in the world, then I needed to respond to the recent changes in Congressional Policy and pursue an appointment to West Point. Because of people like Marion, willing to challenge the status quo, I had the opportunity of choice. It galvanized for me what was a pretty fuzzy future. The day I received her letter, I applied for admission to the United States Military Academy.

Lissa received Marion's letter during the spring of her sophomore year at New College, then a private liberal arts university in Sarasota, Florida. With only two years remaining in her undergraduate program, Lissa was contemplating her future career prospects. Marion's letter proposed a career she had never considered.

Within two months, Lissa received an appointment to West Point. On the same day that she received her acceptance letter, she also received an offer to become a water ski instructor in the Bahamas. These were strikingly different alternatives: become a professional water skiing instructor, bask in the sun and surf while teaching others a new sport, or face the possibility of being in harm's way leading soldiers serving one's country. She chose the profession of arms.

Lissa entered West Point in July 1982, beginning again as a freshman. She flourished in the classroom, on the athletic field, and in the military environment. She majored in Comparative Literature with a focus on psychological aspects of modern British Literature. This course of study complemented her affinity for reading and nurturing her imagination. Lissa said that she liked the more liberal arts approach, "I laugh at the irony of attending an engineering school to get a literature degree." Literature helped her develop a context in which to analyze various aspects of culture and to better understand the values that inform and shape our nation. In addition to developing her critical thinking, it also nurtured her creativity and self-directed learning, skills that the Army considers essential characteristics of 21st century officers.

She enjoyed studying the human condition through the lens of various authors. Among her favorites was Virginia Woolf. Lissa was intrigued with Woolf's feminist themes, her extraordinary ability to relate women's experiences, and discover her alternatives to male-dominated views of reality. In *A Room of One's Own* (1929), for example, Woolf addressed the obstacles and prejudices that have hindered women writers. A decade later, in *Three Guineas* (1938), Woolf wrote about the necessity for women to define their own history and literary style. Writings such as these provided Lissa a context to study gender identity and a framework for exploring her own sexuality.

A natural athlete, Lissa played on the women's soccer team, a club sport during her years at the Academy. During a particularly grueling soccer match against the nationally ranked University of Maryland Terrapins, in double overtime with just seconds remaining, Lissa experienced an event that became a lasting memory. She recalled:

> Lynn Sprague and I found a break. She stole the ball from a formidable Terrapin forward. We worked it down the field together; I found an opening to the left front of the goal. Lynn was racing up the middle of the

field; she too had an opening. But she looked up, made eye contact with me, and passed the ball. In that moment, everything I had learned to stand for, in terms of courage, grit, hard work, selfless sacrifice, and teamwork, came together. She passed the ball, I shot it, and we won. It was the first time we ever had beat a nationally ranked team. The win secured us a spot in the post-season tournament. That, for me, remains my fondest moment—not because I shot the ball, but because Lynn passed it. In that single act rests the confluence of all that makes West Point great.

This season and win helped establish women's soccer as a varsity sport the following year.

Lissa's most significant challenges at West Point occurred outside the classroom. Nearing the end of her junior year, she was selected to participate in the cadet emerging leader boards. These consisted of a series of rigorous interviews by many of the Academy's staff and faculty to determine the cadet leadership and chain of command for the summer training months and the following academic year. As one of five cadet finalists from among the 100 or so who started the process, Lissa was asked which cadet summer command she most wanted. Being more comfortable in a field setting than a garrison one, Lissa asked for the command of Camp Buckner, the summer training of the rising yearling cadets.

Camp Buckner then consisted of an eight-week regimen of rigorous military and physical training, emphasizing crew and squad tactics, and platoon-level soldier skills. Introduced to armor and mechanized infantry operations and equipment, during this period the cadets fired various weapons.

Lissa wanted to have a direct effect on the yearlings. For the majority of cadets, Camp Buckner was their introduction to the field Army, their chosen vocation. Lissa recalled her rationale, "The second summer at West Point is a critical time for cadets, as they transition from being a follower, during a stressful plebe year, to a leader in their second year. I wanted to impact this group as they began to assess West Point from a new perspective."

At the time, Lissa was dating a classmate also among the five finalists vying for the same command. Selected to command Camp Buckner, Lissa's cadet boyfriend was to be the commander of the Armor Training (TCAT) at Fort Knox, Kentucky. While a prestigious position, the TCAT cadet commander was subordinate to the overall commander of Camp Buckner, Lissa.

A few days later, he ended their relationship, explaining that a professional and personal relationship between a commander and subordinate, even though they were cadets, was not appropriate. While initially stunned, Lissa came to the understanding that his view was correct and mature. She remembered, "The lesson for me was the importance of order and discipline taking precedence over all else. Relationships are subordinate to the betterment of the Army."

All eyes focused on Cadet Lissa Young as the first woman to lead Camp Buckner, and she did not disappoint. Lissa led from the front on road marches and physical training runs. She led her staff as they developed the training plans and coordinated the resources for all the military activities. She learned how to train soldiers from the non-commissioned officers of the 101st Airborne Division assigned to West Point to assist in cadet summer training. This leadership experience confirmed her own decision to become a soldier and secured her a senior leadership role during her final year at the Academy.

As summer training at Camp Buckner ended in August 1985, Lissa earned selection as the Deputy Brigade Commander, the second highest-ranking position in the academic year cadet chain-of-command. The first woman to achieve this rank in the Corps of Cadets, Lissa's proven leadership ability, judgment, capacity to handle competing demands, and engaging personality accounted for her appointment.

Excited about the opportunity, Lissa was eager to make a positive impact in the cadet leader development arena. On paper, the plebe leadership development program, known as the Fourth Class System, was the Deputy Brigade Commander's responsibility. Lissa soon learned, however, that it was the company tactical officers who owned and administered it. While she had a highly visible position on the eight-member cadet brigade staff, she found that she had the least amount of responsibility among her peers. She was a figurehead. Other than filling in for the Brigade Commander during his absence, she was responsible for little more than escorting Academy visitors. To her chagrin, the Deputy Brigade Commander was a title without a role. Lissa recalled, "I just hated it. And my classmates thought I got the position because of my gender."

Lissa wanted to lead. Determined to prove her competence, she looked for other opportunities to demonstrate excellence and confirm that she was the most qualified cadet selected to wear this rank. One of the defined responsibilities of the Deputy was to lead parades when the Brigade Commander was not available. This potentially daunting task of leading the Corps in front of thousands of spectators required a voice that projected crisp, authoritative orders without sounding feminine. Lissa's tactical officer enrolled her in voice lessons to prepare her for the first parade and to minimize any chance of the commands delivering in a high-pitched voice.

All eyes focused on Cadet Young's every move as she led her first full brigade parade of the Corps of Cadets. That day, the parade reviewing party included New York State Senator Daniel Patrick Moynihan and West Point's Superintendent. When Lissa visited the reviewing stand after the parade, Senator Moynihan smiled and told her it was a "dandy" parade and congratulated her on a job well done. Although she did a good job, Lissa was still uneasy about what was happening around her. She described:

> I felt like a science project. USCC was learning along with me.[95] The institution did not want me to fail. I had

---

[95] Although USCC refers to the United States Corps of Cadets, it generally refers to the non-cadet governance structure that oversees the academy.

difficulty developing my own identity and questioned whether I could become a respected member of the profession of arms. Everything always seemed connected to gender and not performance.

Lissa led several parades her final year at the Academy, all executed with discipline, precision, and excellence. Her performance nudged the Academy along in its path of evolution.

There was another episode that again caused her to question her ability to become a soldier because of her gender. At request, Lissa was the cadet escort for a visit by retired Major General George S. Patton III, Class of 1946, the son of legendary General George S. Patton Jr., Class of 1909. When Cadet Young and an accompanying officer greeted the general near the bronze statue memorializing the elder Patton, his son looked at Cadet Lissa Young and asked, "What do I call one of these?" Without hesitation the officer responded, "Sir, this is Cadet Young, and she is the Deputy Brigade Commander of the entire Corps of Cadets." Patton's flippant and dismissive comment, while possibly generational, had a philosophical impact. Lissa said, "Here I am, a cadet, performing well among my counterparts, the second highest ranking cadet in the Corps, but my gender still disqualified me from acknowledged membership in the institution by a respected general officer." She would deposit this incident in her store of experience and focus even harder on improving her individual performance.

Nearing graduation, Lissa selected the Aviation branch. Since childhood, she had wanted to be a pilot. "Growing up near a small airport in Florida, I often went to the field to watch the airplanes take off and land. I always liked looking up towards the sky." Army Aviation was one of the few combat arms branches available to women.

Following graduation, Lissa moved to Fort Rucker, Alabama, for the Aviation Officer's Basic Course and the Initial Entry Rotary Wing Course. Even though women could fly, institutional policies at the time did not authorize two women to take to the air together in flight school. Initially, the women accepted this operational policy as a condition of membership in the branch. Many of the women pilots believed this specific regulation contributed to a perception of lower qualification standards for women. As flight school neared completion, Lissa and the other women in the class challenged the policy of not permitting two women to fly together as a clear case of gender bias. This direct challenge led to the review and quiet elimination of the policy. Lissa graduated with her pilot's wings, qualified to fly two types of helicopters.

Lissa developed a serious relationship with another pilot, a Georgia National Guard Officer, in the training program during flight school. His feelings for her were strong, and when Lissa headed for Fort Carson, Colorado, this lieutenant decided to follow her in anticipation of securing a position, even though he had no assignment there. Lissa began her initial troop assignment with the 4th Infantry Division, leading soldiers in a general support aviation battalion as a UH-1 Huey pilot section leader. Her responsibilities included airlifting soldiers and supplies in garrison and in the field.

Not able to find a suitable assignment in Colorado, Lissa's boyfriend returned to his home state and a local reserve unit. In the end, the geographical distance proved to be too much an obstacle, and their relationship eventually faded. Lissa again understood that personal relationships are subordinate to the demands of the military.

Within the battalion, there was a platoon of OH-58 Kiowa observation helicopters whose purpose was to assist the division cavalry squadron in performing reconnaissance, surveillance, and security operations. As one of the Army rapid-deployment divisions at that time, the 4th Infantry Division spent much of the year practicing their wartime missions at the National Training Center (NTC) in the desert of Fort Irwin, California. With three ground maneuver brigades in the division, one was usually in the maneuver box at the NTC or at a training and maneuver site. Lissa was asked to be the Target Acquisition and Aerial Reconnaissance Platoon Leader for the OH-58 platoon. This unique flight assignment involved calling for field artillery support during combat operations as well as flying the maneuver brigade commanders and the training evaluators around the mock battlefield. Lissa began quietly developing a high level of strategic and tactical understanding of military operations, as it was only her and the maneuver commander in her helicopter, and she benefited greatly from watching him command the battle from the air. She attended all battle briefings and reviews, often as the only female soldier present. Lissa remembered:

> The experience was tremendous because it laid the groundwork for me to be recognized as a well-qualified observation helicopter pilot in command, and when I was asked to go through the cavalry squadron's aircraft mission qualification course, I was able to do so with confidence and ease.

As the first woman certified through this program, Lissa became a pilot in command of an OH-58 Kiowa observation helicopter. This required certification in calling for fire, flying and maneuvering as part of an air-ground gunship team, and conducting battlefield reconnaissance. During one NTC rotation, Lissa went from the general support platoon directly to the cavalry squadron, a rare opportunity afforded to seasoned pilots. Lieutenant Colonel Fritz Treyz, 2-7 Cavalry Squadron Commander, had a reputation as a stern disciplinarian, and as battle commander, would have to approve her for the mission. Much to her surprise, he did. With his authorization, Lissa became the first woman to fly a "Cav" mission at the National Training Center. This opportunity gave Lissa a sense of her potential but also served as a reminder of the restrictions the Army then placed on women. The Army trained women aviators to be haulers and not fighters. Women could not fly cavalry squadron missions in a deployable combat unit. Lissa said:

> This assignment completely changed my view of myself as an Army aviator, as my capabilities and

skills were enhanced. It made me a better officer and pilot. It again reminded me of the limitations based on my gender, and just how different my opportunities would be if I were a guy.

Along with struggling with the institutional restrictions, Lissa continued on her journey of self-discovery. She re-read many of Virginia Woolf's essays provoking her to reconsider her own sexuality. At the same time, she involved herself in the local civilian community of Colorado Springs, volunteering for several organizations, including the American Society for the Prevention of Cruelty to Animals (ASPCA), a soup kitchen, a nursing home, and a recreational soccer league. Through these various community activities, Lissa began to meet women officers from the other federal service academies. Besides their military affiliations, some of them shared the secret of being lesbians and eventually developed their own informal network. Interacting with these women proved powerful. Lissa explained,

Up to this point, I myself believed all the stereotypes that others do about lesbians. Interacting with these professional soldiers helped me affirm how I was feeling. Most of us had spent our time at our respective Service Academies isolated and deliberately ignoring our sexuality. As I came to know other women in the community, I learned that homophobia and stereotypes exist everywhere, not just in the military. I understood that heterosexual people do not have to announce publicly their sexual orientation. It sets up an interesting discord and reinforces the difference in a way that is unfathomable for straight people to consider. Yet this difference often becomes an obsession for young gay folks. Everyone assumes you are straight until you proclaim otherwise.

Through this group, Lissa developed a strong association with a similar-aged artist working in an established jewelry shop. While a sculptor, this young professional woman, Paula, made her livelihood designing jewelry. The bond they developed helped Lissa confirm her own sexuality, which she found liberating. A dilemma existed, however, in that being gay in the military was more than unacceptable. It was a violation of the Uniform Code of Military Justice (UCMJ). She knew that she could not introduce her as her partner, nor could they openly display affection for one another. Constantly aware of the potential consequences of her sexual orientation on her professional life, Lissa was discreet in her relationship with Paula.

Years before Lissa had received a letter from West Point inquiring about her interest in returning to West Point as an Assistant Professor in the Department of Behavioral Science and Leadership. Intrigued by the opportunity to attend a top-notch graduate school, she completed the required questionnaire. The prospect was several years in the future, as for consideration, Lissa needed to complete two more assignments, including a successful company command.

Fortuitously, a neighbor introduced Lissa to the Center for Creative Leadership, a not-for-profit focused exclusively on leadership and leader development. She became the subject of a case study about the development of a young lieutenant at the outset of a professional career. Her exposure to leadership development as an academic discipline and how organizational policies affect leader development piqued her intellectual curiosity.

Similar to many young professionals, Lissa began to feel the demands and opportunities of her career pursuits introduce competing interests into her personal relationships. Lissa's partner was comfortable in Colorado Springs, as her artistic talents became more refined and her work recognized. Lissa's future was everywhere but Colorado Springs. The two eventually ended their relationship. Once again, Lissa learned that personal relationships are subordinate to military duty.

Lissa returned to Fort Rucker for the Aviation Officer Advanced Course. She became qualified as a CH-47 Chinook pilot because she had always wanted to be part of the Chinook's unique and challenging mission profile. The Chinook is the largest helicopter in the Army inventory, and its size and strength enabled it to conduct a wide variety of missions, and that excited Lissa.

Her next posting took her to Fort Bragg, North Carolina, as flight platoon leader in a Chinook company. During this assignment Lissa played a pivotal role in standing up forces in south Florida in the wake of Hurricane Andrew in August 1992, organizing and coordinating efforts to fly supplies and personnel into and out of the region, and clearing debris. Following this mission Lissa received an opportunity to command the XVIIIth Airborne Corps' Command and Control UH-1 "Huey" Company.

Offered her first command of A Company, 1-159th Aviation Regiment, this was notable because of her rank. Lissa was still a captain, but most company commands in aviation went to majors, the next higher rank. She accepted the responsibility for the 150-person, 6-aircraft combat aviation organization in the Army's premier quick reaction division, the 82nd Airborne Division— deployable to anywhere in the world in just 18 hours. She did the job well, and at the conclusion of the company command received the Meritorious Service Medal for creating the best command in the battalion.

During her 18 months of command, West Point officially selected Lissa to return to teach. Excited, she looked forward to attending graduate school, but in the aftermath of the Gulf War and the lessons learned about the lack of wartime preparation of the Army's reserve units, many of the Army's highest potential active duty captains and majors with successful company command behind them received assignments to reserve component units in rural locations. The Army removed Lissa from the graduate school selection list, but West Point, still wanting Lissa, asked Army Personnel not to fill Lissa's now empty slot. They indicated their continued desire for Lissa and encouraged her to pursue her master's degree during her reserve assignment.

In Olathe, Kansas, Lissa became the Chief of the Regional Heavy Lift Training Team for the U.S. Army Reserves in the Fifth Army Region. In her first year, she succeeded in transforming a Heavy Lift Chinook Reserve unit from combat-ineffective to combat-effective by developing and implementing a comprehensive, battle-focused training program tailored to the 25 different occupational and functional specialties in the unit. She was also accepted to a graduate program at the University of Kansas.

In class, she pursued a Master of Arts degree in Social Psychology to prepare for her return to West Point as an assistant professor. Although very disappointed in not being able to attend graduate school full-time, Lissa focused her energy intensely in order to keep up in the demanding program without threatening her unit's training and improvement. Lissa studied organizational theory and group dynamics with regard to interpersonal and intrapersonal assessments of leadership effectiveness.

In her research with the Army Research Institute at Fort Leavenworth, Kansas, she concentrated on understanding the impact of stereotypes and prejudice of leader demographics on leader effectiveness. Fascinated by the statistical evidence that supported the contrary position, Lissa hypothesized little effect. Her research concluded that the Army's calculated assignment of officers into small groups during military courses, to ensure diversity of military occupational specialty, gender, and race, actually amplified the stereotypes and prejudices of others within the group. In a pre-designated group, members would pre-judge the leadership effectiveness of others as lower based on their race, gender, and branch before giving those individuals an opportunity to demonstrate actual leadership competencies. As time passed, and the individuals in each group worked closely together, the initial impressions remained, even when the stereotyped group members demonstrated disconfirming evidence. The primary predictors of an officer's perceived leadership effectiveness unfortunately was found to be in gender, race, and branch of service.

The outcome of Lissa's research included a set of recommendations that the Army assign groups at random, abandoning the practice of trying to make each group as diverse as possible. *The Journal of Personality and Social Psychology* published Lissa's masters thesis, entitled "All That You Can Be: Stereotyping of Self and Others in a Military Context," two years after its completion. As Lissa looked back at her time in Kansas, she said,

> While my thesis was a homerun academically, it was a big downer personally, and a very challenging time for me professionally. My research concluded, and I realized, that as a woman, my peers would not perceive me as a great leader even in spite of being a great officer.

As she continued to mature professionally and personally, Lissa became more comfortable with her sexual orientation. She grew more active in defending homosexuality by writing letters to newspapers and magazine articles under pseudonyms. Lissa walked a tightrope as she strove to be the best officer she could be. And, surprisingly there was an upside to being gay. She found that as others, especially soldiers in her units, learned of her orientation, the dynamics between them changed. Being gay, Lissa was a not a sexual target for men in the unit, and she was not a threat to male soldiers' wives. While many people knew Lissa was gay, none of them cared. They saw her as a professional soldier and leader.

Nearing the completion of graduate school, a West Point professor from the department she would be joining contacted Lissa. This faculty member was the officer sponsor of a female cadet who was being investigated at the Academy after several women cadets were reported for being gay. This faculty member, aware of Lissa's sexual orientation, wanted to provide the cadet with another officer as a sounding board and advocate.

Under federal law, openly gay people are prohibited from serving in the United States Armed Forces.[96] The military's *"Don't Ask, Don't Tell"* policy is the only law in the country that allows for the firing of a person based on sexual orientation alone. The policy, issued during Bill Clinton's presidential term, promised no investigations into the sexuality of service members unless they divulged they were homosexual.

Lissa advised the cadet to contact the Servicemembers Legal Defense Network (SLDN) for counsel, as well as seek out other woman graduates who had since left the service. In the end, the cadet chose to remain quiet, neutralizing the need for any continued effort.

Lissa graduated with her master's degree anxious to return to West Point. She looked forward to being in an academic environment with many smart and intellectually curious people, yet concerned and cautious because of the recent investigation that had expelled several cadets from West Point.

Lissa arrived at West Point in the summer of 1996 amazed at the difference between the military academic garrison and the field army. She found it to be very collegial and less rank-conscious than she had anticipated. As an assistant professor in the Department of Behavioral Sciences and Leadership, she taught the department's core course in Military Leadership, becoming its course director and leading the effort to overhaul the course content. Lissa said, "I was honored, thrilled, and anxious to return to the grounds that provided me such wonderful opportunities. It was an honor and joy to work with cadets, as well as my former mentors, Colonels Joe LeBoeuf and Barney Forsythe."

Lissa also developed close friendships with many of the women stationed at the Academy as tactical officers and professors, eventually coming to learn that some were homosexual. Through these newly established relationships, Lissa began to feel as if she were cut from the same cloth as other educated, patriotic, social, and career-minded military professionals. She again found it reinforcing

---

[96] Policy concerning homosexuals in the armed forces § 10 U.S.C.§ 654 (1993).

to be facing so many similar challenges with fellow professionals who truly understood her. Among this group, Lissa could relax. This was a privilege straight people enjoy daily. Lissa explained,

> There is a tremendous amount of bandwidth required of men and women officers who are gay to always be aware of their orientation. I often wonder what it would have been like to focus that bandwidth and energy in other areas.

At West Point Lissa became more open about her sexuality. She said, "People knew I was gay and never questioned it. I focused on my responsibilities as a teacher and role model to the cadets, and was praised for doing a great job."

As she got to know the cadets outside the classroom, she came to understand some of the issues the women at the Academy faced. Among the most prevalent were eating disorders, possibly stemming from the strict weight standards for cadets. She found West Point open and willing to make positive changes if one presented data to support the proposed change. Lissa knew that the continued presence of an eating disorder would prevent a cadet from commissioning as an officer upon graduation. Lissa said, "If we are in the business of producing officers, we need to ensure their health." Lissa brought in an expert on eating disorders who shared findings and empirical data from various colleges and universities across the country. After two months of investigation and research, assisted by the expert consultant, the Academy established the Eating Disorders Task Force, chaired by Colonel Maureen LeBoeuf, the first woman department head at West Point. The task force eventually designed and implemented a comprehensive program to detect, address, and treat eating disorders in the Corps of Cadets.

Lissa was also involved in the development of training materials for the identification and prevention of sexual harassment among the staff, faculty, and civilians at West Point. She felt valued in the way she had the opportunity to make decisions and generate solutions to problems, much more so than expected. She developed a desire to return to West Point as a permanent Academy Professor, and perhaps to compete one day to be the head of an academic department. It was during this time that Lissa developed the dream of maybe one day earning the honor of becoming the Dean of the Academic board.

There are many lasting memories Lissa took away from her time at West Point. One was a trip to Washington, D.C., for the unveiling and dedication of the Women in Military Service to America Memorial at Arlington National Cemetery. Lissa wanted to take a group of cadets to march in the military parade honoring women veterans. Some at West Point did not believe this particular event was of sufficient importance, however, and denied her the funding and support for the field trip. After challenging the opposition, Lissa received permission and allocated the resources. Lissa recalled, "It was a wonderful opportunity to connect cadets to a fundamental and often overlooked aspect of their military history and heritage."

Excelling in a teaching environment, Lissa was asked to consider returning to USMA as a permanent faculty member after a field grade command assignment and completion of a doctoral program, some five to seven years in the future. Her continued future at the Academy depended on time back on the flight line in the Army along with a successful battalion command. The time at West Point galvanized Lissa's desire to return as a permanent professor.

In between West Point and her next field assignment, Lissa attended the Army's Command and General Staff College[97], a highly selective yearlong, graduate-level program for the United States Armed Forces and foreign military leaders.

Upon completion, Lissa moved to Fort Wainwright, Alaska, to serve in a Heavy Lift Aviation Battalion of the Pacific Region. This

---

[97] The U.S. Army Command and General Staff College (CGSC) educates and develops leaders for full spectrum joint, interagency and multinational operations; acts as lead agent for the Army's leader development program; and advances the art and science of the profession of arms in support of Army operational requirements. http://usacac.army.mil/cac2/cgsc/about.asp.

remote battalion was the most diverse rotary wing unit in the Army with its four types of aircraft. In July 2000, Major Lissa Young accepted the command of B Company, 4-123rd Aviation Regiment. As commander of a high altitude search and rescue heavy lift unit, the "Sugar Bears North," she had the responsibility for the tactical war fighting response force for both mountain and arctic environments as well as for civilian emergencies above 10,000 feet in Alaska and Western Canada. With its unique mission and challenging environment, the United States Army Aviation Center designated this unit primarily for its most qualified instructor pilots, typically senior warrant officers.

This command was three times as large as her first command, and included the responsibility for 300 soldiers, 18 aircraft, 66 vehicles, and an operating budget of more than $25 million dollars. There were only nine Chinook companies in the active Army, making the command selection for such a unit extremely competitive.[98]

After responding to a high altitude rescue on Mount McKinley, Young explained to reporter Amy Mayer of the Weather Notebook Radio Show the challenges of flying these enormous birds.

> The liability of having an aircraft that has rotor blades this large and this much power is that you blow the snow so much. Landing on a snow-covered glacier is like sinking into a bag of powdered sugar. Typically, at about 40 feet, you'll begin to kick up a lot of snow cloud, and then you begin to just slowly lower while you still maintain visual reference on the horizon, but you stop every five or ten feet, using the radar altimeter, so that you can continue to allow that snow cloud to settle. And what you're actually trying to do is blow out the snow. And then if you have blowing

---

[98] Aviation Systems Capabilities Analyst Rick White, Force Applications Division, Capabilities Developments Directorate, Army Capabilities Integration Center, HQ TRADOC, Fort Monroe, VA 23651.

snow and flat light, it's very, very, exciting. It's challenging and exhilarating. It's absolutely breath taking in both terms of fear and awe.[99]

In the summer of 2001, Lissa was contacted by Dr. Roland A. Gangloff, the Curator of the Earth Sciences Museum at the University of Alaska in Fairbanks, to assist in his quest to recover the 90 to 230 million-year-old remains of a long extinct sea creature, the Ichthyosaur, located in the Brooks Range, north of the Arctic Circle. Excited and thrilled at the prospect, Major Young began a year of extensive planning, reconnaissance, and coordination to execute this mission. The Army finally granted permission to support this historic undertaking. The crew extracted the fossil successfully and delivered it to the University of Alaska museum, where it is on display today.

In between various tactical missions, Young often flew the two-star commanding general of Fort Wainwright. Impressed with her flying skills, depth of strategic knowledge, and curiosity about leadership, he wrote a letter of recommendation on her behalf for assignment as a permanent faculty member at West Point. As her outgoing battalion commander neared the end of his command, he provided Lissa a glowing officer efficiency report, also strongly endorsing her selection as a permanent faculty member to USMA as well as early promotion to the rank of lieutenant colonel.

Nearing the end of her two-year command of the Sugars Bears North in July 2002, Major Young was to receive a promotion and official nomination as a permanent professor at West Point. Sixteen years of commitment and dedication to the service of the nation was bearing fruit. Then her world turned upside down.

Investigated and charged under the *"Don't Ask, Don't Tell"* policy, Young was asked to resign her commission. There was no change of command ceremony, only a final Officer Efficiency Report extolling her as a great commander with exceptional strategic and

---

[99] Lissa Young, interview by Amy Mayer. Weather Notebook Radio Show. 30 September 2002.

www.weathernotebook.org/transcripts/2002/09/30.php.

tactical skills, yet not fit to be in the Army. These comments inflicted a deep wound, and yet she reluctantly realized that the *"Don't Ask, Don't Tell"* policy had teeth, and that she would never be considered an acceptable officer as long as the Army embraced that policy.

On August 28, 2002, Major Lissa Young signed out of the 4th Battalion, 123rd Aviation, and the United States Army after serving 16 years on active duty and slated for promotion to lieutenant colonel and permanent assignment as an Academy professor. Now she had to start over.

> My sexuality put me in violation of an Army policy, and I had no recourse for appeal, other than to launch a campaign against the policy, which I refused to do. I was 40 years old, and half of my life had been spent dedicated to serving this institution. I did not want to spend the second half of my life attacking it. I also knew that I didn't want the rest of my life to be defined by this single moment. I wanted the chance to reinvent myself, and so I chose to treat this tragedy as a gift – an opportunity to do all of the things I would never have been able to do, if I had remained in the military.

Two years later, in an article for *Compass: A Journal of Leadership Magazine,* a publication of the Kennedy School of Government at Harvard University, Lissa addressed the failure of the *"Don't Ask, Don't Tell"* policy. She wrote:

> We are afraid to challenge the assumptions of our institutions even as we respect their foundations. A notable example of our failure is the unwillingness to lift the unconstitutional and incoherent policy, commonly called 'don't ask, don't tell,' that prohibits homosexuals from serving openly in our armed forces. They are told they can serve only if they treat their

sexuality as a secret they must hide from the world. And in the next breath, they are told that a soldier never lies.

The irony is that the military places a high value on integrity and honor, yet undermines these values by forcing and encouraging soldiers to lie about their personal lives.

Historically, the United States Army has been on the leading edge of social change and diversity with the integration of women and minorities. That is, except for those soldiers and citizens who are gay.

The United States promotes its position and stature as the world's only superpower, a beacon of freedom, and a land of opportunity. The military is the organization charged with protecting both this freedom and opportunity. Its foundations for effectiveness are integrity, honor, and respect for others, regardless of a difference—except for sexual orientation. Paradoxically, denied to homosexual soldiers are all the freedoms and opportunities for which they take an oath to serve and protect.

The failure and shame is that our country and our military are losing, by forcing out great leaders and soldiers like Lissa Young. It is apparent that the private sector values Lissa's talents far more than the military.

In the summer of 2003, Lissa started over, and began a corporate career in the Defense Industry. She joined the Raytheon Company as the Six Sigma Lead expert for the Navy's DD(X) guided missile destroyer class ship design program,[100] the centerpiece of the Navy's newest surface combatant family of ships. Responsible for creating and implementing a myriad of process improvements across the program, she reduced the program's cost overrun by $40 million that same year. The following year, selected to be the Raytheon Lead

---

[100] This is now the DDG-1000, USS Zumwalt Class.

on a program at the United States Air Force Academy, Lissa helped reconstruct the leader and character development systems after a series of highly publicized NCAA violations, academic cheating, and sexual harassment cases. Simultaneously Lissa established a relationship between Raytheon Company and the John F. Kennedy School of Government at Harvard University and began working part-time with Ronald Heifetz's and David Gergen's Center for Public Leadership. Over several years, Lissa assisted the Center by co-developing leadership programs for their graduate program scholars. Asked to serve on the John F. Kennedy School of Government's Women's Leadership Board, Lissa gladly accepted.

In early 2006, she received a call from her former cavalry squadron commander, now retired and working for Raytheon, Fritz Treyz. Spearheading Raytheon's move to become a significant player in the airspace management and homeland security arena, Treyz looked for a few talented people to help develop this business. Remembering her role in pioneering women's flying in the cavalry, one of the first people Fritz called was Lissa Young.

Lissa's primary role was the Middle East sales lead for Raytheon's Air Traffic Control business. She dove into her responsibilities with enthusiasm, spending the better part of the next few years traveling her region and meeting with customers in Kuwait, Bahrain, Qatar, Oman, the United Arab Emirates, and Jordan.

She found herself drawn back to school. Lissa remembered the defining moment well. Sitting in a café on the shore outside of Abu Dhabi, looking at the reflection of the moon on the water while absent-mindedly listening to the conversations around her, she overhead two men talking about their college semester and one of their favorite professors. One recalled how that professor had changed his life, forever.

That comment drove right into Lissa's heart, and instantly reawakened her quest for a place in academia so unexpectedly interrupted by her expulsion from the military. She remembered the years she spent in the classroom at West Point, and all of the reasons she wanted to return and teach there permanently. In that moment, Lissa realized her destiny would be to return to graduate school to earn her doctorate degree, enroute once again to becoming a professor. The next day, she returned to the United States and announced her intentions to her boss at the Raytheon Company. He was both disappointed and delighted. He grabbed her, gave her a huge bear hug, and told her, "Go get 'em, Tiger!"

After careful calculation, Lissa decided to try a "Hail Mary" pass and apply to Harvard University. Much to her delight and surprise, Lissa was accepted and awarded a prestigious Presidential Fellowship.

In her first year of the doctoral program in 2007-08, she co-developed and co-taught a graduate course entitled "Leadership, Entrepreneurship and Learning" with her advisor, Professor Monica Higgins. In addition, Lissa was asked to serve on a curriculum design committee for a specifically tailored doctoral leadership program for students in education leadership.

Given the time and investment Lissa has devoted to leading, teaching, leading teaching and teaching leading, she cannot think of a better time, than the second half of her life to bring it all together as a student, scholar, and practitioner. Lissa said,

> I owe a debt of gratitude to that institution for instilling that understanding and igniting that fire in me. It is a lifelong commitment I have made to myself, and beginning the quest to earn my doctorate at 44 years of age, is simply a testimony to that. I owe a debt of gratitude to those two young men in that hookah café overlooking the Persian Gulf, who unwittingly allowed me to eavesdrop on their conversation that fateful night.

Lieutenant Lissa Young does a pre-flight check in a Kiowa OH-58 helicopter. (*Photo courtesy of Lissa Young*)

Major Lissa Young and Emmy Lou Hairy on the stairs of a Chinook helicopter. (*Photo courtesy of Lissa Young*)

Major Lissa Young commanded B Company, 4-123rd Aviation Regiment. The unit had the responsibility for the tactical war fighting response force for both mountain and arctic environments as well as for civilian emergencies above 10,000 feet in Alaska and Western Canada. (*Photo courtesy of Lissa Young*)

Lissa Young as a doctoral student at the Graduate School of Education, Harvard University, Cambridge, MA. (*Photo courtesy of Lissa Young*)

Cadet Anita Allen, USMA 2000, enters the final lap of a 5,000-meter race at West Point, NY. (*Photo courtesy of Anita Allen*)

YOU NEVER KNOW UNTIL YOU TRY | ANITA ALLEN, CLASS OF 2000

"Upon the fields of friendly strife are sown the seeds that, upon other fields, on other days, will bear the fruits of victory."
— General Douglas A. MacArthur

Anita Allen grew up on a 1900-acre farm in Star City, Indiana, far from any big city. She knows a lot about cattle and hogs, having shown them in county fairs and 4-H contests throughout grade and high school. At Pioneer High School, Anita was an A-student, four-sport athlete, cheerleader, and trumpet player. Running was her passion. She competed in five track events running the 3200-meter, 1600-meter, 800-meter, 400-meter, and the 4 by 400-meter relay. She hoped to continue running in college, possibly earning a scholarship based on her academic and running records.

During her junior year, Anita received a letter from the Army Track & Field Office at the United States Military Academy at West Point, New York. Seeing the Army logo in the upper left corner of the envelope, she threw it on the back seat of the family's car. She was not interested in joining the military. Her father, Dean, immediately urged her to open it and see what it said. Anita recalled, "My parents always reminded us that if you discount something without trying, you will never know if that something is good or bad for you." Retrieving and opening the envelope, she learned of West Point's interest in her as both an athlete and student. A little research piqued her curiosity. She found the Academy's low student-to-teacher ratio of 15 to 1 appealing, as it emphasized access to instructors and personal attention in and out of the classroom. The goals and ideals of West Point were noble and Anita sensed the environment demanded excellence in all areas. The fact that the alumni created modern military history and tactics that were part of the course of study were both of interest. Most alluring was the opportunity to run and compete in a Division I track and field program.

In the summer of 1995, West Point announced that Jerry Quiller, the head coach at the University of Colorado, had accepted the top coaching post at Army. In just two short seasons at Colorado, Quiller led the Buffaloes men's and women's cross-country squads to second and fourth place finishes, respectively, at the 1994 NCAA Championships and that fall Quiller was named national "Coach of the Year."

Anita decided to complete the application process and began her final year in high school. During her senior year, she made two visits to West Point as she seriously considered an offer of admission, weighing it against scholarship offers from two other colleges. The meeting with Coach Quiller assured Anita that West Point was the place for her. Impressed with Quiller and that his entire staff focused on providing his athletes the resources and mentors they needed to succeed on and off the track, Anita accepted an appointment in the Class of 2000. Anita said, "I was a part of 'Q's' first official recruiting class." Coach Q or Q were the nicknames his athletes used for their coach.

Early in her plebe year at West Point, Anita embraced the notion and practice of teamwork on and off the track. Anita remembered:

> West Point is definitely not an effortless endeavor for most. You rely on those close friends to get you through the tough times and celebrate the little victories from getting all the laundry delivered plebe year to doing well on a group engineering project. On the track, you could not have had a better group of teammates and friends. Learning to lean on one another was a method of survival, and success was measured by group accomplishments.

As a competitive runner, Anita fought through a series of typical training injuries—sprained ankles, pulled hamstrings, stress fractures, and shin splints. Vigilant about minimizing her recovery time, she faithfully did her prescribed rehabilitation exercises. When she was not able to run on land, she would "run" in the pool. Rarely able to get through a season injury-free, she endured many disappointing finishes. Anita felt that she was squandering her innate talent with lackluster results. She struggled with a widely fluctuating appetite and an eating disorder attributable to the daily stress most cadets experience and the Academy's constant emphasis on weight management. Anita attributes many of her poor performances to this combination of variables. She explained,

> The injuries and eating disorders wreaked havoc on my body. I was always first string, but never was able to put it all together for a great season. With support from my family, I focused on my firstie year and had a fantastic injury-free cross-country season. I think the fuel for my dream was the fact that I had never put it together and I knew that I was capable of so much more.

Like many athletes, Anita dreamed of competing in the Olympics. With Q as a coach, she had a chance to realize that dream. United States Track and Field named Quiller assistant coach for the 2000 Olympic Games in Sydney, Australia. Anita loved running for this coach. She said,

> Q is one of the most charismatic people I have ever met. He has a way with people and is always able to stay light-hearted regardless of the situation and circumstances. If you want results, it is up to you to seek his guidance. You have to have the desire and he will make himself available. He had this saying— 'super-do!' That's how you know you are on the right track.

Anita's final collegiate cross-country season appeared to be the breakthrough season she had been working toward. She was winning all the dual and three-way meets, and firmly beating many All-Americans. Then, during a typical fall afternoon workout that involved running sprints up the ski slope, just outside West Point's back gate, Anita lost her footing and slipped on the grass. Her ankle turned and made a popping sound. Immediately, it swelled. The Patriot League Championships were only two weeks away and the Eastern Coast Athletic Conference Championships (ECAC), a mere three weeks. Again, Anita began her recovery with training in the pool. However, this injury took much longer to heal than prior sprains, and her dream began to fade. At the ECAC competition, Anita finished fifth.

Anita's overall collegiate athletic resume includes 11 varsity letters for her cross-country, indoor and outdoor track seasons, and five Patriot League Championships. But the disappointing end of her last cross-country season left her wanting another opportunity to compete. However, it was time to focus on her future as an Army officer.

At the start of her final semester at West Point, Anita was having difficulty deciding a branch of the Army in which she wanted to serve. She never liked shooting and her hands always trembled pulling the trigger of her M-16 rifle. Anita explains, "I struggled because most branches' ultimate mission is to inflict harm or deliver things that harm. The Medical Service Corps, however, was about keeping people alive and that was how I made my decision. Despite all the military training, I wanted to keep people alive."

Six months later, in May 2000, Anita graduated and became a commissioned second lieutenant in the Medical Service Corps. Within sixty days of graduation, the majority of new lieutenants begin Officer Basic Courses at various military posts across the United States. Offered the opportunity to remain at West Point as a graduate assistant coach of the women's cross-country team, working under Coach Q, Anita remained at West Point. Accepting this assignment postponed her attendance at her basic course until the following January. Had it not been for her decision to remain at West Point, her Olympic dream might have been extinguished.

Late that summer, Second Lieutenant Allen took Army's cross-country team to Colorado Springs, Colorado, for a high-altitude preseason training camp. The team stayed at the Army's World Class Athlete Program (WCAP) facilities. This program takes elite Army athletes and trains them for international competition. There Anita met Rob Coley, the sports specialist recruiter for WCAP. Knowing Anita's running prowess, Rob asked her if she had ever jumped horses. Curious about the question, Anita answered that she had ridden horses a few times, but had never jumped. She told him that she was more familiar with cattle and hogs as she showed them in 4-H. Rob asked her if she was a good shot. Anita replied that she was a qualified expert on the M-16 rifle. He then asked her if she ever fenced. "I have built several fences!" Anita exclaimed, having grown up on a farm. "I kept wondering where all these questions were leading."

In fact, Rob was talking about the five sports that make up the modern pentathlon: pistol shooting, fencing, equestrian, swimming, and cross-country running. This multi-discipline event was the brainchild of Baron Pierre de Coubertin, founder of the modern Olympics. Athletes who participate in this event must master all five disciplines and develop the endurance to compete in all of them in one grueling day. De Coubertin believed such an event would test an athlete's moral qualities as much as his or her physical skills and attributes, thereby producing the ideal complete athlete. After initially laughing at Anita's responses, Rob explained his questioning. He had succeeded in sparking Allen's interest, and Anita accepted his invitation to a mini tryout the following week.

Interestingly, De Coubertin anticipated that the modern pentathlon would appeal to the military, and held the belief that it would foster peace by ensuring that the world's soldiers could engage in friendly competition.[101] Embraced by the military, this

---

[101] www.modern-pentathlon.com.

multiple-discipline sport demands soldierly competence: courage, coordination, flexibility in changing circumstances, physical fitness, and discipline. Beginning in 1912, and for the next 44 years, the United States Army had the sole responsibility for training and developing modern pentathletes at its facility in Fort Sam Houston, Texas. It was not until 1956, that civilians were invited to enter the Olympic Trials for the sport.[102]

Anita said, "I was introduced to pentathlon in July, and Q was leaving for the Sydney Olympics in August. While there, he watched the entire pentathlon for me and returned to share all the details with me. He said 'I watched it, and you have to have guts.'"

For the next few months, Lieutenant Allen wrestled with the decision either to join the Army's World Class Athlete Program (WCAP) or to begin her military profession as a Medical Service Corps officer. She remembered the words of her parents about her decision to go to West Point—you never know unless you try something. If accepted into the WCAP and she did not like it, she could easily go to Korea and catch up with her West Point classmates. She recalled,

> I spoke with a few graduates who had previously faced the same decision and came to understand that I had been given an opportunity. I questioned my purpose thinking I was destroying a military career. Being a soldier was a sure thing whereas there were no guarantees about making an Olympic Team. I allowed myself one four-year period to make the Games. I was going to work my ass off to do it.

Anita joined the World Class Athlete Program following completion of the Medical Corps Officer Basic Course at Fort Sam Houston, Texas, the same post in which the Army had trained it's pentathletes in the first half of the 20th century. On her first day, she

---

[102] IBID.

received an immediate reminder that she no longer had a viable military career. Anita remembered,

> The Commanding Officer of the post came to our training unit. He asked me 'Do you understand second lieutenant that you are ending your career the moment you sign into this book?' Frequently, I was called to various officers for counseling sessions reminding me of the consequences of my decision. I think all the attention I received was because I was a West Point grad. It begins to make you question your decision when you are trying to focus all of your physical, mental, and emotional energy into effective training and recovery regimen.

That summer of 2001, with less than 30 days of training, Anita competed in her first modern pentathlon competition. A few days later, the world changed drastically. The terrorist attacks of September 11, 2001, occurred, sending the U.S. Armed Forces into action to wage and fight a global war on terror in Afghanistan and eventually in Iraq. Again, Lieutenant Allen confronted the same decision—continue training and competing or join her classmates in the war on terror. After many phone calls and several days of agonizing, Anita decided to pursue her Olympic goal and continue training. She wrestled with the decision, knowing that most of her classmates and friends from West Point would soon find themselves in harm's way.

Competing on the international world cup circuit, the following year, Anita had clinched the 4th place ranking on the U.S. pentathlon team. Instead of cheering and supporting her success, many athletes and coaches felt threatened by her rapid rise in the sport. Other athletes had been training many years and were the favorites to represent the United States in Athens.

With one year to go before the opening ceremonies of the 2004 Summer Olympic Games, Anita was coming close to realizing her dream. As training intensified, Anita absorbed everything she could about every discipline, each competitor, and each teammate. She placed 4th in the U.S. Championships. Two American women would make the Olympic Team. She was another step closer. The next major competition was the Pan American Games in Santo Domingo, Dominican Republic. A win would earn Anita one of two spots on the 2004 Olympic Team. Once again, she confronted the decision to compete for her country or to fight for her country. Twelve hours before her scheduled departure to the Dominican Republic, Anita received an email from her former Tactical Officer at West Point. Her company mate and friend, First Lieutenant Leif Nott had been killed on July 30, 2003, in Belaruz, Iraq. Only twenty-four, Nott died of wounds received from hostile fire. Anita remembered:

> I was grieving, angry, and felt extremely guilty. I went through every emotion. My friends were in harm's way and I was training for the Olympics. I was feeling that I should be there too. So I gave myself an ultimatum. If I won the Pan Am Games, I would continue my pursuit for the Olympics. If I did not win, then I would stop training and return to the fighting Army. I was going to give it my best shot. I owed the Army nothing less, especially when my friends were being killed.

Anita thought her training and sacrifices seemed trivial compared to those of her West Point classmates and other service members fighting on various fronts. "I questioned my self-worth," she said. "Am I making a difference? Am I doing something that's going to be good for the future? Am I doing the right thing?"

With a nation at war, athletic training and competition for an Army officer just did not seem appropriate. However, sports, ingrained in our society, reflect our national character. We tend to identify athletic competition as a rallying point of unity, especially as a country. The decision to compete in a global athletic competition or serve on the battlefield is deeply personal. We need soldiers and we need athletes.

At the Pan American Games, Anita drew a balky horse from the random selection. Very concerned with the draw, her coach advised her to growl at the horse throughout the ride. At each fence, she growled and the horse jumped, knocking off only one rail. Anita entered the last event, the 3000-meter run, nearly a minute behind the leader Katia Rodriguez of Cuba. The total points scored in the first four events determine the starting order for the final event so the cross-country running becomes a handicap event.

Anita ran fast. She not only erased the 42-second deficit, but went on to win the competition. With the win, she became the first athlete named to the Summer Olympic Team who would represent the United States in Athens the following year. There were many tears—tears of joy and tears of sorrow. She explained:

> Winning the Pan Am Games was possibly my greatest self-epiphany. Lief was telling me it was OK to compete. Within hours of winning, I received five congratulatory calls from friends in Iraq. They set up communication channels and spread the news of my victory by any means possible. There they were fighting a war, yet finding the time to send me congratulatory wishes. It was incredibly humbling and very motivating. It was a positive story our soldiers needed in the war zone.

When she returned to the states, Anita received a photo of soldiers from Iraq, displaying a sign with the words *Congratulations, LT Allen*. Somewhat emotional, Anita said, "My victory mattered to them. They were fighting for their lives and the freedom of Iraqis, but found the time to sign the photo and send it to me. These were my friends and they were behind me 100%."

Anita's victory mattered to others. She had inherited a legacy when she made the Olympic team. Anita explains,

I received an email from a West Point graduate and member of the 1956 Olympic Pentathlon Team. He wrote, 'Are you aware you are the first woman graduate to compete in the pentathlon? We graduates have a bronze and silver, but no gold. Go get 'em.'

Then she learned that from 1912 through 1952, every U.S. Olympic pentathlete was a West Point graduate, including General George S. Patton. In 1912, then a lieutenant, Patton participated in the first Olympic pentathlon competition in Stockholm, Sweden. Patton's glory on the battlefield is legendary. His 5th place Olympic finish is less famous. Although known for carrying pistols with ivory handles as an officer, the shooting event kept him off the podium as an athlete.

After returning from the Pan American Games, Anita anticipated that her sole focus for the next year would be the physical and mental training in preparation for the Olympic competition. However, new and previously conquered obstacles reappeared. She continued to have problems with a nagging foot injury and had surgery on that foot in November 2003. After eight weeks on crutches, the recovery from this operation did not progress as effectively or efficiently as anticipated. Unfortunately, the first world cup competition of the 2004 season was scheduled in Mexico in mid February, with the second world cup a week later in Brazil. Anita learned she would have to defend her Olympic team spot. She recalled, "It was a disappointing start to the season—injured and defending a spot I earned." Because she could not run, bike, or even aqua jog, she went back to West Point intent on devising an alternative training regimen. For two weeks, she worked with laser-like focus with Dr. Nate Zinsser, a world-renowned Sports Psychologist and deputy director of the Center for Enhanced Performance. Together they visualized and affirmed her performance and outcomes. Slowly she found that she was able to shoot and fence standing on one leg. Her right leg got very strong, but she was not able to move back and forth quickly, so she focused on reaction time and fencing by touching quickly on the hand. This touch to an opponents hand would eliminate them from the fencing competition. She swam with a buoy. She tried riding without stirrups but quickly realized this was too dangerous, so she stopped riding for three months.

Then the psychological competition began. Anita heard rumors that her sport's National Governing Body (NGB), U.S. Pentathlon, headquartered in San Antonio, Texas, had put their support behind two hometown athletes to compete in the Olympics. Anita had come on the scene and performed so well so quickly, that the NGB was trying to figure out ways to award the two Olympic berths to other athletes who had been competing in the sport for several years. While Anita's coach defended her performance and her spot on the Olympic team, the NGB continued to erect more hurdles in the remaining competitions in hopes she would stumble and fall.

At each competition, Anita proved the Olympic berth hers. But even though she placed higher than the other two athletes did in every competition, she found a legal defense required to protect the Olympic spot she had earned the previous summer. Anita recalled:

> I came to realize others were trying to break my spirit. My parents and family became my support chain. They allowed me to focus on the physical and mental training. I hired a lawyer. Because I had an injury, others thought I was not physically fit to compete. This was a low point and something I just never anticipated.

Two months before opening ceremonies, Anita was still competing for her spot on the team. Now it came down to the Pentathlon World Championships in Moscow. She says,

> It was a very strange and disconcerting time for me. The Executive Director of U.S. Pentathlon told me 'we are going to order your Olympic uniforms, but you

never know. It still depends on the World Championships.' He just made me want it even more.

More determined than ever to go to Athens, the remarks and actions fueled Anita's fire. At the World Championships in Moscow, Anita secured her spot for the fourth and final time.

Anita arrived in Greece three weeks before the Olympic competition to acclimate and complete some key workouts. Although exhausted from the physical and emotional impacts of her struggle, Anita could now focus solely on the Olympic Games. Walking into the Olympic Stadium on opening night, Anita said is unforgettable and nearly impossible to describe. Anita wrote in her electronic Olympic journal to family, friends, and supporters on August 18, 2004:

> We were eight in a row, nearly 40 deep, walking in darkness. In the distance music was blaring, crowds were chanting, and bursts of fireworks were everywhere in the sky. As a sea of blue snaking from the parking lot into the tunnel, we paused one final time...then you saw us and I was waving to you.

> Walking into the Olympic Stadium last night with USA on my shoulders was a dream realized. It has been a long road...literally. From my familiar gravel road near Star City, Indiana, to the paved mountains of West Point, NY, to the real mountains and gravel roads in Colorado Springs, Colorado, some of you have been with me all the while, some of years, and some of lately. Regardless, your support and friendships have meant a lot. Thank you.

> I may never have the chance to express my gratitude in person, so I am attempting to thank you electronically. My plan is to keep a journal throughout the Games,

'Anita's Athens.' From the opening ceremonies, to the Modern Pentathlon competition, to closing ceremonies, and everything else in between, my goal is to bring you along for the ride.

Since I can't explain what walking in opening ceremonies felt like, here are a few pictures and background that hopefully will be worth thousands of words.

Anita placed 18th in a field of 32 competitors in the Olympics. Although she struggled in some of the events, she won the equestrian portion of the competition. Fondly recalling the experience, Anita said, "Winning the equestrian event was the highlight of the competition for me. Prior to the Olympics, I was having a difficult time recovering from a foot injury, and defending my Olympic berth. Somewhat frustrated with my pre-Olympic performances, my confidence was low. Some said I drew an easy horse. I know I rode well."

Anita credits her training at West Point for helping her meet and surpass the physical and mental challenges. She said:

Things can upset you, break your spirit, but the job has to get done. I kept thinking back to MacArthur's words and message that we memorized as plebes, *'There is no substitute for victory.'* I reflected regularly on 'his opinion on athletics' that is carved in the portal of Arvin Gymnasium that I entered every day for nearly five years:

Upon the fields of friendly strife are sown the seeds that upon other fields, on other days, will bear the fruits of victory.[103]

---

[103] Bugle Notes, 1983-1987. (United States Military Academy), West Point, New York. 238.

Unfortunately, I came to understand that the fields are not so friendly. Occasionally it is war; and I chose to fight. There was no substitute for victory. I had hoped to bring home a top 10 finish, but did not. I had amazing support from professors, military friends, and even soldiers I didn't know. So many soldiers took the time to write me words of support, encouragement, and inspiration. It meant a lot to me.

After returning to the U.S. following the Olympics and the media tour of WCAP athletes, Anita returned to the Army as a staff officer in a military hospital ready to be a soldier. Anita said, "I was tired and burned out of the Olympic movement, and was more than ready to start working." Assigned as an assistant operations staff officer, Captain Anita Allen arrived at a unit not used to having extra personnel. She explained:

Unfortunately, I missed much of the on-the-job-training you get as a lieutenant and platoon leader as well as the guidance you get from experienced non-commissioned officers like squad leaders and platoon sergeants. Everyone at this post knew about me and only thought of me as an Olympian. I wish I could have been anonymous going into the unit. Since I did not have the typical platoon leader and executive officer time, I was labeled as the captain who was really a second lieutenant. I got a little discouraged, needing to fast-forward four years in an Army career.

Anita once again contemplated her prospects:

I really did give the Army an honest chance, but I had a difficult time because I had not really served as a soldier's soldier. I was branded. In WCAP, while training for the Olympics allowed me to pursue my dream, the Army experience was not all positive. Despite taking on several leadership positions of other WCAP athletes, which I continued to do repeatedly throughout my training. It was never acknowledged. My military ratings did not reflect this aspect of my leadership nor my success in being ranked as one of the top two pentathletes in U.S. and the current Pan American Champion. It was time for me to move on.

Completing her service obligation, Anita resigned from the Army in June 2005. She had prepared for medical school by taking several pre-requisite classes and the Medical College Admission Test in early 2004. However, Anita was not ready to make the commitment to years of schooling. Not focusing on a goal for the first time in her life, she began looking for opportunities in Colorado, where she was living. Lara Hammerick, an Army teammate, mentioned El Pomar, a Colorado-based organization that trains the next generation of leaders for the nonprofit sector. Recognized as one of the most creative, diverse, and effective training programs in this sector, the two-year program selects highly qualified individuals to develop their leadership skills in a dynamic, active and hands-on program designed to provide participants with a 360 degree view of and education about the nonprofit world. The core of the experience is the opportunity to staff and lead the foundation's various community stewardship programs, thereby providing a thorough education in the nature of the nonprofit sector and the role of foundations.

As one of the largest and oldest private foundations in the Rocky Mountain West, with assets totaling $500 million, El Pomar's mission is to "enhance, encourage and promote the current and future well being of the people of Colorado through grant making and community stewardship in health, human services, education, arts and humanities, and civic and community initiatives."[104]

---

[104] www.elpomar.org.

Intrigued by the idea and ready to set and meet a new professional goal, Anita applied and was accepted for the two-year fellowship program. Anita said, "The people are amazing. It is a very positive and creative environment and exactly what I needed." During the fellowship Anita worked with three specific programs: one that recognizes excellence in Colorado not-for-profit organizations, the Penrose Non-Profit Institute, an outreach program, and making grants to fire departments to prepare and fight wild land fires.

Anita's journey has taken her around the world. More than anything, she realizes the importance of never giving up on a dream. She said, "Never let anyone compromise your self-worth along the journey of life you have chosen. Dream BIG! And go for it because you (and they) will never know until you try."

One of Anita Allen's highlights of the 2004 Summer Olympic Games in Athens, Greece was being on Team U.S.A with her childhood sports idol, Martina Navratilova. This photo was taken just prior to the Opening Ceremonies. (*Photo courtesy of Anita Allen*)

Anita Allen and her horse, Dino, clear a jump in the equestrian event, the 4th of 5 events in the Modern Pentathlon. Anita won the equestrian portion of the pentathlon, and placed 18th in a field of 32 competitors in the 2004 Olympics. (*Photo courtesy of Anita Allen*)

Cadet Holly Hagan, USMA 1987, receives her West Point diploma from General John Wickham, Chief of Staff of the Army, May 27, 1987. (*Academy Photo*)

NEW LIFE | LIEUTENANT COLONEL HOLLY OLSON, MD, CLASS OF 1987

"Avoid having your ego so close to your position that when your position falls, your ego goes with it."

— General Colin Powell

As twilight arrived on February 12, 2001, in Mililani Town on the Hawaiian Island of Oahu it brought with it a thick blanket of gray-black fog. A storm brewed slowly as the rain fell. Major Holly Olson and her two children, Brittany, 12, and TJ, 7, sat in the living room of their home, catching up on the day's activities while finishing that evening's schoolwork. At 9:00 P.M. they heard the familiar sound of the rotating blades of helicopters overhead. "Maybe that's Dad's chopper," Holly said, knowing her husband's mission today had included the rigging and transporting of some Army vehicles by air.

Rob was due home later that week following the completion of a two-week field training exercise. As the operations officer for his Field Artillery battalion, Major Rob Olson had responsibility for the planning and conduct of the exercise. His family eagerly anticipated his return from the exercise.

Holly, a doctor who specialized in Obstetrics and Gynecology, had called Rob that morning on his cell phone from her office at Tripler Army Medical Center shortly after completing her rounds and prior to reviewing her resident's patient charting requirements. Earlier that day, all three Olsons had spoken to Rob at various times. Brittany and TJ each talked with their dad in the early afternoon to tell him about school and soccer. All calls ended with a mutual and heartfelt, "I love you."

Classmates at West Point, Holly and Rob began dating their final semester at the Academy. After three months, Rob asked Holly's best friend, Kim Randall, to go shopping with him for an engagement ring. Holly laughed,

Of course, I found out that he was going to ask me to marry him, because Kim is my best friend. I just knew that if I did not marry Rob, I would spend the rest of my life looking for someone as great as Rob. It was graduation week, a week filled with a lot of excitement and anxiety. After all the festivities of graduation and commissioning, we had a huge tailgate with our families and friends in A Lot. After the party, when everyone left, he asked me. I just knew it was meant to be. May 27, 1987 was one hell of a day—graduation, commissioning, and getting engaged.

Holly's decision to pursue admission to West Point and a subsequent life as a soldier and doctor arose from her desire to try something outside the usual college and business paths. "It sounded both challenging and intriguing. It provided a sense of security about the future by having a guaranteed job for five years, the federal service obligation upon graduation. While the education is financially free, there's a significant payment with physical and mental energy," recounted Holly. "I was pretty much a geek at West Point."[105]

Holly's most significant challenges at West Point were not in the classroom but on the pavement of the Central Area, the quadrangle surrounded on all sides by six stories of cadet dormitories known as barracks. On most days, the Area fills with cadets in various uniforms walking to and from class, lining up for meal formations, or playing pick up basketball games. But each Saturday and Sunday, cadets walk punishment tours in this "Area." These tours result from the accumulation of excess demerits for a spectrum of infractions of the cadet rules and regulations. Cadets walk them off in hour units in dress uniform with parade weapons and spit-shined shoes, marching back and forth, for three hours at a time, with a 10-minute break each hour.

---

[105] Lieutenant Colonel Holly Olson (interview with author), March 2004.

During her second and third years at West Point, yearling and cow years, Holly accumulated more than a hundred hours of punishment tours. Her first major infraction resulting in a "slug"— the award of multiple hours—was after she attended a movie on a weeknight. Only cows[106] and firsties could see movies during the week. Her second and third "slugs" came from drinking alcohol during the academic week, a major violation of cadet regulations.

While varsity athletes typically work off their tours by sitting room confinement, Holly's antics earned her 134 hours of walking back and forth in silence on the cold, black asphalt of Central Area because soccer was not yet a corps squad sport.[107] As intended, walking punishment tours are an enormous waste of time. With little spare time in cadet life, this type of discipline is effective and frustrating. In addition, while cadets have outstanding tours to walk, they are confined to specific locations on the West Point installation, the academic buildings, the library, the mess hall, and their Spartan rooms in the barracks. "During my last set of tours, I got a 4.0 that semester," said Holly.

> I had nothing else to do but study. I was very concerned about grades and my academic standing. I had chosen chemistry as my major and I just knew for certain that everyone else at West Point was smarter than me, so I studied my brains out first semester of plebe year. After that semester, I realized that I could make it here.

Midway through West Point, Holly began looking at how to use her chemistry degree in a way that would both benefit the Army and offer her career satisfaction. Graduating in the top 5% of an

---

[106] Cows are third year cadets or juniors.

[107] At West Point, intercollegiate varsity sports are known as corps squad. Women's soccer became a corps squad sport in 1986. Corps squad athletes, who amass punishment tours, typically sit room confinement in lieu of walking off the hours. Given heavy competitive travel schedules, this allows the athlete to use the time to study.

academy class of 1014 cadets at number 37, she excelled in academics as well as athletics where she was now a starter on the Women's Soccer Team. Not drawn to a specific military branch of service, she pursued a pre-medical course of study. Holly was accepted into medical school as one of fewer than 2% of her graduating class permitted to attend medical school immediately out of West Point.

Engaged on graduation day, Holly and Rob decided they would wait until August 1988 to get married, allowing Rob to complete his officer basic class and a few specialty courses, and Holly to focus on her first year of medical school.

The first year of marriage, they lived apart, with Rob residing in Oklahoma, and Holly in medical school in South Carolina. When Rob arrived at his first troop assignment at Fort Campbell, Kentucky, Holly applied for a transfer to Vanderbilt Medical School, 60 miles to the south, so they could live together. Medical schools typically do not accept transfers from other programs, making the process extremely difficult. Holly was then six months pregnant, so the day after the medical board exam, she moved to Fort Campbell and took a year off to care for her newborn daughter.

In January 1990, she interviewed with the Vanderbilt Medical School admissions department and was accepted as a 3rd year medical student. By the time she returned to school later that summer, Rob's unit deployed to Southwest Asia as part of Operation Desert Storm. Brittany was 10 months old.

The next challenge was finding appropriate day care for Brittany. She recalled,

> I just started working the phones, turning over every stone and investigating every possible option. I had no family in the area. Besides having an infant, I needed extended hours of care because of school and the commute to Nashville. Unfortunately, every person and every place I called only offered care from 6:00 A.M. to 5:00 P.M. The very last name of my list was Patty. I called her, exhausted and desperate. When I

asked her hours, she responded, 'I'm always open, 24/7/365.' When I described my situation and the various scenarios of dropping Brittany off at 4:30 in the morning and picking her up at 7:00 in the evening, Patty said yes to everything. I then told her the amount of my medical school stipend and what I could afford to spend. Patty said we will make it work.

Rob's homecoming after seven months in Kuwait was exciting and challenging. While grateful Rob was back and safe, Holly needed to adjust to having someone else around the house. Holly said,

> I would pick her up, feed her, read to her, bathe her, put her to bed and then begin to study. Now it all changed. Every marriage has moments you grow together or apart. We were just so excited to finally be together again that we looked at the opportunity as the first day of the rest of our lives. With every scenario we encountered, we made the decision that we were a team, and we were going to get through it. I was on my medical school OB/GYN rotation, and I knew this was the specialty I wanted to pursue, so I had to perform well.

USMA had prepared Holly well for the rigors of medical school and residency training. The curriculum was tough and demanding. Time management skills, ability to multi-task, attention to detail, and being able to go for long periods with limited sleep sustained Holly.

After Holly graduated from Medical School, and Rob finished his Officer Advanced Course, the Olsons moved to Hawaii, where Holly began her training as a medical resident and Rob commanded a Field Artillery battery. The Olson family grew with the birth of TJ, their son, in November 1993.

Nearly a decade after their graduation, the Olsons returned to West Point in 1996, as members of the Academy's staff and faculty. Holly reported to Keller Army Hospital as an obstetrics and gynecology staff physician, and Rob as a tactical officer for a company of cadets. Rob had served in Army Artillery units in various leadership positions for nine years, including seven months in Kuwait during Operation Desert Storm. Based on his performance in all these assignments, he was promoted to the rank of major a year ahead of most of his classmates. Holly would become a major in 1998, two years after completion of her residency training.

Holly outranked Rob in the Class of 1987. He stood 1,004[th], just ten from the bottom. Academic standing at graduation greatly influences where one lives, if selected as a member of the West Point faculty or staff.

Prior to the electronic age, the "housing draw" was an official and mandatory event for officers newly assigned to the garrison of West Point. It was at this notorious event that officers selected which houses they would call home for the next 3 to 4 years based on their graduating class rank within a year group. For married couples of the same graduation year, the couple drew a home based on the higher class rank of the two. When Rob stood up to select their quarters early in the housing draw, other classmates jeered and joked with him to sit down, knowing how low he ranked. He offered his classmates and others in the audience his typical wide, toothy smile and reminded everyone that he was married to Holly Hagan. Holly, lest anyone forget, graduated 37th in the class. With that remark, he chose the house on the corner of Merritt Road with the fenced-in backyard and lots of parking for the many tailgates he anticipated hosting the next few years.

For the next three years, many classmates and their families stopped by the Olsons to reminisce and recount their antics as cadets. During that time, Holly touched the lives of many of her classmates in a profound and memorable way by bringing their children into the world as their obstetrician.

During a visit she made to my own home in Park City, Utah, in March of 2005, I recalled just how many lives Holly had touched. Each year, as the Christmas holidays approach, we clear our refrigerator of all of the previous year's pictures and begin anew with the large, blank white metal backdrop. By March 2005, the refrigerator was covered with an impromptu collage of all the 2004 Christmas photo cards. Holly began pointing to various children, 13 on the refrigerator in all, she helped bring into the world. One classmate, Christine Voisinet Bender, had Holly deliver three of her four sons. Unfortunately, Holly and Chris were not at the same Army post for the birth of Chris' fourth son, much to Chris' dismay.

Among the photos on the refrigerator was a picture of the Holland family—Marty, Anne, Erin, and Christopher. The Hollands and Olsons have been friends since Rob and Marty met as cadets during their first summer at West Point. Since that time, they were nearly inseparable. Upon graduation, the two newly commissioned lieutenants attended Officer Basic Class at Fort Sill, Oklahoma together, shared a house at their first duty station at Fort Campbell, Kentucky while assigned to the 101st Airborne, and remained roommates until they married within two weeks of each other. "We deployed to the desert together," Marty said.

> After the desert, Rob followed me to the Officer Advanced Course and lived in the house that we had rented during the previous Officer Basic Course. Next, we went to Hawaii, where we served together and where Holly delivered our first child, Erin. After Hawaii, I spent two years in Chapel Hill, North Carolina, while Rob remained in Hawaii (our only active duty separation). We got back together at West Point, where Rob served as a TAC and I was an instructor in the Department of History. While at West Point, Holly also delivered our second child, Christopher.

One of my favorite memories of our time at West Point was a night when Rob was the Tactical Officer in Charge at the Cadet Central Guard Room, and I was the Academic Officer in Charge; we both had a good laugh, and we were sure that Sylvanus Thayer himself would be shocked to think that Rob O was in charge of 'good order and discipline' for the corps while I was in charge of study conditions. Truly, the inmates had taken over the asylum. In 2000, the Hollands and Olsons moved together once again, to Fort Leavenworth, and continued to enjoy many good times together.

After the year long Command and General Staff College Course, Rob and Holly headed back to Hawaii while Anne and I returned to Fort Campbell and the 101st. Rob and I joked that the only rationale for taking different assignments was that we were both returning to previous duty stations where we knew the lay of the land.[108]

In 2000, Rob received orders to attend a yearlong course at Fort Leavenworth, Kansas, Command and General Staff School. Holly fought hard for assignment with Rob in Kansas, but knew that she could not attend since the course is for line officers only. In her profession as an Army doctor, the personnel rules stated that she needed to be at any given location for more than one year. After much persistence, however, Holly found an exception to the rule, which allowed the Olsons to move as a family to Kansas and then back to Hawaii the following year.

Upon their arrival in Oahu, Dr. Holly Olson became the director of ambulatory care and the associate program director for residency training. After a short stint as the 2nd Battalion, 25th

---

[108] Written by Marty Holland on 21 February 2001 on west-point.org and Rob Olson Eulogy page.

Aviation Brigade Fire Support Officer, Major Rob Olson became the operations officer of the 2-11 Field Artillery Battalion, a position that carried significant responsibility for the training and readiness of an 800-person military unit. It required that he spend a lot of time in the field ensuring that the unit remained prepared for deployment anywhere in the world.

One such exercise came in February 2001, in a mountain training area on the north side of the island, and lasted two weeks. One evening, about 10:30 P.M., the phone rang. It was one of the wives from Rob's unit, calling to initiate an emergency phone chain.

Holly asked, "What's the situation?"

The woman answered, "The information given was that they were calling all the families to request they not overwhelm Tripler hospital by showing up there and asking questions."

Holly responded, "Why would anyone do that?"

She said, "Haven't you heard about the helicopter crash?"

There were no more details at that time, except to wait for further information after all the families of the casualties had been notified. Holly's heart sank. She immediately called Rob on his cell phone, and left a message asking him to call at the first opportunity. "At that moment, I just knew Rob was dead. I asked God for the calmness to sleep, because I knew I would need my strength later on," she said. At 2:00 A.M., the phone woke Holly. It was Colonel Mike Yancey, Holly's boss, telling her to go to her front door. When Holly arrived at the door, her best friend and colleague, her boss, his wife, and her pastor were standing in the rain. She knew. The helicopter she and the kids had heard earlier that evening was indeed their Dad's helicopter, but it was the medical evacuation helicopter carrying Rob and others to the hospital.

That night, February 12, 2001, two U.S. Army helicopters crashed, killing Major Rob Olson, and six other soldiers, during a night exercise, 15 miles from their home base at Schofield Barracks and a few miles from the world famous surfing spot of Sunset Beach. The accident occurred when the two Black Hawk helicopters—660 feet shy of the landing zone and about 100 feet off the ground—

slowed for a landing and became entangled. When the call of duty in peacetime is fatal, the shock is extreme. No words can express the grief one feels at losing one's husband, friend, and soul mate.

Holly remains steadfast in her commitment that the grief will not ruin their lives. "I'm so thankful for the short time we shared our lives," she said.

> During the first few months following Rob's death, a quickly moving fog blanketed our existence. Although the emotional support of family, friends, and colleagues was amazing and so critical, I'm not sure if I will get those months back in terms of my memory. In a very short time period, I experienced major epiphanies and struggles in my individual grief and the grief of our children.

Holly decided that someone simply had to take charge and run the house and that she was that someone. "It was a decision, plain and simple," she said. "You go on autopilot."[109]

Three months after Rob's death, I had dinner with Holly at a classmate's place in Honolulu. Standing on the 31st floor lanai looking out over Diamond Head, Waikiki beach, and Pearl Harbor as the sun lowered, I offered the only words I could muster, "I am not sure what to say."

"Don't worry," Holly responded compassionately. "Not an hour goes by in which I don't think about Rob. I'm just so thankful and lucky that I had the opportunity to share some of my life with him. He was my best friend."

"How do you get through each day?" I asked meekly.

Holly responded, "I focus on the kids and my job. It's most difficult and trying at the times I least expect. A few weeks ago, TJ and I were going to a Boy Scout award presentation. When we arrived, TJ didn't want to get out of the car. He just wanted his dad.

---

[109] Lieutenant Colonel Holly Olson (interview with author), March 2004.

What I am to do? I just cry with him and hug him. We didn't go inside."

The days that are the most challenging are the annual anniversaries of Rob's death, his birthday, Memorial Day, and Veteran's Day. Holly makes a significant effort to spend these days as a family in an activity such as hiking or going to the beach.

Coping with the loss of her soul mate, best friend, and husband, Holly continues to excel in the two areas most important to her—taking care of her family and practicing medicine. She explained,

> Rob's death totally changed everything. On the surface, it all looks much the same; but I have become a different person over the last several years. I may have the same job, and I may get stressed about some things; but in general, I have a better perspective on what is important. I've spent much more time developing my faith as a Christian. This has helped me deal with the unanswerable question of how do I continue without my best friend?

Holly's ability to hold everything together in a delicate balance, while raising two teenagers, seeing to the affairs of a home, managing a medical resident program, and caring for patients makes her the personification of selfless service. Being able to share even a few years with someone you love so much is priceless. Holly remembers many of the wonderful experiences they had together and holds Rob in her mind in a loving, caring, and even peaceful way. "Rob was one of the most emotionally mature people," she said. "He truly believed marriage to be a team effort. The mutual respect we had for each other was the key to it all. It applies in all the relationships we have, especially in positions of leadership."

As head of the residency program, Dr. Olson cares for patients and counsels young doctors. She focuses on mentoring physicians whom she is confident to send into the Army to care for women. Holly is their disciplinarian as well as their advocate. As a physician, she is well aware that the residents watch everything she does. Leading, practicing, and caring by example from patient interaction through charting is paramount. "They use that information with what they do," she observed.

> So I try to have meticulous attention to detail, an enthusiastic and welcoming bedside manner, be available in an emergency, and practice proper preoperative procedures. Equally critical is interaction with the staff, especially nurses and medical assistants. I try to model behaviors they will pick up and, hopefully, imitate. We all learn from each other every day, regardless of rank or age.

Throughout the cadet experience at West Point, the principles of leadership are taught, practiced, and reinforced. The first principle, "know yourself, and seek self-improvement,"[110] is one that Holly looks to and strives for each day.

"One does not anticipate becoming a widow at an early age," she said. "There have been major struggles over Rob's death. Early on, I decided that the grief would not ruin our lives. It's just a choice and a fairly simple one at that. I am grateful to have shared part of my life on earth with Rob."

---

[110] Bugle Notes 1983-1987 (New York: United States Military Academy, 1983), 63.

Vanderbilt Medical School graduation. Dr. Holly Olson and daughter Brittany. *(Photo courtesy of Holly Olson)*

Majors Holly and Rob Olson at the Field Artillery Ball. *(Photo courtesy of Holly Olson)*

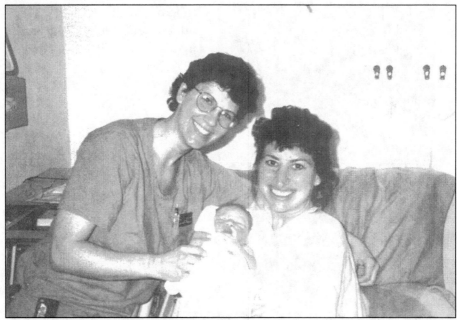

Dr. Holly Olson shares a moment with Lieutenant Christine Voisinet Bender, a West Point classmate, following the birth of Michael Bender. (*Photo courtesy of Holly Olson*)

First Class Cadet Nancy Hogan, USMA 1995, poses with her godson, Robert Hogan. (*Photo courtesy of Nancy Hogan*)

Against All Odds | Captain (retired) Nancy Hogan, Class of 1995

"We do not know of the future and cannot plan for it much."
— Joshua Chamberlain

Growing up on Long Island, Nancy Hogan was familiar with West Point. Her two older brothers attended the Military Academy, and her family made regular trips there for football games, tailgate parties, and cadet parades. Dan, the oldest brother, graduated in 1984, and Chris graduated in 1993. Although not certain that West Point and military service were for her, when Nancy received an appointment to the Academy, she felt it was an opportunity that she should seize.

Her many visits to West Point and numerous conversations with her brothers, familiarized Nancy with the regimentation of daily cadet life. She had seen the Spartan living arrangements in the barracks and listened to both brothers describe the intensity of the intellectual, physical, and mental demands of each year at the Academy. When she reported to West Point in early July 1991, she seemed less apprehensive than some of her classmates. She tried to find some humor in that first day of Cadet Basic Training, the initial summer program of military indoctrination known as Beast Barracks.

"The cadet in the red sash" is the dominating figure at each in-processing station that first day. These first class, or senior, cadets wore a distinctive maroon sash around their waists as highly visible marks of their leadership positions within the cadet chain of command. Reporting to the cadet in the red sash after each station was a process designed to dehumanize, shock, and educate the new cadets. Despite repeatedly being reminded of her four responses "Yes, sir," "No, sir," "Sir, I do not understand," and "No excuse, sir," she tried to laugh beneath her breath, heeding the advice from her brothers to maintain a sense of humor and perspective about the day and the ensuing summer training. Amongst the yelling, correcting, and directing, Nancy, disciplined often when the inner amusement became an external "nervous" giggle, found that the internal laughter made the shock of this particular day more bearable. That night, as taps sounded over the loudspeakers, Nancy fell asleep thinking the day was not too bad, she was not "dead," and it probably would get easier going forward. The following days brought a significant increase in the physical demands placed on new cadets. It did not get easier, at least not right away.

The challenge of running in a group formation during Beast Barracks was new to everyone except those cadets who had been enlisted soldiers or who had attended a military preparatory school. As a sprinter on her high school track team, Nancy thought she was in relatively good shape, having posted numerous track meet wins in the 100-meter and 400-meter hurdles and the 4 x 400 relay races. She had played volleyball throughout her high school years. She "fell out" of the formation runs the first week of training, completing them behind the group. There was a pervasive belief among the faculty and upper class cadets that if one could run one could lead. Any cadets who fell out of runs were the object of sharp comments, " 'how can you expect to be a soldier, if you can't run,' and 'do you think anyone is going to follow you if you fall out of a run?' " It was the first time Nancy had truly faced such a challenge.

Assigned into the Gold running group (a euphemism for the slowest runners who required additional physical training), Nancy had never before "failed" at anything. Wanting to quit, she recognized that if she left West Point so quickly it would reflect poorly on her and her family. She decided to gut it out.

The mandatory assignment to the Gold group required Nancy and other new cadets undergo extra training that consisted of running uphill sprints from the banks of the Hudson River to the Eisenhower Hall Theater. The summer heat and humidity, and the steepness of the 20% grade eclipsed the beauty of the majestic river setting. Nancy said,

> I remember my lungs burning, and gasping for air, as
> the cadet cadre would make us run what seemed like

dozens of sprints up that hill each day. I just hated running, particularly under duress. I knew I needed an attitude adjustment if I was going to get out of this group before the end of the summer. I just convinced myself that I would give running everything I had. By the end of that summer, I was completing the runs comfortably. By the time I was a firstie, I ran often and confidently. Little did I know how valuable this mind over body phenomenon would later become.

Nearing the end of the six weeks of summer training, Nancy passed the physical fitness test and the running portion with a respectable time and score. After that first summer, she scored the maximum number of points on the running portion of all of her Army Physical Fitness Tests (APFT) during her time at the Academy and her career in the Army. She recalled, "I learned quickly the importance of developing a positive frame of mind and setting goals. You have to set your sights on being successful. If you don't think you can, you won't."

As a plebe, Nancy played volleyball on the Academy's intercollegiate women's team. The team traveled to the University of Connecticut in Storrs to play in an invitational tournament. Assigned a locker room in the Connecticut gymnasium, the Army team discovered a bulletin board displaying a posting, "Hey Class of '92— Looking for a job after graduation?" Nancy immediately thought to herself and smiled with pride about her future, "No. I have one." From that point on, she never again thought about leaving West Point.

During the first semester of her sophomore year, Nancy began dating a senior or first class cadet, John Sarabia, who had an easygoing personality and a smile that Nancy said would light up any room. They met through one of Nancy's volleyball teammates and began spending the little free time cadets have together. They dated for a short period following John's graduation in the spring of 1993 and spent a portion of their summer leave together before John reported to his officer basic class, and Nancy returned to West Point. Considering Nancy had two more years of school and neither had been in a serious adult relationship before, they mutually decided to remain friends and date other people. They did spend time together when John returned to West Point for the Homecoming football game weekend in October 1993.

A few weeks later in early November, while studying for a mid-term exam, Nancy heard a knock on her door. Intently engaged in the text for a required course, History of the Military Art, she instructed the visitor to enter. She turned to see one of John's best friends standing in the doorway. As he spoke, tears welled in his eyes. John had been involved in an accident earlier that evening while riding his motorcycle home from a local gym. The other driver ran a stop sign; John did not survive. Nancy shared,

> From what I can remember, I just lost it. My roommate, Tara hugged me, and we stood there crying in each other's arms. The next morning, after being granted emergency leave, my dad picked me up and drove me to our family's home in Long Island. My mom went with me to our travel agent and bought a ticket for me to fly the following day to San Antonio, John's hometown, for his wake and funeral. Chris, my brother, was one of John's classmates. He drove from Oklahoma to San Antonio to be with me at the funeral and pay his respects. Many of John's classmates drove and flew to San Antonio for the memorial service. That day I lost my first love and best friend. It is a day that is hard to forget.

Returning from the funeral, Nancy had a difficult time re-adjusting to the routine of cadet life. She had trouble concentrating in class and studying in her room without her thoughts wandering to John and the shock of his accident. At 22, he had his whole life ahead of him. Her tactical officer recommended she seek grief counseling.

While initially reluctant, Nancy admitted that it was an important part of the healing process. She said,

> I think I was in denial the first couple of months following John's death. He was all I could think about. The counseling did help because it gave me someone to talk to as everyone around me continued with the daily routine. Although time heals many wounds, I didn't think this was going to be one of them.

Nancy really does not remember the remainder of that academic year. "I was there physically, but emotionally was somewhere else," she recalled. It took most of the semester for Nancy to refocus on academics and duties of cadet life. Again, she needed a change of attitude if she was to pass her classes, graduate, and become a commissioned Army officer. "Once again it was about a mindset to achieve my goal. I did not want to go to summer school. I wanted to graduate."

During her final summer at the Academy, Nancy was appointed as executive officer of a Cadet Basic Training company. This leadership position provided her an opportunity to influence the incoming cadets in their transition from high school graduates to military officers in training. In addition to developing the daily training schedules dominated by physical and military activities, she was in charge of the Gold running group for all of basic training. The importance of her own struggles and small victories during Cadet Basic Training three years earlier provided a solid foundation for Nancy's own personal leadership development. The new cadets in the Gold group could not believe that their leader had once been assigned to the slowest running group. Nancy told them that people could do anything if they put their minds to succeeding. They had to believe in their ability to run. She ran every hill sprint with her group, leading them by her own example. She joked and laughed with them. She made the training intense and fun. Sometime between assignment to the Gold group and leading the Gold group,

Nancy discovered she actually enjoyed running because she was not doing it under duress. Nancy recalled,

> It came full circle. I could help those who were now struggling with what I had experienced three years prior. When you have something to work on you have to develop some form of motivation. You need to be able to embrace it and love it, and make it your motivation. If you have to do it, there is really no point in hating it. We were running on the banks of the swiftly flowing Hudson — there are plenty of less attractive locations.

As the academic year began, Nancy struggled with the selection of the branch of the Army in which she would serve. A Military Police officer in the National Guard, Nancy's sister-in-law encouraged her to consider that branch. There appeared to be many opportunities available within this specialty as well as the logical fit with her academic major, American Legal Studies. So Nancy opted for the Military Police branch.

Soon after her selection, Nancy learned about the 298th Military Police (MP) Company based at Fort Meyer, Virginia, and attached to the 3rd United States Infantry Regiment, "the Old Guard" — the group assigned to Arlington National Cemetery. This company's mission was to provide ceremonial and tactical support to the Old Guard. Not only allowed in this company, regulations stated that the platoon leader attached to the Old Guard had to be a female whose height was between 70 and 74 inches. Nancy stood 5'10". During many trips to Washington, D.C. in high school as well as visiting her brother Dan at the Pentagon, she made several visits to Arlington National Cemetery and to the Tomb of the Unknown Soldier. Nancy found the solemnity of each visit to the tomb poignant and inspirational. The Old Guard soldiers were sharp. The unit's history, tradition, and discipline attracted her.

Nancy deeply admired the sentinels of the Old Guard as perfect soldiers. With precision and reverence, these soldiers stood steadfast in their mission of guarding and honoring the Tomb of the Unknown Soldier regardless of weather conditions, 24-hours-per-day, 365-days-per-year. She wanted to be part of this elite honor guard. She wanted to be the MP platoon leader attached to the Old Guard.

In June 1995, Nancy and her classmates threw their white cadet caps into the air when the Cadet Brigade Commander issued his final command, "Class Dismissed!" on graduation day. Later that summer, Nancy attended the Military Police Officer's Basic Course at Fort McClellan, Alabama en-route to her first unit as a platoon leader in the 988th Military Police Company in Fort Benning, Georgia. Shortly after her arrival, she contacted her branch human resources manager about her interest in the Old Guard Military Police Company, an assignment reserved for a first lieutenant. Nancy felt there was no harm in communicating what she wanted to do and where she wanted to be. She learned, from her brothers, the importance of proactively managing one's own career.

Nancy fell in love with the tactical work at Fort Benning. She and her platoon were often in the field practicing their wartime missions of unit maneuver and mobility support, area security, police intelligence operations, and resettlement and internment operations on the battlefield. During this assignment, she met a member of the Silver Wings, Fort Benning's skydiving team—the feeder squad for the Golden Knights, the Army's world-renowned skydiving team. As their interest in one another grew, he introduced Nancy to sport parachuting. She enrolled in a skydiving school owned and operated by a military veteran. The two spent many of their free weekends skydiving together.

A little more then a year into her platoon time, Nancy was selected to lead a direct support platoon working with the 3rd Brigade of the 3rd Infantry Division. The Army recently had allowed women to serve in platoons that directly supported combat arms teams consisting of infantry and armor units. While Nancy enjoyed the missions and the challenges, she came to learn that few infantry and armor commanders understood how best to utilize a platoon of military police soldiers in executing their own tactical missions. To compound the problematic situation, the brigade commander was not interested in the advice of his MP platoon leader on how her soldiers could provide rear area security of his tactical operations center or assist him as his units maneuvered across a battlefield. Nancy remembered,

> On numerous occasions, the commander would try to either use my platoon as a scout reconnaissance or engineer unit, both of which have distinctly different missions. I would continually try to help him understand the role of the military police on the battlefield and how to use my platoon to leverage his own organic capabilities.

> He was not interested in anything I had to say or offer. At first, I thought it was because I was a lieutenant. But he seemed to listen intently to his scout platoon leader, also a lieutenant, I assume because he understood their purpose. On one exercise at the National Training Center (NTC), I remember an engineer battalion commander advising the brigade commander that MPs should not be used in a particular way. It was at this point, the brigade commander heeded this officer's advice. Ironically, it was the same advice I had been giving all along.

Establishing credibility as an officer, who just happened to be a female, at Fort Benning, the home of the Infantry, was at times entertaining for Nancy. There were few women stationed there, and many of the men she had to work with had never served with women. To make matters more challenging, this was just a few years after the infamous "Tailhook" sexual harassment scandal, and many male soldiers were not used to being gender neutral and "politically correct." Nancy recalled two specific instances in which she had to deal with the inexperience of others. The first was during a pre-deployment briefing for all the officers of the battalion. A major from the brigade operations (S-3) office swore in the middle of his briefing. He then immediately looked at Lieutenant Hogan and apologized directly and only to her. Nancy said,

> I went up to him at the end of the meeting and asked that he never do that again. If he did not feel the need to apologize to the male officers present, he should not apologize to me. I was a soldier and wanted to be treated like one. He wasn't sure how to react, but I'm pretty sure he never did it again. Unfortunately, this happened regularly as other officers felt the need to apologize only to me and not their colleagues.

The second occasion was a remark from her company commander who stated bluntly that the only reason she was regularly invited to tactical planning meetings was because she was single and attractive, and the Brigade Commander was single. Nancy said,

> I had to continually remind others that I was a soldier like them, not just a female soldier. It always took me by surprise when it happened because it didn't happen in the MP units. But after working along side me for a while, the combat arms guys started to get it.

In early January 1998, prior to a routine four-month unit deployment to Kuwait, Nancy received a call from a major assigned to the Old Guard asking her if she was still interested in applying for the platoon leader's position now that she was a first lieutenant. He had received her name from the branch manager and a recommendation from an infantry major in the S-3 operations office of the 3-3rd Infantry Battalion. He listed all the documents she needed to send him immediately: all her officer evaluations, an official photo, and a personal essay describing why she wanted the position. He said she needed to call and interview with Colonel Gardner, the Regimental unit commander, first thing the next morning, the same day she was to fly to Kuwait with her platoon.

With little time remaining, Nancy finished packing for Kuwait and wrote the composition in her head. She stayed up all night transcribing and editing her essay, knowing she had only one opportunity to make a great impression. The next morning, she faxed and shipped the documents to Fort Meyer. Excited and nervous, she called the officer-in-charge. As Lieutenant Hogan recalled, Colonel Gardner had a strong and commanding voice, just as she had anticipated. It was a routine interview about why she wanted the position, and knowledge of the Old Guard and its mission. The Colonel thanked Lieutenant Hogan for her interest in the position, and informed her that several others were in consideration. He would be in touch in a few weeks. "That was it. It was a routine interview with no indication of how I interviewed or where I stood. The good thing was that I had made my interest known at branch and I had to take my soldiers to Kuwait. This helped the time pass and kept my mind off the possibility of getting the one job I wanted during my military career," said Nancy.

Three weeks later, while in Kuwait, Nancy got the phone call she had anxiously awaited. She had been selected to be the platoon leader for the 298th Military Police Company. Upon completion of the deployment to Kuwait and return to Fort Benning, she processed out of her unit and prepared to move north to Virginia.

Nancy spent her final weekend in Georgia skydiving across the state border in Alabama. That Saturday, on her third jump, Nancy's main parachute malfunctioned. Instinctively, she quickly "cut away" her main chute and pulled her reserve parachute. She steered her reserve chute to a safe landing on the drop zone. Relieved that she had performed as she had trained, she did not want to end the day with that particular jump experience. She explained her desire to make one more dive to the jumpmaster. He agreed.

Nancy returned to the school building to get a new parachute rig, and had it checked and fitted. As she exited the building, the skydiving school owner approached her and gave her a different rig to use for her final jump. Together, they exited the building and walked to the waiting plane. She, two others, and a jumpmaster boarded the plane. Once the plane leveled off, at 10,000 feet, the pilot signaled the jumpmaster that it was safe to begin the voluntary exit. Upon receiving the verbal commands and hand signals, Nancy, the lead jumper, dove out of the plane.

She enjoyed the contrasting adrenaline rush of a mid-air free fall with the peace and silence that followed when the parachute deployed. "Holy crap, I love this sport!" she thought. After nearly 60 seconds of free fall, approaching the earth with a speed of nearly 120 miles per hour, with her body parallel to the ground, Nancy arched her back, reached down, and pulled the ripcord to release the main chute. The main canopy deployed as expected. A second or two later, Nancy felt something bump her backside and the heels of her feet. She turned her head to look at her back and saw her reserve chute had also deployed. It was at a 90-degree angle to her body. Although she had once seen someone land with two fully expanded parachutes, this was not a good situation.

She focused on maintaining control of one parachute and maneuvering it to a safe landing. She left the second one alone. Descending rapidly, Nancy remembered time slowing. A split second later, the wind filled one of the parachutes, wrapping it around her neck and flying downward to her left side. The second one pulled in the opposite direction, nearly choking her. Her body and both parachutes were perpendicular to the fast-rising earth just 1,500 feet below.

For the first 500 feet, Nancy yelled for help as if Superman was somewhere nearby and ready to fly in and catch her. The next 500 feet, she envisioned herself as MacGyver using an imaginary knife to cut one parachute away. She feared that if she cut away the reserve, it would interfere and become entangled with the main chute leaving her with less than what she had. With the ground approaching and the thought of death probable, she prayed. She remembered a feeling of peace and calm traveling through her the remaining 500 feet as there was nothing she could do physically to untangle herself. She thought that she had led a good life, loved her family and friends, and had no serious regrets. She looked toward the clear blue heavens and called out to John, the closest person she had to guardian angel, and said, "Get me out of this, or I will see you in a minute!"

Nancy hit hard and lay motionless with no feeling below her neck. "I landed in the middle of a bunch of trees. When I saw the sun filtering through the leaves of the trees, I knew I was not dead. I had that going for me which was nice," Nancy recalled. Almost immediately, rescuers ran toward her. They worked carefully and quickly to secure her to a backboard and carried her to an awaiting ambulance. The jumpmaster in the aircraft had radioed the ground control to get an ambulance and medical team on site immediately, indicating they had just a few minutes before the jumper crashed. Amazingly, Nancy sustained no visible physical bruises to her body.

The ambulance transported Nancy to the civilian hospital near the drop zone in Alabama, where the staff took a series of x-rays and tests. Immediately put back into an ambulance and driven 40 minutes, she arrived at Martin Army Hospital located at Fort Benning, Georgia, on the other side of the drop zone.

At Martin Army, a second series of x-rays revealed burst fractures of Nancy's T-12 and L-1 vertebrae. That evening, Nancy's company commander came into the room and learning that Nancy's parents had not yet been notified of the accident and Nancy's injuries, he contacted them. Again, the medical evaluation team stabilized her and loaded her into an Army Black Hawk helicopter and flew to Augusta Veterans Administration Medical Center, a regional facility specializing in back and spine injuries. She arrived close to midnight, nearly 11 hours after her crash landing.

Lying on a gurney in the third hospital's emergency hallway, the attending physician asked Nancy if she had "voided." Under the influence of various pain medications, Nancy replied, "No, and that's weird because I am famous for always having to go to the bathroom." Immediately the doctor's expression changed. He suspected she sustained a severe spinal cord injury. More x-rays and another battery of tests confirmed this diagnosis.

Nine hours of surgery followed. When Nancy awoke from the anesthesia, two of her friends stood at the foot of her hospital bed. One friend commanded the 988th Military Police Company at Fort Benning. The other was her boyfriend, a member of the Golden Knights, the Army's elite parachute team. He arrived from Fort Bragg, North Carolina, his home post. Not able to speak because of the tube down her throat connected to a respirator, Nancy suspected one of the members of the parachuting school had called her boyfriend to notify him of Nancy's accident, as he knew many of those at the school.

After driving through the night from Long Island, Nancy's parents arrived in Augusta, Georgia. At her hospital bedside, Nancy's parents met her boyfriend. It was a somewhat tense and awkward first meeting, as he had introduced Nancy to skydiving and felt responsible for her accident. In all her previous jumps, they had been together.

Nancy spent the next week lying on her back in the intensive care unit, slowly coming to learn more about the extent of her spinal cord injury, although never once doubting she would eventually heal. She had fractured several of her vertebrae, specifically T-12 and L-1, affecting both skeletal and neurological movements. During the lengthy surgery, the doctors removed one of Nancy's floater ribs, and her T-11, T-12, L-1, and L-2 vertebrae. They crushed the removed bones and put them into a mesh titanium cage that the surgeons molded around her spinal cord and fused to the spinal column. Next, they inserted three screws and a plate to provide stability, strength, and protection to her damaged spinal cord.

The second week post-surgery, Nancy was moved to the acute ward and fitted for a body brace, a turtle shell-like support extending upwards from her hips to her shoulders. Then the true challenges began for Nancy—learning how to perform basic tasks of daily life. It took her the following weekend just to be able to sit up on her own in the brace without losing consciousness.

Initially, Nancy's doctors explained to her parents that they expected paralysis from the accident to prevent her from walking freely again. If she did regain the ability to walk, it would be possible only with the assistance of crutches or a walker. This became their goal–to get Nancy to walk assisted. Fortunately, no one shared this prognosis with Nancy, who always thought she would eventually walk and run normally.

Carol and Dan Hogan remained with their daughter at the Augusta VA Medical Center for two weeks as she began rehabilitation therapy in the spinal cord unit. They provided the encouragement, love, and support to help Nancy on her long road to recovery and healing. Told that she would be in the body brace for at least three months—six weeks too long for Nancy—she was determined to walk again sooner. She had plans. The maid of honor in her sister Kathleen's upcoming wedding, Nancy remained determined to walk down the aisle in front of her sister. The wedding was in six weeks.

Nancy found rehabilitation physically demanding and exhausting. She had to relearn the most basic activities of every day life: how to sit, stand, walk, bathe, dress, and relieve herself all in a turtle shell that significantly restricted her mobility. Following the weekend of learning how to sit up and lie down on her own, the therapists assisted her in her first step. The focus of that week's work was to begin connecting steps—first two, then three, and then four. Nancy remembered sucking wind, just as she did that first summer at West Point. "It was incredibly unsettling having to hold onto two therapists as I tried to literally step and slide. It was as if I had vertigo, as my sense of balance and stability was gone. I could not feel my feet underneath me," she said. She remembered the importance of mindset and belief in herself that she would recover. At the end of her second week of rehabilitation, Nancy was only able to walk three feet before needing to sit down and catch her breath. Most frustrating, however, was the lost control of many of her bodily functions. She thought these functions were temporarily dormant due to spinal cord shock. "At 25 years old, wearing a diaper and having someone assist you is most humbling. The challenge with a brace was that I could not twist my torso to take care of myself," she said.

As an inpatient, rehabilitation therapy in the spinal cord unit continued with various therapists for seven to eight hours a day. Once able to walk slowly, Nancy had to relearn how to walk on various surfaces, such as tile, grass, carpet, and hardwood. Twice a week, she engaged in aqua therapy wearing flotation devices. Nancy's recreational therapist would toss very light balls to Nancy to make her move in different directions, trying to regain comfort with lateral flexibility and re-establish her balance, coordination, and stability. She performed exercises with light weights and on exercise balls. Nancy shared,

> Throughout my life, I had been athletic. Rehab is frustrating and humbling, because you know you used to do so many things unconsciously, and now everything was a challenge. But you really have two choices: be frustrated and depressed or to get motivated and get better. I think my whole experience that first summer at West Point really helped me through this period, as I once again needed to channel my frustration into motivation. But I never thought that I would not recover. I wanted to be independent.

Climbing stairs was one of the most trying and painful activities to re-learn. Because Nancy's apartment near Fort Benning had 47 steps between the parking lot and her front door, she had to learn how to negotiate stairs. The first attempt involved just one flight.

> It probably took about 15 minutes for me to get up those 13 stairs. We then had to come down. Both directions were difficult as I realized so many difficult muscles were in use or in my case not functioning. I felt so weak. But the next week, I was determined to add another flight and continue that progress throughout my time in the hospital until I could climb up all eight flights. As we were fond of saying as cadets, each task was an opportunity to excel.

Nancy continued to work with dogged determination to prove to her doctors that she would be self-sufficient when she traveled to her sister's wedding.

> Originally, the doctors told me that I couldn't go to the wedding because most of the activities of daily living cannot be accomplished while wearing the turtle shell. I worked with the therapists and nurses on creative ways to do these tasks. I wanted to be independent and get back to my life. I thought things were temporary and that I would be 100%, and good as new in a few months. Although frustrated, when reality hit, I tried hard to be as 'whole,' for lack of a better term, as possible.

Although it is difficult to prioritize the common activities of daily living, controlling one's bowel movements is one of the most critical and the most humbling that many able-bodied people take for granted. Eager to regain her previous level of independence and get out of a diaper, Nancy needed to learn how to manage her bodily functions. As her injuries sustained were below the T-12 vertebrae, the paralysis that occurred resulted in a loss of sensation in the perineal area. Nancy had to learn how to use and employ a urinary catheter as well as develop a schedule for relieving herself. Various health care professionals in her rehabilitation helped educate her on sterile techniques, anatomy, catheter insertion, and proper catheter care. Nancy approached this learning with mission-like focus. "I just knew that I did not want to be dependent on others and I wanted to get to my sister's wedding."

A week before Kathleen's wedding, the doctors approved Nancy's travel to Massachusetts. Once at her destination, Nancy wheeled herself into an airport bathroom and entered the handicap stall. She proceeded to put on gloves and begin the catheterization process. Unknown to her, the door had opened and a woman stood there staring at her while she prepared to perform a sterile catheterization. To a registered nurse, what Nancy was doing would be obvious. This woman was not in the medical profession based on the horrified look on her face when she finally closed the door for Nancy. Nancy recalled, "It was by far the most traumatic and humbling part of the trip. I saw my folks for the first time in several weeks shortly after that and I started to cry hysterically for the first time in public. Reality of my injuries was starting to settle in."

Flanked by her two brothers and holding them for support, Nancy preceded Kathleen down the aisle on her sister's wedding day.

> I convinced myself that I would walk. You have to do it. Like running, I knew I had to, so I embraced it and gave it my all. I chose an option to focus on the good and the fact that I was alive. I always told myself that it could be worse. Focusing on how bad it was would only drain my energy.

Nancy's rehabilitation continued for the remainder of that summer.

Although Nancy is now able to walk, not all of the muscles in her legs function properly. Without the use of her calf muscles, she is unable to push off with a forward step. She is not able to run.

Permanently bent at the middle joint, the injuries left her with "hammer toes." The nerve damage she sustained led to a condition known as "drop foot." This is a simple name for a complex problem, which in Nancy's case was caused by damage suffered to the neural pathways that supply the dorsiflexors. Essentially, when Nancy walks, her foot slaps down onto the ground. To compensate, she has to raise her thigh as if walking up stairs. She wears ankle foot orthotics, although they do not fit in all her shoes. She cannot walk on her toes, perform calf raises, or walk with a normal heel-toe pattern. She laughed, "I can trip myself at anytime and often do." The nerve damage limited her sense of feeling in parts of her lower body. She cannot sit or stand for long periods due to pain and in fact states her chronic pain "is like breathing—it's always there but after a while you get used to it." Released from the hospital after three months as an inpatient, Nancy returned to Fort Benning reassigned to the garrison military police company to allow her to focus on continuing her daily physical therapy.

Beginning in August 1998, and for the next six months, Nancy went through a series of medical tests to assess her functional abilities and her capacity to return to military duty. Numerous appointments with doctors and therapists contributed written summaries of Nancy's condition and capabilities to the review board. In March 1999, a Physical Evaluation Board Liaison Officer (PELBO) notified Nancy of a forthcoming appointment to provide her the findings and conclusion of the medical board. At this meeting, the PELBO gave her the medical review board's evaluation and asked her to accept their decision to medically retire with a series of signatures on various documents.

The disability rating conferred by the medical review board was significantly lower than Nancy knew to be correct for her condition. Having performed her physical rehabilitation in a Veteran's Administrative Medical Center, she met a service officer from Paralyzed Veterans of America (PVA), an advocacy organization for military veterans benefits and rights. Initially she rated at a 60 percent disability based on each individual doctor's analysis. The Army Medical Evaluation Board had rated her injuries under a degenerative disk disease, not a spinal cord injury, which had maximum medical benefits of 60 percent. Because she could walk, as explained to her, her condition seemed more like degenerative disk disease than a spinal cord injury with residuals. She believed the Army medical evaluation board failed to consider that each of the individual body functions that had been traumatized by the accident were independent of each other, and therefore should not be grouped together under one diagnostic code.

Nancy refused to sign the disability ratings determination and requested an appeal through a formal hearing with the Physical Evaluation Board (PEB) located in Fort Sam Houston, Texas, the home of Army medicine. Nancy recalled,

> I was advised, by the PEBLO and later by the JAG attorney assigned to represent me, I should accept the rating of the medical evaluation board as I risked total loss of any and all disability benefits if I went before the physical evaluation board and they found I deserved a lower rating. My argument was that the Board had rated me applying an incorrect code. I didn't have a degenerative disk disease; I had a spinal cord injury with residual neurological and muscular effects. The PEBLO told me she had been in this position for 14 years and had never seen the PEB change a rating code once it assigned one. I didn't care what I could lose, only what I could gain.

A hearing date was set for two weeks. Nancy quickly learned that soldiers medically retired for a disability have few alternatives in the adjudication of their cases. There are two options: take the disability rating assigned by the board or appeal the decision with a high probability of a lower rating. This piqued her interest in disability law.

During her rehabilitation at the Augusta Veterans Administration Medical Center, she got to know several medically-retired soldiers with a wide range of disabilities. Curiously, the Army had not updated its disability codes and ratings in more than a decade. She came to learn that the medical evaluation board's decision is entirely based on how the doctors evaluating the injury wrote the description and to what code they assigned the injury.

In the two weeks leading up to her appeal, Nancy researched the diagnostic codes and faxed multiple medical and occupational evaluations to San Antonio. They included several doctors' statements and the summary of a decision of another case in which the soldier had sustained a similar spinal cord injury. The Board had adjudicated this soldier's case under a different set of ratings.

Nancy's last hope was the doctor who originally evaluated her at Fort Benning. She asked him to write a detailed description of her condition as a "walking paraplegic" for submission to the Board. On March 22, 2001, the day prior to her appellate hearing, Nancy flew to San Antonio and met with her JAG attorney to prepare for the next day's in-person hearing. The attorney told her that the PEB reconvened and changed her disability rating code. The paperwork processed for full disability and medical retirement from the Army. This negated the need for the hearing the next day. Nancy was medically retired from the Army at a 100% disability. She concluded,

> Unfortunately, many soldiers do not know what to expect or understand the system, and they take the first decision handed to them. It is often less than what they deserve. This was one of the main reasons I decided to purse a law career with a focus to practice disability law specializing in veteran's benefits. If I could no longer serve on active duty, I wanted to do something that served those in the military.

In the fall of 2001, Nancy entered Roger Williams University School of Law in Rhode Island. It was a typical law school experience, with lots of late nights reading case after case. The summer before her third and final year of law school in July 2003, she began to have some abnormal feelings in her stomach. Because of the internal injuries she sustained in the skydiving accident, she was not sure if the pain was an indication that she was regaining some of her internal functions that had been paralyzed or if something was wrong. A year earlier, Nancy had a three-millimeter kidney stone passing through her ureter for eleven days with very little pain. Her body alerted her that something was wrong by breaking out in cold sweats, moments of total fatigue, but little pain. Therefore, when she felt pain in that area, she became alarmed. The pain intensified throughout the next two days and Nancy took herself to an emergency room at the Providence Veteran's Administration Medical Center. X-rays revealed she had a blockage in her large intestine. Somewhat relieved, she returned to her student apartment. After "cleansing" her system, she returned to the emergency room as instructed for an ultra sound and check of her appendix. This test revealed that her right kidney was larger than her left one. When told this, she said, "Well, it shouldn't be!" This second visit to the emergency room led to a subsequent CAT scan that exposed a tumor in her kidney.

Two months after celebrating the fifth year anniversary of what Nancy called her "Alive Day," the day she did not die skydiving, she was diagnosed with cancer in her right kidney. "It was a shocking discovery, to say the least, but I was more concerned about the affect this diagnosis would have on my parents," remembered Nancy. She decided to wait a few hours before breaking the news to her parents. She called Chris, her brother, first. He worked for a pharmaceutical company and had many medical contacts in New York City. Chris immediately took the lead in helping her secure an appointment for a second evaluation at Memorial Sloane Kettering Cancer Center in New York. "When I finally decided to call, it took me a few minutes to dial their number. My mom answered and I asked her to get my dad on the phone. I told them that I had an abnormal mass in my kidney and that I was not, nor should they get too excited, concerned, or worried until I got a second opinion. I remember they were quite calm, which really helped me."

Within a week of the confirmation of the presence of cancer in her kidney, Nancy underwent surgery to remove the tumor at Sloane Kettering. With most kidney surgeries of this type, patients are typically released from the hospital in three or four days. Nancy, however, remained in the hospital for 11 days. She was not able to have a bowel movement, which was of great concern to her medical team. The doctors at Sloane were not used to dealing with spinal cord injured patients and the normal means to the end here weren't working. Nancy finally called her spinal cord doctor to help them understand the internal paralysis and explain what care was necessary.

Nancy took a leave of absence from the first semester of her final year of law school to recover. For the first week at home, Nancy had to bring in a home health aide nurse to assist her in her personal care. "This was like losing a level of my independence I worked hard to gain after the accident," said Nancy. She was not able to drive for a month.

Once more victorious against all odds, Nancy walked in her law school graduation exercises in May 2004, and finished her Juris Doctor in December. Two months later, in February 2005, Nancy passed the bar exam, on her first attempt, and was admitted into the New York State Bar that fall. Staying true to her commitment to help those who served in the military, Nancy applied for an open position with the Paralyzed Veterans Association (PVA). Hired immediately as a service officer, Nancy worked in PVA's Newark, New Jersey, and Manhattan, New York, offices.

Within the year, promoted to an Associate Director in the Field Services Program, Nancy's responsibilities increased to include PVA services offices across the nation and in Puerto Rico. The promotion involved a move to PVA's headquarters in Washington, D.C. A year later, Nancy, again promoted, became the Associate Executive Director for the Veterans Benefit Department (VBD),

PVA's largest department, with 175 appellate, field, medical, and vocational rehabilitation staff dedicated to serving paralyzed veterans by providing free, comprehensive benefits and medical counseling, assistance, and representation. VBD works through a national network of National Service Offices to answer questions and offer support from on-site quality care reviews of health care facilities to guidance through the VA claims process to legal representation for appealing denied claims. Nancy's department has the ability to directly affect medical care as well as benefits provided to veterans. In this role, as part of the senior management team she is typically the lead person for developing PVA's positions on various issues involving benefits.

Nancy met with former senator Bob Dole, the co-chair of the President's Care Commission for America's Returning Wounded Warriors, and discussed the changes needed in the current DOD and VA systems. She and others in her department regularly conduct site visits to Veterans Administration Medical Centers to ensure that employees are providing the quality of care needed by patients. What she finds most challenging is the media focus, particularly regarding facilities and the condition of Walter Reed Building 18. She said

> While the systems are not perfect, Walter Reed Building 18 is not part of the VA system. Politicians are eager to fix system problems with 'band-aid' legislation. The systems can be improved and need to be improved. But it cannot happen over night. The key for fixing the problems lies in the funding for the VA. The fixes should benefit all veterans, not just the ones returning from Iraq and Afghanistan. We are constantly thinking and evaluating how changes and improvements in the VA system will affect those we serve. The rewarding and satisfying part comes from helping vets. We successfully helped a Korean War Veteran receive 55 years worth of benefits

retroactively. This veteran had a case that had never been pursued. He was a vet living in a FEMA trailer after Hurricane Katrina.

Nancy's next challenge is learning how to run again. Nancy said, "If amputees are able to run with prosthetic devices, I want to figure out a way that I too can run again."

The Hogan family following Nancy's graduation and officer commissioning on June 3, 1995. *Left to right*: Dan Sr., Carol, Kathleen, Dan Jr., USMA '84, Chris, USMA '93, and Nancy, USMA '95. (*Photo courtesy of Nancy Hogan*)

Nancy Hogan skydiving pre-accident. Hanging off the wing of a Cessna 182 airplane, she is waiting for the jump master to give her the "green light" to begin the jump. (*Photo courtesy of Nancy Hogan*)

In July 2008, ten years after her skydiving accident, Nancy Hogan returned to the air. Here she is in a tandem free-fall with a member of the Army Golden Knights parachute team. (*Photo courtesy of Nancy Hogan*)

Following the July 2008 jump, Nancy and two members of the Army Golden Knights parachute team. (*Photo courtesy of Nancy Hogan*)

Cadet Jackie Stennett, USMA 1990.
(*Academy Photo*)

SOWING THE SEEDS OF EDUCATION & SERVICE
| JACQUELINE E. STENNETT, CLASS OF 1990

"It is one of the most beautiful compensations of life that no man can sincerely try to help another without helping himself."

— Ralph Waldo Emerson

Jacqueline E. Stennett has a fundamental belief about the importance of service, particularly as it relates to the education of children. "Every child, not just those born into privilege or wealth, should have a role in defining the course of their nation and their world. Their words should be heard, and through advocates' involvement, we can help to amplify their voices."

Jackie Stennett, the youngest of three siblings born in Jamaica, is an advocate whose actions speak volumes. When Jackie was eleven months old, Marjorie Stennett, her mother, left her philandering husband and her beloved Caribbean island to create a new life for her three children. Jackie's mother believed that, through education, all things were possible. She came to the United States with few possessions, a technical school degree in business and big dreams for her children.

As a child, Marjorie had grown up in what she recalls as "humble" conditions, losing her home and possessions in 1951 as a result of Hurricane Charlie's devastation to the island of Jamaica. Though Marjorie's external environment was not abundant with what others would consider necessities, she relishes the memories of her childhood. She recalled, "We were happy children who were industrious in taking advantage of the natural beauty that surrounded us on the island. We studied hard, played hard with our friends, and took advantage of every opportunity that life presented."

Through the care and concern of her teachers and community, Marjorie excelled in school and envisioned a better life for herself. When it came time for her to leave high school, Marjorie earned a competitive scholarship to attend a prestigious technical school where she learned skills in business and accounting. Through the kindness of her uncle, she was able to afford the books and uniforms required to attend, and through education, she was able to build a better life for herself. She passed this reverence for education on to her children. Jackie recounted the quotation her mother would recite throughout her youth, "Silver and gold may vanish away, but a good education will never decay." To her children, education was the key to success and leveler of the playing field between "the haves" and "the have-nots".

Jackie recalled her mother describing her memories of life in the Caribbean. Her mother reminisced:

> In Jamaica, our national motto is 'Out of Many, One People.' Jamaica is a beautiful mixture of all different races and nationalities: white, black, Chinese, East Indian, and Syrian, multi-racial, you name it. When you asked someone what they were, they didn't say 'white' or 'black,' they said, 'I am a Jamaican.' The color of your skin wasn't important. Status was most important. And everyone knew that education was the key to attaining that status. This encouraged many people, especially the poor, to seek and view education as a valuable asset. Many of our doctors, lawyers, teachers, and public officials were black. Many of the people that I admired looked just like me. Because of this, I didn't personally feel the effects of racism until I came to the United States.

Marjorie relished the opportunities and vibrancy afforded by a big city and decided to start a new life for her family in New York City. Returning from work one evening to find strangers dealing drugs in the stairwell of her Bronx apartment building, she relocated her family to South Florida. For Marjorie, the presence of a large Caribbean population, lower cost of living, and availability of single-family homes with yards were more conducive to raising a family and a safer environment. Marjorie easily found work with a top corporation, thanks to her technical school training and strong work ethic. As a black divorced woman, finding a home to accommodate her three children, however, would prove more difficult.

Though Marjorie had saved enough to make a sizeable down payment on a home, she had difficulty obtaining a larger mortgage from the banks because of her marital status and race. Classified as a "high risk," many realtors showed her homes in areas that were racially segregated or disheveled, but Marjorie persisted until she found a beautiful, yet modest home in a safe and integrated family community.

Because of her frugal upbringing in Jamaica, Marjorie was able to "stretch a dime into a dollar." She provided for her children in seemingly effortless fashion and grew several of her own fruits and vegetables in an abundant backyard garden. Her children were unaware of the sacrifices their mother made to create a better life for them. While Jackie and her siblings did not grow up with a wealth of unnecessary material goods, their home was filled with much more. Jackie remembered:

> We never, for a moment, considered ourselves less privileged. Quite to the contrary, we felt as if we were advantaged because we always had what we needed and our home was filled with love, support, and encouragement. Rather than shower her children with material goods, my mother showered us instead with her time. She found time to participate in the PTA, as a band parent, a scout chaperone and in a myriad of other activities throughout the course of our lives. Because of my mother's diligent savings habits, we were able to travel together as a family each year, sometimes internationally. My mother was frugal, but we always had plenty. When we were adults, my mother often joked that in our early years she would make one chicken last for a week. We felt privileged to

be a part of "the greatest country" in the world. Every day she instilled in us that we lived in the land of opportunity and all things were possible if we applied ourselves to the best of our abilities, made no excuses, studied hard, and pursued an education.

Jackie's mother made it a point to teach her children the consequences of choices early in their lives. One year she worked part-time for the census bureau going door-to-door to collect population information, often from families in low-income housing projects. Marjorie decided that each child would accompany her for one day during her census taking. On her day, Jackie remembered arriving at an apartment project occupied by a father and his adult daughter. She described:

> As my mother began to ask questions for the census, the daughter who was put off by my mother's Jamaican accent, became very upset. She accused my mother of stealing jobs from 'the Americans' and began to berate her loudly. The woman's father quickly intervened and scolded his daughter, stating that she was ignorant and was so because she made many bad choices instead of pursuing her education and elevating her life. My mother couldn't have planned it any better. Her beliefs about education were further cemented in my mind.

Marjorie lived her own creed that "knowledge is power." She set the example by finding time to attend night classes weekly to pursue her Associates degree. Marjorie expected all her children to excel in school and use each educational opportunity presented. A firm believer in and an advocate of public school education, Marjorie sought out the best available public schools in Broward County, specifically looking for schools with college preparatory curricula in math and science. She believed in the opportunity public education provided to all members of the community and the diversity of its students and faculty. Ely High School, now known as Blanche-Ely, a magnet school, fit her criteria. Located in an inner-city neighborhood, Ely had a stellar reputation for its focus in pre-engineering, math, and science. The school attracted a myriad of students across the normal geographical boundaries defined by the local school board. Children from all socio-economic backgrounds attended the school. Some, like Jackie, bused from miles away to attend the magnet program. Others merely walked to school. Ely was a wonderful amalgamation of cultures: the affluent, the poor, the middle-class, the under-class, gay, straight, Haitians, Cubans, South Americans, Asians, East Indians, West Indians, Africans, African-Americans, Caucasians, Christians, Jews, Muslims, Buddhists, Agnostics and Atheists were all drawn to the school because of the outstanding quality of its college preparatory curriculum. Jackie recalled:

> My lessons learned at Ely were an extension of the values taught in my home. I was able to continue and expand my exposure and involvement with an ethnically and culturally diverse student body. I was fortunate to have teachers who were willing to nurture students in and outside of the classroom. The demanding and focused curriculum prepared me for the challenges of both college and post-graduate education. These collective experiences helped to deepen the roots of the seed of life-long learning planted by my mother.

With a solid foundation in math and science, Jackie earned high PSAT scores, and various colleges began to solicit her interest. Jackie set her sights on attending the best undergraduate college that could prepare her to become an architect, a dream born from a mandatory drafting course in the pre-engineering curriculum at Ely.

During a routine search through her children's garbage bins to ensure "all was right" in their worlds, Marjorie found an unopened envelope bearing the crest and return address of the United States Military Academy, and recommended that Jackie open the envelope before throwing away an opportunity. Ely had several graduates who had attended West Point, so Jackie was familiar with the program, but the Military Academy was not in her plans. The idea of eating her meals with precise military movements and total strangers yelling at her was not appealing. Marjorie encouraged Jackie's brother to explain the opportunity in greater detail. Jackie remembered:

> My brother, then in college, called me one day under the guise of catching-up. When the topic of college selection arose, he explained that West Point was an opportunity worth considering. He spoke to me about the lineage of leaders that West Point produced and the responsibilities I would be entrusted with as a leader of men and women once commissioned as an officer. Much to the delight of my family, I began to conduct more research about West Point. What I began to discover, I liked and I applied for early admission into West Point. Serendipitously, a Junior Reserve Officer Training Corps (JROTC) program was being created at Ely. The school's leadership circulated my name as a possible candidate to lead the program.

As a senior, Jackie became the first cadet battalion commander for Ely's JROTC program. Jackie had assumed leadership roles in various student activities throughout her years at Ely, but JROTC was unfamiliar territory. At times, Jackie was unsure of her own ability to rise to the challenge, but the master sergeant and lieutenant colonel in charge of the new program had confidence in her. Like all good leaders, they enhanced her strengths while coaching Jackie through her areas of weakness. It was through the tutelage of Master Sergeant Granville Scott and Lieutenant Colonel Sellers that Jackie first understood what she described as the "special privilege of being led by individuals with formal military leadership training." Jackie recalled,

> I was confident I would excel in my role as battalion commander, as I had with most leadership roles before. I was firmly corrected when needed, and warmly supported when necessary. At 16, they instilled in me the professionalism and leadership traits that had to be projected in front of a group of individuals who expected the presence of a confident leader.

Jackie earned a nomination to attend West Point. She credits the support of her family and community, the rigors of her high school curriculum, and her leadership experience in JROTC as key factors. This was yet another step toward the fulfillment of Marjorie's dream of an exemplary education for her daughter.

Excited, anxious, and nervous, Jackie and her family arrived at West Point on July 1, 1986, Jackie recalled:

> Told to say our goodbyes, parents were directed to move to the left and new cadets to the right. I was petrified, but I kept remembering my Master Sergeant's advice 'not to take it too seriously'. So I didn't...and on the five-minute bus ride from Michie stadium to the cadet barracks, I earned the label of 'attitude problem' because I kept laughing at the senior cadets while they glared and yelled at me. This label would stay with me throughout my entire plebe year. I thought those cadets were the strangest people I had ever met and, though I couldn't tell them so, my body language said it all. I became a challenge and a project for certain cadets who needed to make my life very difficult while I was there. I had to quickly release the notion that we all were viewed equally. We were not. I

had to overcome not just the academic and physical challenges, but the various social undercurrents that were prevalent throughout my years at West Point.

Although West Point attracts and recruits candidates nationally, and seeks a student body representative of the Nation, not all those who matriculate have been exposed to people of differing ethnicities, nationalities, religious traditions, and ideologies. For many cadets, those first months at West Point challenge their stereotypes and the accompanying notions about interacting with someone who is different. In 1986, the entering class of 1990 had 1,307 new cadets; of those nine were African-American women. Four years later in 1990, 931 cadets graduated. Among them were six African-American women who received their commissions as officers.[111] Retrospectively Jackie wrote,

> In 1986, at age 17, when I entered the Academy, I had not personally experienced the prejudices and preconceived notions about African-Americans and women emplaced by society. It had been ten years since women were first admitted into West Point. Ten years seemed like an eternity to me, as it was more than half my life. I expected that ten years would be enough time for West Point to have worked out the disparities between men and women, and their views of each other. However, I learned that ten years is a short span of time when compared to the history of an institution that had been in existence for 192 years; and even less significant when compared to the legacy of barriers, which existed between the sexes and races throughout history.

---

[111] United States Military Academy, Office of Admissions.

During the final training exercise of cadet basic training, new cadets spend a week in the field with few facilities in which to practice extensive personal hygiene. This environment is especially challenging for the hair care of African-American women with relaxed or chemically treated hair. Once subjected to moisture, the application of heat is essential to restore smoothness and to seal the cuticles of the hair. Left unsealed, it becomes frizzy. Jackie, like her eight other African-American classmates, had less than attractive and stylish hairstyles after extended time in the field. Some believed that this detracted from their military bearing and presence. Jackie shared:

> One upperclassman crudely asked why my hair looked the way it did and gave me the name 'Buckwheat' because he thought I bore a resemblance to the character parodied by Eddie Murphy on *Saturday Night Live*. Hair challenges persisted during the academic year even when we did have access to the hair salon and all manners of styling implements. I chose to curl my hair every night in rollers to maintain the health of my hair. The nightly entertainment for some of the upperclassmen would be to come by my room just to look at my hair in rollers. One even took a picture of me with rollers in my hair, standing at attention, braced against the wall of the hallway in my cadet robe. Though at times I was their source of comic relief, it was just as comical to me when I realized how misinformed and culturally sheltered many of these upperclassmen were. I knew most meant no harm, but I always laughed to myself at the thought of how the enlisted soldiers they would soon encounter would quickly re-shape their culturally insensitive behaviors. I knew many of these upperclassmen would be in for a rude awakening. The active duty military is a wonderfully diverse environment, filled with

individuals of all races, socio-economic backgrounds, and cultures. In the military, when you respect and take care of your soldiers, your soldiers take care of you. But when you don't, your soldiers will definitely take care of you...in assisting you in your failure as an officer.

Jackie's greatest challenge during her plebe year was running. Combined with her apparent "attitude problem," Jackie became an easy target for a few upperclassmen in her company. During the first half of her plebe year, she spent numerous weekends walking punishment tours, while her classmates got to enjoy the little free time allowed for first year cadets. Fortunately, for Jackie, she was well liked, supported, and respected by her classmates. With each challenge Jackie faced, she always returned to the constancy of the support of her family and friends. Their love and support served as Jackie's internal compass. Jackie recalled:

On the days where others wanted me to feel less than worthy, I reflected on my past, on what my family overcame to make a life in this country. I reminded myself that I was worthy to compete, worthy to stay, and worthy to claim my spot on the soil of West Point. It mattered not to me what a handful of ill-informed upperclassmen thought about me, but rather what my family and community at home had invested in helping me to become a cadet. Failure was not an option.

Many times during Beast Barracks, I had four or five upperclassmen surrounding me as I stood at attention in formation. This certainly wasn't unusual for new cadets, but I seemed to receive an inordinate amount of 'attention.' With their faces a few inches from mine, they yelled a series of questions in rapid succession that they expected a response to. Their intent might have been to have a little fun or perhaps to break me down or perhaps to simply remind me that I was a 'spaz' in their eyes. From my standpoint, the only thing they were successful at accomplishing was pissing me off...and it showed in my eyes. What I couldn't say, I conveyed with my eyes.

My bravado was apparent. To some it was interpreted as an unearned arrogance and attitude. To most, it was defined as confidence. In my refusal to break in front of these upperclassmen, I garnered respect from some of those around me. I simply wanted to do the best I could, and when my best was not good enough, I kept trying.

Jackie applied the same deliberateness and consistency in her choices for an academic major and an officer career field. China used to be called a sleeping giant. Now, as the world's fastest growing major economy, it is awake. Nearly 20% of the world's population speaks Chinese. The rise of China's economic, political, and cultural power, as well as Mandarin being the most widely spoken first language in the world, led Jackie to select it as her academic major. She believed understanding of another culture, particularly one of the most ancient in the world, and its language, would benefit her both in and out of the military. The same applied to her selection of the Quartermaster Corps, a branch she selected based on the notion that logistics management would be useful in any career endeavor.

Following her branch-specific officer courses, Jackie reported as a field service supply platoon leader in Wiesbaden, Germany. The platoon's mission was to provide water purification, laundry, bath, and graves registration support for V Corps units. This was no easy task given the platoon's infamous nickname within the company as "the field circus" platoon. The platoon suffered from poor morale, low physical training scores, and the perception of favoritism and inequity on the part of platoon's former leadership. Jackie began by instituting a junior leader development program for the squad leaders and section chiefs. She changed the platoon's physical fitness training, using the skills gained when she received her Master Fitness Trainer certification from West Point. She set high standards for her platoon's performance and held them accountable for their results. For one of the most significant training exercises for U.S. Army units based in Germany, REFORGER, Jackie's platoon provided all water and field service support to more than 45,000 soldiers dispersed throughout the country. Jackie took charge of her soldiers and their mission and transformed a splintered, demoralized platoon into a cohesive unit.

Jackie would continue to lead in the company, later becoming a supply platoon leader. Eventually, the group commander selected her to serve as battalion Adjutant and restructure the failing personnel system of the largest battalion in the Army.

In 1993, while still a first lieutenant, West Point selected Jackie as an Admissions Outreach Officer to recruit high school students to the Academy. Assigned the eight-state region of the southeastern United States, Jackie's mission was to increase minority enrollment. She created a marketing and advertising campaign to reach her target market, and briefed more than 10,000 students, parents, educators, and congressmen about the opportunities offered by West Point, and the procedures to gain admission. During this assignment Jackie began to discover that not all children had access to the outstanding education she was afforded. "Far too many of the schools I visited had neither the appropriate curriculum nor the faculty required to propel students into the next century." She explained:

> I found guidance counselors overwhelmed and some apathetic to the students they were supposed to be serving. Most sadly, I found bright, young minds that weren't fully engaged and challenged. My role quickly evolved into a personal campaign to educate and

inspire these students. Though I had not fully realized it yet, my role as an Admissions Officer was a key starting point of my journey to help underserved youth develop their ultimate potential.

While her focus was on high school students, she visited elementary school children. During one visit, a young boy, no more than ten years old, approached Jackie, who was wearing her Army green dress uniform with various awards and medals. He asked her where she was going. Jackie told the boy that she needed to return to West Point that day and was taking a plane to New York. Astonished, the little boy questioned, "You came here just for us?" It was in that moment that Jackie realized how even the smallest gestures meant so much to a child.

Her military career reinforced her confidence, at an early age, that the world was hers to conquer, and that when placed in any leadership role, she could have a positive impact in the lives of others. Jackie was at a critical decision point in her military career, having completed her active duty service obligation of five years after graduation. Largely influenced by the downsizing of the Army at the end of the Cold War, although Jackie felt she had experienced great assignments, concerned and strong commanders, and a professional trajectory that would be difficult to match in the civilian sector, she made the difficult decision to resign her commission and leave the military.

Jackie joined General Electrical (GE) Capital Corporation as a financial analyst in the well-regarded entry-level Financial Management Program (FMP) that combines work assignments with a formal financially focused business school curriculum. She chose GE because it was a highly respected company that understood the value military veterans brought to the business world. She needed to develop her business and financial acumen in areas such as profitability analysis, variance analysis, asset allocation, budget forecasting, and preparation. Jackie explained:

While I was intellectually challenged in my assignments and in the classroom, I felt no connection to the work and I missed the inherent sense of importance and fulfillment I experienced while in uniform. Though it was a time of continued professional growth, I didn't feel my talents were being best utilized in the position I had chosen for myself. It wouldn't be until years later that I finally understood that what was missing from my life was the service aspect I had grown accustomed to as a military officer.

Accepted into Harvard Business School after one year in the FMP program, Jackie entered the MBA program in 1996. Once again, the same feelings of unease began to surface and manifested themselves in a manner to which Jackie was not accustomed. She shared:

> It was a surreal experience. I was totally disconnected from the curriculum. I was frustrated and displeased with myself that I did not feel more appreciative of the opportunities that I was being blessed with. Yet I was not happy. I was not engaged. I felt lost.

Jackie took a leave of absence from the school after completing the first year of the program and returned to South Florida. At first, Jackie explored her more artistic side as an intern at a modeling agency in South Beach. There, after discovering an advertisement for an organization that worked with abused children, Jackie recalled the satisfaction and joy she experienced when working as an outreach officer and decided she wanted, once again, to reconnect with underserved youth. Jackie became a "teaching parent" for Kids in Distress (KID) a nationally accredited South Florida agency committed to the prevention of child abuse by providing care and treatment to abused and neglected children.[112] The combination of emergency shelter, group home, and foster care services along with programs geared toward academic success, behavioral therapy, and relationship building between children, adults, and peers resonated strongly with Jackie.

The unique component of this setting was the group home as it provided a safe and supportive environment for these children to address their needs outside of the classroom. For the next two years, Jackie worked with nine emotionally and behaviorally abused children ranging in age from 5 to 11. The children lived in group homes on one of the agency's complexes and attended the local public schools. As a teaching parent, Jackie was an educator, parent, advocate, and role model. She described:

> KID provided a wonderfully nurturing, healing environment for these children. Academically, I found that because of these children's label as 'special needs foster children,' at times, they were quickly grouped as special education students and dismissed as underachievers. As their advocate, I fought to ensure their academic needs were met both in the classroom and at home. These were bright children who deserved the opportunity to be challenged to the extent of their abilities. Sadly, they were not. For these children, it was imperative that education be their tool to break the cycle of poverty, drugs, alcohol, and abuse that had ravaged their families. They had endless capacities to assimilate in diverse environments, and their minds were open and eager to learn. I saw the brilliance in each of these children, and I believed there was no limit to their potential, given the proper support. It was at this time that I gained an interest in opening my

---

[112] www.kidsindistress.org.

own college-prep boarding school for underserved youth.

A calm and firm, yet loving demeanor, along with a strong belief in what these young boys were capable of achieving, helped Jackie persevere through some challenging times. Most of the children were prone to severe verbal and physical outbursts, likely due to previously experienced abuse and neglect. Jackie and her colleagues at KID worked slowly to undo the painful damage of their relatively short pasts by modeling appropriate, nurturing, and loving adult and parent-child behavior. She ensured they were well fed, socially conscious, culturally stimulated, physically engaged, and properly educated. Jackie and the team of teaching parents took them to museums, plays, and ballgames. She helped them learn to care for their surroundings both inside and outside of the home. She coordinated their sessions with therapists and social workers to ensure that they received the appropriate counseling and treatment services. Truly, Jackie cared for these children as if they were her own.

In her time with KID, three of the children were successfully placed in loving foster homes, and two began the process of returning to their own biological parents. Jackie said,

> The benefit to these children is that they are happier, healthier boys who are better equipped to enter into young adulthood to become productive citizens. The benefit to our society is that hopefully, the circle of chronic abuse, anger, and neglect has been eradicated from their own lives.

Now armed with a greater sense of purpose, Jackie returned to HBS and focused her academic coursework on business leadership in the social sector. She graduated in 2000 and accepted a management consulting position with Accenture in their federal government practice to gain a perspective of the role of government in education and social services.

Shortly after graduation, however, Jackie learned that she did not walk across the stage alone to receive her graduate diploma. She was pregnant, but there would be no fairy-tale ending. She would be raising her child alone. While her immediate family rallied to her side and continues to support her decision to raise her daughter alone, it became very clear to Jackie that there were those in her inner circle who did not approve of her as a single woman becoming pregnant. This was not the caliber of decision-making expected from a woman educated at two of the country's most respected institutions. Jackie said,

> I made the decision to have my child, knowing full well that this decision would shatter my image (and the illusion) of a woman who made all the right choices. I cannot intellectualize what would have, could have, or should have been. Becoming pregnant while unmarried was definitely not in my plan, but I will not torture myself over the decision I made to take full responsibility for the outcome. It has no benefit. My mother, with far fewer means than I, made raising a family on her own look effortless. She reared us with love, encouragement, and discipline. I was determined I could do the same in rearing my daughter on my own. I absolutely know now that raising a child is not effortless. It is an extremely consuming, yet worthwhile endeavor. Rather than dwell on the past or on others' disapproving criticisms, I choose to focus on raising my daughter to become a confident and productive citizen of this world.

Jackie gave birth to her daughter while working as a new manager. Accenture was wonderfully accommodating to her needs as a new mother and agreed to her move from Atlanta to Virginia to eliminate the travel required to meet with clients in Washington, D.C. They offered to place Jackie on a flexible four-day work schedule. Nevertheless, these gracious accommodations were still not enough to fully thrive in her dual role as consultant and mother. Although involved in what she called socially conscious consulting engagements, Jackie still felt unfulfilled in her daily work. She began to explore her earlier notion of creating a college-preparatory boarding school for underserved children.

During her research of various college-preparatory schools, Jackie discovered the School of Educational Evolution and Development (SEED) Public Charter School in Washington, D.C. Founded in 1998, SEED was a public boarding school preparing students from urban communities for success in college. Located in one of the District's most underserved and crime-ridden neighborhoods, Anacostia, the school enrolled more than 300 students from the inner city of the nation's capitol.

Jackie contacted the school and interviewed with the now former Head of School, Charlsie Biard and its founders, Eric Adler and Rajiv Vinnakota, both former management consultants turned social entrepreneurs. The three believed that the integration of an academic program and a boarding environment was essential for success. Without a boarding component, they would not be able to control what happened to students once they left school grounds. Many of the students had at least one parent who was incarcerated, absent, or deceased. Providing a safe, secure, and nurturing atmosphere 24 hours a day during the school week could only contribute to a child's growth and development.

SEED received many accolades as a unique charter school that provided consistent holistic education and life-skills training in a nurturing environment. Jackie was anxious to both learn and contribute to the success by bringing the SEED model to other locations or possibly opening her own college prep boarding school.

Jackie accepted a position as the Director of Boarding Programs in 2002 as SEED's inaugural class was beginning its junior year in high school, its members having entered five years earlier as seventh graders. Jackie became the fourth boarding director in the school's short history and knew that the turnover was indicative of systemic issues within the organization.

This innovative and controversial approach to urban education brought together a diverse set of people—business professionals, social entrepreneurs, academic faculty, boarding faculty, counselors, and therapists. While SEED's model had two equally important components, academics and boarding, several academic faculty and school leaders did not view them as equal. The boarding component had been neglected and under-funded. Jackie said:

> I had inherited a program where the budget had been cut by 40% from previous years' numbers. There was no money in the budget to provide part-time relief to my staff in the direct care of students. Salaries for the boarding faculty were significantly lower relative to their academic faculty counterparts and did not reflect a professional's compensation. Important services for the program were sorely lacking relative to the robust and developed programs of the academic component. When I first arrived on campus, there was a stark contrast between the brightly lit halls of the academic building and the then dark dorms where the students resided. Even my office was located on the first floor of a very noisy boys' dormitory versus in the administrative suite where all the other directors were housed.

The boarding program was the key differentiator in this public charter school and, as such, Jackie believed the program required a new pragmatic approach. She explained:

> I approached the design of the boarding program model as if my own child would be attending the

school. The boarding program had little credibility and had lost the trust and faith of key stakeholders. To restore credibility to the program, I needed to recoup the dollars that had been previously cut from my budget. During a two-year period, with the full support of Charlsie, Raj, Eric and the school's board of directors who understood the imperative for change, I managed to increase funding for student programs, faculty development and boarding infrastructure by 68%.

Goals and objectives, which were previously non-existent, were established for the boarding program. The boarding curriculum, Habits for Achieving Lifelong Success (HALLS), was integrated with the academic curriculum to offer SEED students a cohesive academic and life skills education. The educational caliber of the boarding faculty hired in the direct care of the students increased dramatically. Boarding faculty with B.S. degrees more than quadrupled, and we recruited some with advanced degrees.

As the learning environment extended outside the classroom, Jackie implemented the HALLS curriculum, which included components of study skills, time-management, communication and other life skills. She then took it one step further, implementing a student boarding program report card and a boarding faculty evaluation system tied to the success of the students. Each student evaluation measured the student against standards in the HALLS curriculum. In turn, the employee evaluation system measured boarding faculty members against their students' performance within the program. Top performers received the highest pay increases, while the lowest performers received none.

The metrics linked how well the students did in the classroom with the life and social skills curriculum they received in the dormitories. Initially met with resistance and skepticism, the new performance standards immediately caused consternation for many with backgrounds in education. Some believed that Jackie was concerned only with the bottom-line and not the children. Many openly questioned the idea of evaluations and pay based on performance. They questioned Jackie's motives because she was a former military service member and business executive and not a traditional educator.

> The boarding faculty was a group of dedicated and idealistic individuals who truly cared about the success of the SEED students. They needed support, they needed guidance, and they desperately needed the resources required to do their jobs effectively. Consistent and clear communication with my staff helped to refocus their concerns and build excitement towards becoming a more mission-driven organization. Town hall meetings were arranged with the founders and Head of School so that boarding faculty could air their grievances and concerns. I was able to fund sizable salary increases and recruit more part-time staff to relieve full-time faculty when necessary. As collaboration between the boarding faculty and academic faculty increased, morale of the boarding staff improved. A staff recognition program was created where boarding faculty members were awarded and honored for outstanding performance. Though some staff members were still disgruntled, as a result of these initiatives, staff morale began to increase and boarding staff turnover was cut in half within a two-year period.

> With the help of the school's senior leadership and my boarding program management team, we increased the resources, budget, visibility, image, and overall

professionalism of the Boarding Program. Ultimately, the improvements made to the Boarding Program dramatically improved the services to our primary client, the students we served.

SEED graduated its first class in 2004. All of the members of this class received offers of admission to various colleges and universities including Princeton and other premier universities. This was quite a feat, considering that most students entered the SEED school six years prior with performance scores two or three grade levels below the norm.

While professionally engaged in her role as Director of Boarding Programs, Jackie had grown weary in her attempt to be both a great director and a great mother. Jackie, along with her 6 administrators, 27 faculty members and 305 students, resided on the campus of the school grounds. Though the founders and the other school administrators embraced Jackie, her daughter and their needs as a family, at times it was very difficult to draw a clear boundary between where professional work ended, and a personal life began. She realized that she could not do everything on her own and was not at a point in her life where she could devote nearly all of her energy and time to her professional endeavors. Her daughter, now three years old, needed her full attention.

Satisfied with improving the boarding program's professional image and having started the process of restoring confidence in the program to its various constituents—the founders, the Board of Directors, the outside community, parents, students and the school faculty—Jackie resigned and returned to Florida, where her mother still lived.

Jackie needed the support of trusted family in raising her daughter. On the occasions when Jackie had to be away from home, she was comforted in knowing that her daughter was in the care of her mother surrounded by a circle of support that freely shared wisdom and guidance from past generations. As her professional experience demonstrated, children need many positive influences in their lives to succeed socially, behaviorally, and academically. Her daughter deserved the same influences and opportunities. Most importantly, she needed a mother who was more present in her life.

Though it wasn't her plan initially, in Florida Jackie realized that she could better balance work and life as a single mother by working as an independent consultant. In this capacity, she had professional growth opportunities and stimulation, while still having ample time to raise her daughter. Jackie now works primarily with nonprofit organizations that serve youth and underserved populations. She advises organizations with socially responsible missions in designing strategies to improve individual and organizational performance.

Jackie continued her own professional development by pursuing a Certified Master Coach credential from the Behavioral Coaching Institute (BCI) in Sydney, Australia. Historically, this credential has been primarily associated with executive, business, and life coaches who typically serve clientele in the senior management levels of organizations. Jackie hopes to introduce the same type of coaching services to underserved youth to help implement behavioral changes at early stages in their academic and social development.

Jackie's ultimate vision is to collaborate with the esteemed organizations she has been blessed to be associated with in her past, to one day develop a world-class behavioral coaching and leadership model for urban youth in the public school system. Jackie said,

> West Point's most enduring impact for me has been as the catalyst of the birth of my service ethic. I have had the privilege to work in a broad array of industries in diverse and challenging roles. Of all the roles I have held, by far I have been most fulfilled while serving those in greatest need. It has become my mission to serve them, to uplift them and to equip them with the tools they will need to lead extraordinary lives of their choosing. Though I am no longer in uniform, I

continue to serve my country by serving those who will carry on this nation's legacy. It is my privilege to expand the reach of the leadership training from the Long Gray Line that I have been so honored to receive.

West Point Class of 1990 Graduation Banquet. Carolyn (Jackie's older sister) Jackie and Marjorie (Jackie's mother) Stennett. (*Photo courtesy of Jackie Stennett*)

Captain Jackie Stennett. (*U.S. Army Photo*)

Jackie Stennett receiving her diploma from Harvard Business School Dean Kim Clark. Unbeknownst to Jackie, she was carrying Alexandra. June 2000, Cambridge, MA. (*Photo courtesy of Jackie Stennett*)

Jackie Stennett and Alexandra, her daughter, in Big Sur, California. (*Photo courtesy of Jackie Stennett*)

Cadet Bridget Altenburg, USMA 1995. (*Academy Photo*)

A Bridge to Cross | Bridget Altenburg, Class of 1995

"You gain strength, courage, and confidence by every experience in which you really stop to look fear in the face."

— Eleanor Roosevelt

Growing up an Army brat and the second of five children, Bridget Altenburg assumed she would have to pay her own way through college, either by working while taking classes or by earning a scholarship. She never considered the military as the source for an education and the foundation for pursuing one's passions.

Drafted into the Army during the Vietnam War, John Altenburg, Bridget's father, served as an enlisted soldier. Upon his return from Southeast Asia, John pursued a law degree using his GI benefits to fund his education. Following his law school graduation, John re-entered the Army as a commissioned officer in the Judge Advocate General (JAG) Corps[113] and served a 28-year career as a military lawyer. John's various assignments afforded him and Diane, his wife, numerous opportunities to live abroad. Both placed strong emphasis on education, stressing cultural and linguistic development for their five children. As each of their children approached school age, the Altenburgs enrolled them in German schools known for their strong emphasis on homework and their classroom discipline.

With three or more hours of homework assigned nightly, the completion of the work became a family affair. While neither John nor Diane spoke German, both understood the importance of raising bilingual children. German came easily to Bridget, who enjoyed the ability to converse in two languages as a child. Her language aptitude provided an early introduction to leadership, as she often served as the translator for her parents. More important, it helped

---

[113] The JAG Corps is a wide-ranging practice that includes military law, criminal prosecution, international law, contract law, and legal assistance to servicemembers in the United States and abroad.

her develop an appreciation for others–especially those who were not like her.

Shortly before the start of her 4th grade year, Bridget's family moved back to the United States for John's next military assignment. Amazed at how few children in the United States spoke a foreign language, she was eager to converse in German. The transition back to an American school ignited a competitive fire in Bridget. Although ahead of her grade school peers in math and science, Bridget was behind them in reading ability. Within six months, she quickly achieved an age-appropriate reading level.

Following two stateside moves in four years, the Altenburgs returned to Germany as Bridget entered 8th grade. During her junior high school years, they lived in Heidelberg, headquarters for the United States Army in Europe. In 10th grade, the family moved to Ansbach, home of the 1st Armored Division. With the frequency of moving every two to three years, Bridget never really felt comfortable. A shy child and one who had difficulty making friends, Bridget turned to books and sports for companionship.

She resumed her language studies, continuing German and starting Russian. She stoked the competitive flame by playing soccer and keeping herself in shape through swimming, biking and running.

Patrick's, one of Bridget's older brothers, acceptance to West Point during her junior year in high school baffled her. His desire to attend the Military Academy did not make sense given his quiet and passive demeanor. She did not think of him as a tough soldier and one to follow in their father's footsteps. She figured it was his way of paying for college.

Bridget knew she would have to pay for college by earning some type of scholarship. She'd applied to a variety of schools. With the encouragement of her father, she applied to Annapolis and West Point. John's rationale was that acceptance at a service academy might help Bridget leverage other schools for scholarship money. Bridget figured an offer at either West Point or Annapolis would be a solid back-up choice if Amherst and Notre Dame, her two top choices, did not accept her.

The summer before her final year in high school, Bridget and her father traveled back to the United States for a college tour. Their trip began in Indiana with a visit to Notre Dame. From there, they headed southeast to Virginia and then north to Massachusetts. Their final stop was West Point to join Patrick on his report date of July 1, 1990. During this brief visit to West Point, Bridget began to understand Patrick was doing something more than going to a university for an education. He had joined a profession. This caught her attention.

Accepted at both Notre Dame (who awarded her a full academic scholarship) and Amherst, Bridget's senior high school yearbook confirmed that her plans were to head to South Bend, Indiana. On December 27, 1990, shortly after Christmas of Bridget's senior year in high school, John Altenburg, then a Lieutenant Colonel in the Army deployed to Saudi Arabia in support of Operation Desert Storm. The deployment of 15,000 soldiers transformed the small post in Ansbach, on which her family lived from a bustling community to a near ghost town. Immediately, the spouses and families of the deployed soldiers came together to support and care for one another in the absence of their soldiers. Bridget recalled her mother helping to care for many of the young wives and children on post who had never been separated from a spouse or parent. She offered advice, counsel, and even home-cooked meals. In the silence of the post, Bridget began to hear and understand the significance of her father's service. It was more than a job; it was a commitment to a greater good and more important than one's self. She wanted to be part of it, not as a family member but as a soldier herself.

With her father's deployment, Bridget began to think of the military less as a way to pay for school and more as a career. Bridget recalled this same sense of importance and purpose when she visited her brother at West Point the previous summer. She talked to her high school soccer coach who put together a letter and video for the West Point soccer coach hoping it might complement her previously submitted application packet. Knowing there was nothing else she could do, Bridget waited to hear if she would be accepted.

An early phone call from the West Point soccer coach to congratulate her and request her shoe size was how Bridget learned of her appointment to West Point. Thanks to some delays in overseas mail during Desert Storm, the actual appointment arrived by mail in April, barely three months before the start of cadet basic training. Attending and graduating from West Point was an alluring challenge that Bridget accepted.

She reported to West Point on July 1, 1991, one year after her brother, and began the rigorous transition from civilian to cadet. As a soccer player, she enjoyed the intensity of the daily physical workouts on the field, and the travel for away games provided a brief respite from the daily grind of cadet life. She struggled academically, however, and did not see much playing time. At the end of her second season, she left the soccer team. It was a difficult decision, but she knew she had to improve her grades if she wanted a choice in the selection of her military branch upon graduation. Bridget came to West Point first to be a soldier.

Bridget joined the triathlon club as a junior and began training in the three events required. In the interim between her junior and senior years at West Point, she spent her vacation time at the Lake Placid Olympic Training Center for a triathlon camp. Surprisingly, she found her triathlon experience invaluable in ways she had not imagined. Bridget explained,

> As a woman in the military, being in top physical shape tended to enhance the respect from male counterparts. If a woman is not in great shape and a strong runner, few men respect her opinion on any subject. She is perceived and often categorized as weak. There seemed to be a double standard, as a man's opinion always carried weight, regardless of his physical prowess.

At West Point, one's ability to run is considered a proxy for leadership ability. This physical manifestation of fitness and strength affected significantly one's standing as a cadet. Physical fitness, along with academic performance and military proficiency, were all inputs into one's cadet class rank and leadership position within the Corps of Cadets.

For more than 200 years, West Point has provided commissioned leaders of character for our Army and our Nation. Within the very rigorous West Point environment is a process known as the Cadet Leader Development System (CLDS). It is by means of this tough and demanding development process that West Point trains its cadets to lead American soldiers in war and peace. This learning is a shared responsibility among the Academy's staff and faculty, but the cadet is the primary driver in his or her own development.

Bridget realized the significance of this process. She learned to be a follower first, accepting individual responsibility and accountability for her actions and commitments, and only then becoming a leader of others. The first cadet leadership responsibility normally is for two or three plebes as team leader. As one matures and progresses in seniority and rank, leadership responsibility increases to include cadets of all ages and ranks. This developmental process helped Bridget to understand the need to learn new skills and refine those acquired previously as she assumed increasing amounts of responsibility. "The same thing happens when you become a commissioned officer. You apply what you learned at West Point to being a leader in the Army. You have to be open to constantly learning and refining," said Bridget.

By her third year at West Point, Bridget changed the way she interacted with the cadets in her unit. She replaced the typical 6:00 A.M. hallway counseling sessions with plebes, rattling off seemingly useless amounts of trivia, with a scheduled weekly one-hour session with each plebe in her squad. While requiring a significant investment of her time in an environment with little time to spare, these sessions provided focused opportunities to concentrate more deeply on topics and issues that directly affected the performance and development of the younger cadets entrusted to her. Bridget recalled,

> I learned not to micromanage my plebes. I like to believe these scheduled sessions helped them take more responsibility for their own knowledge and actions. They learned that others were counting on them. This is where I learned about the importance of delegating responsibility and setting clear expectations. By giving others increased responsibilities, it helps them to better understand what they can expect in the future.

Rote memorization and on-demand rapid recall of various facts, figures, and news items was a widely used tool among upper class cadets to help enhance a plebe's ability to perform under pressure. Bridget's own leadership epiphany was that if she set clear expectations, clarified potential outcomes, and trusted her subordinates to take care of basic tasks, she could help them focus on other aspects of their cadet development. The more interest she took in them, not just as plebes, but as leaders, the more they responded with an eagerness to learn.

During her final year at the Academy, Bridget focused on getting her teams to understand real Army knowledge, to learn their tactical responsibilities, and to prepare them for their next cadet leadership assignment. She explained, "I think my leadership helped the cadets in my company to use their experience at Camp Buckner to evaluate the missions of each branch of the Army and select a branch they understood and one in which they were excited to lead." Bridget helped her cadets understand the importance of self-evaluation and reflection in the selection of one's military occupational specialty. Often, factors other than self-assessment influence cadets' branch selections. These include faculty, staff, and graduates the cadets they know on active duty, follow-on military schools, and even future location assignments.

A significant portion of military education and socialization during a cadet's four years at West Point emphasizes the combat arms branches, specifically the infantry, metaphorically and ironically known as the *Queen of Battle*. The infantry is the main land combat force and the backbone of the Army. Its mission is to "close with the enemy by means of fire and maneuver in order to destroy or capture him or to repel his assault by fire, close combat, and counterattack."[114] The Infantry, Armor, and Special Forces are three of the seven combat arms branches under the combat exclusion rule.[115] The other four branches Field Artillery, Air Defense Artillery, Aviation, and the Engineers are open to women in limited capacities. As Engineers have the primary responsibility to assure the mobility of the force, Bridget found the challenge of building and destroying structures, as the mission dictates, both exciting and interesting. As a combat arms branch, the secondary mission of the Engineer Corps is to fight as infantry. Either way, Bridget figured, with a commission in the Corps of Engineers, she would be in the action.

During Bridget's four years at West Point, a war raged on in Europe with Bosnian Muslims, Croatian, and Serbian forces brutally attacking one another in a country formerly known as Yugoslavia. As they began their final semester at West Point, Bridget and her classmates talked a lot about the Balkans, particularly those who selected a European post as their initial assignment. This was the first time since Operation Desert Storm in 1990 that West Point cadets felt that they could be involved in ground combat shortly after graduation.

Although the United States negotiated an end to the fighting between the Bosnian and Croat forces, the Serb forces continued to fight. NATO initiated a series of air strikes against the Serbian rebels,

---

[114] Department of Defense, Department of the Army. "Army Field Manual 7-20, The Infantry Battalion." April 6, 1992.

[115] Department of Defense, Department of the Army. "Army Regulation 600-13, Army Policy for the Assignment of Female Soldiers." March 27, 1992. Located at www.army.mil/USAPA/epubs/pdf/r600_13.pdf.

following their attack against Gorazde in what is now the Republic of Bosnia and Herzegovina. The United States continued to pursue diplomatic initiatives to bring the warring ethnic factions to the bargaining table. The diplomatic delegation successfully mediated peace talks between Serbian and Bosnian forces and persuaded both to sign a truce on New Years Day, 1995.

Five months later, Bridget and Patrick graduated West Point and commissioned as second lieutenants in the United States Army. (Patrick, originally a member of the class of 1994, had been turned back for a year for an academic deficiency, requiring him to repeat a year at the Academy and graduate with the class of 1995.) John and Diane Altenburg smiled proudly as two of their children entered the profession of arms. After a short graduation leave and some time with their family, both of the new lieutenants attended their respective officer basic courses. Bridget went to Fort Leonard Wood, Missouri, for the Engineer course, and Patrick went to Fort Benning, Georgia, for the Infantry course.

Then the war in the Balkans escalated. The New Years Day truce was short-lived as the Croat Army violated it with a strike to re-take land held by the Serbs at the outset of the war. Following seven months of sporadic fighting, all sides returned to the negotiating table. A second set of peace talks, held at Wright-Patterson Air Force Base in Dayton, Ohio in November 1995, yielded results. The Dayton Peace Accord signed formally in Paris on December 14, 1995, by Presidents Franjo Tudjman (Croatia), Aliji Izethbegovic (Bosnia), and Slobodan Milosevic (Serbia)[116] ended the Balkans conflict that had claimed the lives of more than 200,000 people and drove another two million from their homes.[117]

As Bridget neared the completion of her Engineer Officers Basic Course, the U.S. and 12 allied nations deployed peacekeeping forces to Bosnia to support Operation Joint Endeavor, as provided for in the Dayton Peace Accords. Twenty thousand soldiers in Task

---

[116] www.globalsecurity.org/military/agency/army/1ad.htmcom.

[117] U.S. Department of State, Office of the Spokesman, November 21, 2005. Fact Sheet "Ten Years of Dayton Progress."

Force Eagle comprised the U.S. element of this peacekeeping force. This operation was significant for two reasons. It was the first commitment of military forces in NATO history and the first collaborative effort since World War II between U.S. and Russian forces.

> Between December 1995 and January 1996, the 1st Armored Division, as part of the NATO's European Allied Command, deployed to Bosnia-Herzegovina. The peacekeeping force arrived during the worst Balkan winter and flooding of the Sava River in 70 years. In that first month, the division's bridge building unit, the 502nd Engineer Company, deployed to Croatia and placed the historic ribbon float bridge over the Sava River connecting Bosnia and Croatia.[118]

In addition to supporting the movement of Task Force Eagle elements and the Implementation Force (IFOR), the 502nd Engineer Company assisted the 38th and 55th Engineer companies in constructing the first fixed bridge over the Sava River in Brcko-Gunja.[119]

> Task Force Eagle enforced the cease-fire, supervised the marking of boundaries and the zone of separation between the former warring factions, and enforced the withdrawal of the combatants to their barracks and the movement of heavy weapons to designated storage sites. Task Force Eagle supported the Organization for Security and Cooperation in Europe's efforts to administer the country's first ever, democratic national elections.[120]

---

[118] IBID.

[119] www.globalsecurity.org/military/ops/river.htm.

[120] www.globalsecurity.org/military/ops/joint_endeavor.htm.

In February 1996, Bridget reported to the 38th Engineer (Bridge) Company, 130th Engineer Brigade, V U.S. Corps in Hanau, Germany. Her platoon had deployed to Bosnia, so she quickly went through orientation, situation exercise training, and finally a 2-day bus ride to Bosnia where she assumed command of a 34-person bridge platoon at Camp Bedrock. Their mission was to enforce the provisions of the peace treaty as part of Task Force Eagle by improving freedom of movement. Bridget was in the action. The 1st Armored Division provided the first movement of United States soldiers into the war-torn country that began with Operation Joint Endeavor in October 1995.

Bridget's platoon constructed the largest Bailey bridge[121] erected since World War II.[122] Given this build was to be completed in three days, careful and detailed plans were developed for the staging and guarding of materials and components. The warring factions had laid significant numbers of land mines throughout the region. To establish a place to put the several hundred pound panels and trusses the platoon had to clear the area of mines. And then provide around the clock guards for all the materials. Bridget recalled, "If something was not protected with armed guards it would disappear. Although stealing an 800 pound panel would be challenging at best, we did not take any chances."

Task Force Eagle's mission was to rebuild the country's basic infrastructure to improve freedom of movement for the former warring factions. It worked closely with Russian units to open supply routes in the Zone of Separation. Bridget recalled,

> It was an exciting time. Our mission had strategic importance for the future of the country. Our presence and accomplishments helped to reduce the tensions

---

[121] Designed in 1910, Bailey bridges are built on site from a pre-engineered system of ready-to-assemble components connected end-to-end. Although construction of a Bailey bridge is labor intensive, the bridge is highly versatile for long spans and heavy loads as it can be assembled in multiple heights and widths.

[122] Department of Defense, Department of the Army. "AE Pamphlet 525-100 Military Operations: The U.S. Army in Bosnia and Herzegovina." 7 October 2003, p.18.

between the warring factions. Today, thousands of people are alive and living in Bosnia because of the success of Operation Joint Endeavor.

With the transfer of command and control authority of Task Force Eagle from 1st Armored Division to 1st infantry Division in November 1996, Bridget returned briefly to the unit's home garrison in Hanau, Germany. She had been in Bosnia-Herzegovina for nine months.

Less than a year later, Bridget returned to the Balkans when the 565th Engineer Battalion deployed to Slovanski Brod, Croatia. The purpose of this August deployment was to conduct bridge building exercises on the Sava River as the 1st Armored Division again assumed command of Task Force Eagle and the 12-member allied nation Multi National Division North Force (MND (N)).

Now a senior lieutenant in the battalion, she was one of only two lieutenants with bridge building experience. The battalion was in the process of certifying the two bridge companies in the unit as float and fixed bridge units. Although in the position of adjutant, or personnel officer, responsible for managing the battalion's soldiers in Germany and Croatia, Bridget used her experience to mentor the new platoon leaders in the bridge-building process. She helped them understand, plan, and coordinate the logistics of a build, learn how to employ the expertise of the non-commissioned officers, and conduct their actual jobs during a build.

Bridget then transitioned to become the V Corps Commanding General's scheduler. She viewed this position as an opportunity to understand better the type of preparation battalion and brigade commanders in V Corps undertook for every type of exercise. It allowed her to develop relationships with all of the senior commanders.

After a year and a half as scheduler, the V Corps Commander, Lieutenant General John W. Hendrix, selected First Lieutenant Bridget Altenburg to be his aide-de-camp. A prestigious position for a lieutenant, it was unusual for a male commanding general to have a female aide, given the professional intimacy of a general and aide. An aide-de-camp is an officer on a general's personal staff who acts as his confidential secretary in all matters.

Shortly after Bridget became the aide, V Corps headquarters deployed an advanced team to Albania to provide a close-air component to the on-going air war. V Corps deployed Apache helicopters and an artillery battalion from Germany into Albania to support the ongoing air war in Serbia. This was the first deployment of Corps assets since Operation Desert Storm in 1991.

As the corps commander's aide, Bridget experienced this deployment from a strategic vantage point. She observed the daily targeting situation and the war planning and preparations for the air war and ground assault in Kosovo from the Supreme Allied Command of NATO and its commander, four-star General Wesley Clark. The command was an alliance of 19 nations. Missions between U.S. Special Forces and the Kosovo Liberation Army (KLA) on the northern Kosovo border helped identify potential air targets. Strategic air power alone won the war without a single allied combat death. The effectiveness of this air power successfully isolated Slobodan Milosevic from his allies and abruptly ended his attempt at driving a million Kosovars from their homes. This was the beginning of the end of the Serbian leader's rule; he was voted out of office and tried for war crimes.

With a successful end to the fighting, V Corps deployed units to Kosovo in advance and anticipation of the passing of U.N. Security Council Resolution 1244, which established the overall political framework for Kosovo. This peacekeeping mission comprised an international security presence as part of the Kosovo Forces/International Security Force (KFOR) recognized to enforce military agreements with the former warring parties and to ensure public safety and order for all.

Bridget's unique vantage point and experiences provided her access to commanders at all levels, but she encountered some surprising limitations. Bridget interacted with the all-male and Muslim Kosovo Liberation Army, the KLA. On one particular day,

Bridget planned to accompany General Hendrix to northern Albania to work with U.S. Special Forces and the KLA on targets in Kosovo. As she prepared to go, a young female sergeant and bodyguard of the V Corps Commander informed Lieutenant Altenburg that they would not be able to go because they were women. Bridget was shocked; she previously had accompanied the Commanding General everywhere. Now, for the first time, she could not accompany him on a mission because of her gender. Bridget had experienced few boundaries because of her gender in the Army since not permitted her choice of infantry as branch selection as a cadet.

When Lieutenant Altenburg approached her boss about the situation, he apologized. General Hendrix explained to her that he had made a significant mistake in not allowing her to perform her job, and he would ensure gender would not be a factor again. Bridget recalled, "His response and acknowledgement of a mistake reinforced the sincerity of his apology and willingness to listen to subordinates and change his actions. He demonstrated strong leadership." Bridget believes General Hendrix's change in position was an important example for the KLA. She explained, "In Albania, the soldiers were fine with us. They were asking for our leadership, so showing them that we have men and women working together was a good lesson for them."

As Bridget neared the five-year mark of her active duty service obligation from West Point, she considered her future in the Army. While she relished in the leadership development and challenges of being an Army officer, she wanted more control in her life. Most importantly, she sought to reconcile her integrity with the Army's policy against homosexuals. Bridget recalled,

> I deployed three times in four years. I knew exactly when I would be promoted and had no say about for whom I would work. More importantly, I could not be open about my personal relationships.

Her lack of control had roots in her sexuality. She was gay and this significant obstacle took an emotional toll on her. Prior to her final deployment to Albania, Lieutenant Altenburg recalled the difficulty in saying goodbye to her partner in the privacy of their apartment. She had to act secretly as other family members, spouses, children, and significant others said goodbye publicly in front of the unit's headquarters before the deployment. Bridget worried constantly that some one would discover that she was gay. She shared,

> The inability to be open about the person I loved weighed heavily. All of these influences contributed to an overwhelming feeling of being out of control, with no true ability to influence my future, regardless of my performance and competency.

Throughout her deployments to Albania and Kosovo, Bridget feared being separated from the Army under the *"Don't Ask, Don't Tell"* (DADT) policy, even though she had never "come out" or confided in anyone besides her partner. She recalled the fateful day in which she made a decision about her future in the Army: "I didn't want to be dishonest and to pretend to be someone I was not any longer. It had taken me several years to acknowledge my sexuality." She explained,

> While I loved the Army and excelled as a junior officer, my military experience was colored by the fact that the federal *"Don't Ask, Don't' Tell"* statute governing military service by gay Americans like me, forced me to lie to my fellow soldiers about my sexual orientation. I played what I call the 'the pronoun game' when asked about my significant other. I maintained an empty apartment to keep up the charade. No one knew I actually lived with my partner. I remember my homecoming from Kosovo;

while other soldiers met their families as soon as they landed, I drove home alone so that my partner could welcome me out of the sight of my uniformed colleagues. For two years I made myself miserable as I tried to reconcile the happiness I had finally found in my personal life, when I met my partner, with the Army I loved and the career I had chosen. I left the Army in 2000 because I could not continue living a lie.

Concerned about their reactions, Bridget hesitated revealing her sexuality to her four brothers and sister. Those concerns were unfounded. Bridget said, "It was a wonderful experience personally to finally understand and accept the fact that I felt so different and more awkward than others. My siblings all responded 'It's about time you figured it out!' "

Bridget always found her parents to be compassionate and embracing of difference and individuality, but she remained apprehensive about revealing her sexuality to them. Bridget recalled,

I was 25 years old. My father was a major general and Assistant Judge Advocate General for the entire Army. I was concerned about the impact on his career more than my own. He had some 26 years on Active Duty. I suspect he must have known, as I frequently asked cause and effect questions about 'hypothetical' friends.

When Bridget told her parents, she recalled their hesitant reaction. She shared, "Mom told me 'love the sinner hate the sin.' Dad told me he'd love me no matter what but then argued with me about DADT. It annoyed me then, but now I know they were worried about the life I would lead—that I'd chosen a difficult path."

With her decision to resign from the Army and the discussion about *"Don't Ask, Don't Tell,"* Bridget's father provided her with a perspective that she had not considered. John compared the integration and acceptance of homosexuals in the military with that of the integration of black soldiers and women into the Armed Forces. As Bridget recalls, he posed the question of the military being a microcosm of society and did it have a role to be the social scientist. She remembers his explanation of the need for the military to be methodical and deliberate in the implementation of policy changes. He reminded her that the Armed Forces were not policy makers, but policy implementers.

In Bridget's experience, she had found few in the military were concerned about working with gay soldiers. She believes that if a gay soldier breaks regulations or acts in an inappropriate manner, that soldier deserves punishment. She said the act of being gay is easy to hide. "Many soldiers play games with the policy; however it affects people's leadership and integrity. When they have to lie to pursue a profession, they are naturally unhappy. The act of lying itself is shameful," explained Bridget. The individual irony with Bridget is that her good character and her desire to serve her country leading soldiers made it impossible for her to do so honestly.

The *"Don't Ask, Don't Tell"* policy states that the regulations apply to sexual behavior and not sexual orientation. "President Clinton wanted to end discrimination in the armed forces, but he has instead presided over the institutionalization of anti-gay animus," according to Law Professor Janet Halley, who wrote the Clinton administration's 1993 regulations for implementing the *"Don't Ask, Don't Tell* policy."[123] Under federal law, that policy prohibits openly gay people from serving in the United States Armed Forces. The military's *"Don't Ask, Don't Tell"* policy is the only law in the country that allows for the firing of a person based on open expression of sexual orientation alone.

More than a decade after its implementation, the policy continues to create anxiety among gay servicemembers. Bridget said,

---

[123] Janet Halley, "Despite Reforms, "Don't Ask, Don't Tell"," Los Angeles Times, August 22, 1999, Op-Ed, at M5.

The policy is bad because it encourages soldiers in the Armed Forces to lie. This is in direct conflict with integrity, one of the Army's seven core values. Integrity means doing what is right, legally and morally, and to be willing to do what is right even when no one is looking. The Army proffers that integrity is its moral compass and inner voice.

The paradox is that the military places a high value on integrity and honor, yet undermines these values by forcing and encouraging soldiers to lie about their personal lives. The military allows gays to serve as long as they do not admit their sexual orientation. According to Bridget,

> The law isn't about sense. It's not about unit cohesion. It's not about military readiness. It's about discrimination. Nothing disrupts unit cohesion like lying. Being in the Army is not like any other day job. You live with other soldiers. You are with them 24 hours a day. They know you. They know if you are lying.

Since leaving the service in 2000, Bridget has worked with the Servicemembers Legal Defense Network (SLDN) to lobby Congress to end the ban on homosexuals serving openly in the military. In 2006, she spent three days training with SLDN and meeting with various congressional aides to encourage passing a house resolution to end the ban. Bridget continues to volunteer her time with SLDN, contacting people, recruiting others for lobbying efforts, and working locally and nationally to bring attention to this discriminatory policy.

The enactment of *"Don't Ask, Don't Tell"* has caused the discharge of more than 12,500 soldiers from the military for being lesbian, gay, or bisexual.[124] According to figures from the General

---

[124] www.sldn.org/pages/about-dadt.

Accounting Office, the cost of training replacements for those soldiers exceeded $360 million from fiscal years 1994 through 2003.[125] Included are soldiers in military occupational specialties with critical shortages, such as pilots, intelligence analysts, and Arabic linguists.[126]

These numbers do not include servicemembers such as Bridget, who complete their service obligations but choose not to continue their military careers because of the *"Don't Ask, Don't Tell"* policy. Bridget says, "I am proud of my service and would have continued serving. But the toll of keeping my life secret was too great. It is a choice many talented, patriotic, and committed soldiers have had to, and continue to, make."

In 2000, Bridget resigned her commission, received an honorable discharge, and entered the Columbia University School of Business in New York City. Graduate school allowed Bridget to combine her competitive drive, discipline, and the team-building skills she had honed in the military with new business acumen. It provided an opportunity to live her life openly without fear of discrimination or involuntary discharge from the military.

Although Bridget chose to concentrate her graduate business studies in the areas of finance and banking, a summer internship with Ford Motor Company reinforced her desire to continue a career in leadership and general management as a civilian. During her second year of business school, several companies in various industries recruited Bridget. All placed a high value on the leadership skills she had developed in the Army. Weighing several employment offers, Bridget joined Bally Fitness, headquartered in Chicago because it promoted a concept she was passionate about— fitness.

Bridget explained, "At the time, working at Bally was my absolute dream job. This was the optimal integration of sports and fitness, language, leadership, management, and challenge. Bally had a general management program geared towards turning around their

---

[125] IBID.

[126] IBID.

operations in an increasingly competitive environment." Bally was in the midst of developing strategic and aggressive plans for a major global expansion into Europe and Asia. As a triathlete, Bridget thought working for a company dedicated to people's fitness was a perfect fit. During this time, Bridget met a new partner, Colleen, a professor at DePaul University.

Initially, Bridget found Bally to be conservative in their human capital management practices and same-sex partners. The company's benefit plans extended only to married couples. Through Bridget's initiative and persistence, Bally became more progressive and changed its policies. Working with the human resources group, Bridget helped the company develop a non-discrimination policy and initiate benefits for domestic partners. Bridget recalled,

> This was an extremely positive and rewarding experience. I learned that often times you just need to ask the question and be willing to take the lead. Generally, most people do not intentionally discriminate. If you challenge them, they usually will step forward. When I asked the Senior Vice President for Human Resources why Bally did not have a non-discrimination policy, he offered me the opportunity to work with his team to develop one. The same applied for same-sex-partnership benefits. I conducted some analysis and put together a proposal. I just had to ask.

As Bridget sharpened her business acumen, she competed in her first Ironman triathlon on November 6, 2004, completing the grueling three-sport endurance race in 12 hours, 51 minutes, exceeding her goal of finishing in 14 hours.

While the opportunity with Bally was a dream, Bridget felt unfulfilled in her professional progression from the military to the corporate world. She had transitioned from a career focused on missions to improve freedom of movement in a country attempting to become a democratic nation, to missions focused on creating and improving shareholder value. According to Bridget, Bally began to change their strategic direction as external pressure for improved stock performance mounted. As part of that change, Bally abandoned their global expansion and brought in a new chief executive officer keenly focused on short-term stock performance. Bridget perceived her work on the operational turnaround to be a very low priority and decided it was time to pursue another opportunity.

She was eager to talk with others who had experienced similar career transitions as well as unmet expectations after various transitions. Through an email, Bridget contacted Janet Hanson, the founder of 85 Broads, a global network of women. Bridget learned of 85 Broads through a conference of women graduates of the five federal service academies. The 85 Broads organization facilitated networking among professional, graduate, and undergraduate women, focused on questions of business, career, and life balance.

Janet Hanson's response was near instantaneous. Bridget said, "Within about 30 seconds, Janet emailed me and exclaimed, 'I will be your employment agent.' " Janet proceeded to contact several women in 85 Broads and learned that Sears Holding Corporation, the retail giant headquartered in Chicago, was looking for candidates with Bridget's experiences and skills. Sears had initiated a new senior leadership rotational program aimed at hiring experienced managers from outside of Sears and providing them with an intensive yearlong apprenticeship with a senior executive. The goal of the program was to develop the company's bench of executive talent. Motivated by Sears' focus on moving successful graduates of the program into senior executive positions Bridget accepted the opportunity. Bridget's initial rotation was with a newly created team focused on improving the customer experience at Sears.

Early in 2007, CBS News and anchor Katie Couric as part of a series titled *American Spirit* interviewed Janet Hanson. The weekly segment highlighted Americans taking risks to solve problems in their communities and the national proliferation of these unique community-based solutions. Specifically, this segment focused on Janet's investment in women through the creation and expansion of

85 Broads. Bridget was asked to be part of this interview to illustrate the reach of the network and her work with Janet.

Couric mentioned briefly Bridget's position with Sears but focused the 30-minute interview on the formation and launch of the West Point Women's Network (WPW) and Bridget's role as a founding member. Bridget recalled, "It was at this point that I articulated my true passion and desire to build a career helping develop women leaders." This was not a newly developed passion. She explained,

> As graduates of the Military Academy, we lacked an alumni network of our own. To me, it's important because WPW are the people I feel most connected to—we share the same values and experiences. I wanted to give WPW the chance to remain connected after they left the service. I remember how much I missed that connection when I went to business school.

The CBS interview opened a window into Bridget's career and her future as well as stretching Janet Hanson's focus. Janet returned to 85 Broads with a laser-like intent to expand the organization. Janet realized that while she had a group of young and committed employees, primarily information technology and web content managers and campus ambassadors, she did not have a strong leader overseeing the day-to-day operation so that she could concentrate on growth and expansion. Janet created the position of Chief Administrative Officer.

Bridget returned to Chicago and Sears. Regularly scanning the 85 Broads website, Bridget saw a posting for the Chief Administrative Officer position and contacted Janet. The following week, Bridget flew to Greenwich, Connecticut, to talk. Both agreed she was the right person to lead the daily operations of the organization. Concerned about leaving Sears within months of joining, Bridget worried how her departure might reflect on the 85 Broads Network. She explained, "Sears made a significant investment in me in a short period of time. I did not want to create the belief or perception that we poach from our own network." With Janet's advice, Bridget spoke with her boss at Sears. She shared with her the opportunity 85 Broads offered and how it correlated with her own passion of helping women develop as leaders. Bridget found her boss not only supportive, but encouraging. Her boss presented a scenario in which Bridget, in the future, would be able to help identify talented women to contribute to Sears. Bridget shared,

> 85 Broads is all about women helping women build businesses, partnerships and a sense of community. While women are making gains in various professions, men continue to play a dominant role in business. Available data shows [sic] that women earn only 76 cents for every dollar a man earns. I was motivated by Janet's desire and personal investment to change this.

Bridget accepted Janet's offer to join 85 Broads as the Chief Administrative Officer. In addition to managing the company's daily operations, Bridget helped Janet create tools and training to assist women in various career decisions at life junctures to help them become successful on their own terms. This appeared the perfect opportunity, working for a network dedicated to helping women become better leaders.

The chance to lead and to develop programs for women intrigued Bridget. However, she failed to clarify Janet's expectations of her. She reflected,

> Unfortunately, the lesson I learned was that when something sounds too good to be true, it probably is. I got sold on the chance to lead a proven website team and turn it into a viable business team. I should have insisted on looking at the budget, learning more about the CEO's plans for the future and talked in much more detail about my day-to-day role. Not only did I

not do proper due diligence on the business, I did not do it on the people already working in the organization.

Bridget found herself flying between Greenwich and Chicago each week, trying to clarify all the messages and intimations about her role and responsibilities. The strategy of the organization was in flux. One day the plan was to develop leadership-training seminars for women, but the next day it was to open campus coffee shops. The organization's budget and staffing models did not support each other. Bridget discovered there was no budget to cover her negotiated salary. Bridget left 85 Broads after only a few months.

Through each of her transitions, Bridget has gained strength, courage, and confidence in facing the unknown. Bridget now focuses on her two passions, sports and leadership. She is again training to compete in triathlons and volunteering her experience with the Chicago Triathlon Club and West Point Women's Network. She and Colleen, her partner of two years, were married in September 2007, in front of family and friends in Chicago. Bridget reflected,

> When I look back, I sometimes miss the Army and having that sense of doing something important in the world. I've had to find that in my volunteer work instead. Even more important to me is the chance to live my life openly with the woman I love. I wouldn't give that up for anything.

Lieutenant Bridget Altenburg in Bosnia serving with soldiers from Russia in the Zone of Separation, 1996. (*Photo courtesy of Bridget Altenburg*)

Bridget Altenburg crosses the finish line of her first Ironman triathlon in Florida beating her goal by nine minutes, 2004. (*Photo courtesy of Bridget Altenburg*)

Cadet Sarah Gerstein, USMA
2007. (*Photo courtesy of Kathy
Gerstein*)

Pursuing the Family Business | First Lieutenant Sarah Gerstein, Class of 2007

"It is our choices, Harry, that show what we truly are, far more than our abilities."
— Dumbledore in *Harry Potter and the Chamber of Secrets* by J. K. Rowling

On May 2, 2003, United States President George W. Bush landed on the USS Abraham Lincoln, arriving in the co-pilot's seat of a Navy S-3 Viking.[127] Shortly after landing, the President, wearing a military green one-piece flight suit and holding a white helmet, climbed off the plane and sharply saluted the sailors on the flight deck of the enormous aircraft carrier. Behind him, the landing tower on the flight deck proudly displayed a banner that read, "Mission Accomplished." Captured and forever preserved in the media, it quickly made its way into news headlines worldwide. Later that evening, President Bush addressed the nation, informing Americans that "major combat operations in Iraq have ended."

* * *

Sarah Gerstein grew up always imagining serving in the military, despite the fact that less than two percent of Americans do so. Dan and Kathy Gerstein, Sarah's parents, graduated from the United States Military Academy in 1980. Born in 1985, raised, and schooled on military bases around the world, Sarah is the oldest daughter of two Army officers. She watched her father leave for work each day in camouflage fatigues. Constantly around people in military service, Sarah liked the attitude of those in uniform. Dan Gerstein deployed for extended periods three times during Sarah's childhood. In 1991, he deployed to Kuwait in support of Operation

---

[127] The S-3 is an aircraft used to identify, track, and destroy enemy submarines.

Desert Storm. When Sarah was 11 years old, her father deployed to the Balkans twice within an 18-month period.

Sarah does not remember the first time she thought about serving her country, as it has always been a part of her life. The Gerstein house was a shrine to the storied Military Academy, with various rooms displaying West Point and Army memorabilia. Sarah recalled, "In nearly every room, there is some picture, print, or item from West Point—pictures of parades, the beautiful landscape, and the famous hat toss at graduation. My mom still has her R-day tags and all her cadet uniforms. I remember one year dressing up as a cadet for Halloween, although I was too old to go out and trick or treat."

Family dinner conversations often revolved around cadet tradition and lore, military issues, foreign affairs, and politics. Her parents often joked at dinner, incorporating etiquette peculiar to cadets, such as the table duties of plebes. Sarah remembered:

> Growing up, typically we had tacos for dinner on Friday evening—that was what my parents had as cadets. Dad would often do the whole cadet spiel if there was one serving of food left. To anyone outside the Army, we sounded as if we were speaking a foreign language with our use of all the acronyms. It was really my younger sister Rachel, who had no interest in the military, who did not find dinnertime entertaining.

Although classmates at West Point, Dan and Kathy first met at the Signal Corps Officer basic course, where they got to know one another because they shared a kitchen in the Bachelor Officer Quarters (BOQ) at Fort Gordon, Georgia. By the end of the six-month course, Kathy and Dan married. The two eventually planned to raise a family. As Signal Officers, they spent long periods in the field for various training exercises. For them, these professional requirements were not conducive to raising a family. Dan enjoyed the Army, and

Kathy wanted to focus on raising a family, so at the end of their five-year active duty service obligations, the two agreed jointly that Kathy would resign her commission and Dan would remain on active duty.

That decision probably influenced Sarah as she grew up in ways she could not imagine at the time. As with nearly all military families, the Gersteins uprooted and moved their home every two to three years. Sarah recalled,

> When you grow up and live in one community, I imagine you have the opportunity to form some pretty strong friendships and bonds with people in your neighborhood. Given the frequency of our moves, I did not really form many strong friendships with other children my age. I actually formed those friendships with my parents and sister. We are all very close. My parents are great role models and friends. I trust them and can talk to them about anything. They have always been there for me, regardless of how trivial my problems might have been. They provided a stable influence in my life, even when we were moving around so much.

Deciding she liked the structure and the opportunities available in the military, Sarah applied to West Point. She said,

> Some of my reasons were a little selfish. I am not sure how many other colleges I could have gone to for free with the vast array of opportunities available at West Point. I wanted to swim on a division one team; I did not have to worry about a job after graduation. I wanted to be part of something greater than myself. My parents inspired me with their cadet and officer stories and experiences.

In June 2003, two months after President Bush's infamous "Mission Accomplished" speech, Sarah entered West Point as a new cadet. She was part of the first class to matriculate after the United States invasion of Iraq. Sarah understood the responsibilities of the profession she was entering, but was unsure whether the United States would still be at war by the time she graduated. Sarah and her classmates of 2007 were the first cadets to enter the Academy in wartime since the Vietnam era. Sarah said,

> I honestly do not think I knew what the invasion meant for the long term. I was accepted to both West Point and Annapolis in September of the previous year. I did not make a decision to go to West Point until April. Although I had read a lot and talked with both mom and dad, I really did not think I would be affected by the situation in the Middle East, as I would be in school for the next four years.

Sarah accepted the appointment to West Point, feeling it was a better fit academically, athletically, and professionally than attending Annapolis and joining the Navy. Sarah said,

> The Army is about leading people. That is what I want to do. I had an interest in International Relations and the curriculum at West Point provided a greater range of options. Being that Army's swim team was a little weaker; I felt I would have more opportunities to make a competitive impact in the pool. Applying to Navy was a little bit more about shocking my parents and less about my interest in being at sea.

From many discussions with her parents leading up to her report date, Sarah thought she knew what to expect. She felt well prepared for the challenges and the intensity of that first summer of Cadet Basic Training. Kathy, recalling her own athletic challenges with running in formation, strongly encouraged Sarah to start running even before she decided to go to West Point. Sarah said, "It was my mom who would give me a swift kick in the butt to go out and run. She emphasized that it was important to put in the mileage now and build a good base foundation. I didn't really enjoy it, but it made sense, and I did start to run." Most important, Sarah said, were her parent's words of wisdom regarding an attitude during Beast Barracks and beyond. Sarah recalled,

> Both my parents told me to take it seriously. They described it as a laboratory where the 'inmates' experiment on you for the purpose of developing leaders. They encouraged me that I needed to keep a sense of humor during the entire experience. They used the analogy of a duck swimming. On the surface of the water, the duck looks like it is gliding effortlessly. Underwater, the duck is paddling ferociously. The message was to keep a calm exterior but work like crazy underneath it all. I continue to draw on their advice.

Despite the challenging formation runs, the mileage and the training Sarah put in before she arrived at West Point paid off, as she completed all runs. What did take Sarah by surprise was what she described as a lack of maturity among some of the cadet cadre that summer. One of the cadet leaders in Sarah's chain of command learned that both her parents were graduates of West Point. He used this to tell Sarah repeatedly how she was "failing her parents as a new cadet." Sarah said,

> I wanted to give him the benefit of the doubt that he was trying to motivate me, but it totally backfired. He always seemed to attack me, and not inspire me. However, I did learn a valuable leadership lesson early on—when I became a leader, I would not place

unnecessary burdens on someone I am trying to develop. I think he was just really immature, because it continued throughout the academic year. Whenever I saw this cadet, he berated me.

Another facet of cadet life Sarah did not anticipate was the reality of being in the military and of hearing the announcements of graduate combat casualties during meals. Three times a day, cadets file quickly, en masse, into the West Point Mess Hall for breakfast, lunch, and dinner. It is a strange combination of order and chaos as cadets enter the building from three different locations and hurriedly scatter to its four wings in four minutes. Painted with a massive mural on its walls, one wing depicts the history of warfare. It is a place where the past is always present and the bridge to the future is under perpetual construction with each incoming and graduating class of cadets.

The high arched ceilings of the mess hall subdue the voices of the cadets to a muffled chatter. Near the conclusion of each 20-minute meal comes the powerful voice of the Cadet Adjutant responsible for delivering a quick litany of important announcements, events, and athletic team scores. On this day of basic training the adjutant said, "Please give your attention to the Commander of Cadet Basic Training." The rumble fell silent and all froze in place. The commander known as "The King of Beast," approached the microphone and spoke,

I regret to inform you of the death of Captain Joshua Byers, Class of 1996. Captain Byers was killed in action on 25 July 2003 when his convoy hit an explosive device in Iraq. Captain Byers was Commander of Fox Troop, 2nd Squadron, 3rd Armored Calvary Regiment in Fort Carson, Co. Please join me in a moment of silence for this fallen graduate.

Less than one month into their 47-month officer-training program, the Class of 2007 heard their first war casualty announcement. Sarah and her classmates would hear this message delivered nine more times before the end of their first year at the Military Academy. Although they did not know personally any of these graduates that year, it was an eerie foreshadowing of what was to come, and a surreal introduction to the sacrifices of those within the profession of arms.

Sarah recalled one particular announcement of a graduate killed in combat during her first semester plebe year. Once again, from the balcony in the cavernous mess hall, the Cadet Adjutant announced the combat death of First Lieutenant David R. Bernstein, killed in Iraq when his patrol was ambushed on October 18, 2003. Although Sarah did not know Bernstein, she did know that he was the former captain of the Army swim team. This time, with the entire Corps of Cadets present, nearly 4,000 cadets fell silent and paused in a moment of thought and prayer. Along with the entire swim team, Sarah attended Berstein's funeral service. It was the first funeral she ever had attended, but it would not be the last. She remembered the service, the reception, and then boarding a bus to attend and compete in her first intercollegiate swim meet. Sarah recalled, "Every death is terribly sad. It made me and my teammates pause. However, it was so early on in our cadet careers and in the war, we did not think we would be attending any more funerals."

Plebe year proved much more trying for Sarah than Beast Barracks. The quantity and rigor of the academic curriculum required the quick development of time management skills. She expected her focus to be on studying and swimming. She did not anticipate her emotional state and the time and mental energy she spent worrying about how to get everything completed. Sarah found herself very unhappy and questioning what she was doing at West Point.

I came to understand that I really did not know what
to expect from the academic intensity and competing

on the swim team. Both seemed all encompassing. Add the required duties and plebe knowledge memorization; I did not like the daily grind of being a cadet. There was just no time for anything else. Every minute of every day was filled with completing some type of requirement and meeting some standard or expectation. I wasted a lot of energy thinking about all this.

As a varsity swimmer, Sarah was often away from her cadet company during both morning and afternoon workouts, returning just in time for meal formations. Many of her company mates thought that she was "getting over" — avoiding plebe duties, such as calling minutes for formation and delivering newspapers and laundry to upper class cadets. Sarah felt her classmates ignored her and she was unable to bond with many of her classmates in that company. She said, "It's a lonely and empty feeling. But I never really considered leaving. I was not going to quit and go home or go to another college. I had too much pride." This is when Sarah sought out her parents. She explained,

> My mother was awesome. She always listened to my complaints. She was very into sending cards. I remember receiving one that said, 'When life gives you lemons, make lemonade, or stuff them down your shirt to make your boobs look bigger.' She provided me another perspective and reminded me to laugh. Each event was part of the lab experiment.

For more than two centuries, West Point has educated future Army officers in the ways of large-scale industrial warfare against defined enemies. It has established a reputation jokingly described by its graduates as having 200 years of history, unhampered by progress. However, the on-going wars in Iraq and Afghanistan have made the Academy's mission even more imperative as it prepares future Army leaders for a completely different type of warfare, one waged by countless insurgents. The Academy's mission is:

> to educate, train, and inspire the Corps of Cadets so that each graduate is a commissioned leader of character committed to the values of Duty, Honor, and Country and prepared for a career of professional excellence and service to the Nation as an officer in the United States Army.[128]

The lieutenants commissioned after 2004 are often in command of soldiers who have previously served two to three combat tours in theatre. This is a significant leadership expectation to hang over West Point's young officers. Having turned into an insurgent-directed battle, Iraq is a platoon leader and company commander's war. Fighting guerrillas means young lieutenants and captains are out in front of their units, executing small unit tactics instead of working as part of larger unit operations typically directed by much higher-ranking officers. Often they hold quasi-governmental positions in the areas where their units operate. Lieutenant Colonel Joe Felter, professor at West Point and director of its Combating Terrorism Center (CTC) said,

> These new lieutenants, they're literally the mayors of towns. They have to work with multiple U.S. government agencies, international agencies, host nation folks, tribal leaders—the threat environment is really complex, and more than ever, they need to be prepared for that.[129]

---

[128] www.usma.edu/mission.asp.

[129] "Progress at West Point. A new, privately funded institution teaches cadets about a new enemy." by Paul McLeary, October 18, 2007, The Weekly Standard.

As a nation at war, West Point has significantly changed the academic, military, and physical curriculum and the way it trains the Army's next generation of leaders. Sarah and her fellow officers-to-be are the beneficiaries of these changes. Shortly after the deadly attacks of September 11, 2001, West Point hired Dr. Jason Winkle as the Director of Combatives as a first step to overhaul its physical curriculum. Winkle had spent the previous two decades training Army Special Forces and Navy SEALs. He said,

> West Point has changed almost everything it teaches about on-the-ground combat in the past five years. In the Vietnam era, we were going into jungle warfare: in the first Gulf War, it was a lot of air strikes. Now we've moved into an era where urban warfare is predominant. I introduced military operations in urban terrain.[130]

The combatives physical education curriculum, spread throughout the first three years, is designed to develop the skills, knowledge, strategies, attitudes, and effect management that will prepare a soldier to engage and defeat an enemy in the last six feet of the battlefield. In other words, it teaches cadets to defend themselves and develop a combative survival mindset using hand-to-hand combat. Sarah recalled the multi-year course,

> While I had to take all these classes, I didn't really enjoy them much. I worked really hard and knew what I should do but wasn't always able to make it happen. No one likes getting beat up, thrown across a room or nearly choked to death. Fighting is a unique skill when trying to develop it along some defined standards and for a grade.

---

[130] "Intro to Warfare—preparing for graduation at West Point, where your first job is the front line." by Chris Smith. June 8, 2007, New York Magazine.

In February 2003, a few months prior to the Class of 2007's arrival at West Point, a privately funded CTC was established to offer instruction about the enemy the cadets will encounter when they become officers. The Center's stated mission is "to arm current and future leaders with the intellectual tools needed to defeat and deter terrorist threats to our nation." Specifically, the Center's focus is on understanding terrorism threats to national security, educating future leaders who will have counterterrorism responsibilities, and providing policy analysis and expertise to counter future terrorist threats. The center's staff (both full-time and non-resident fellows) are leading thinkers and researchers on terrorism. Together they have published twelve books and multiple articles that have greatly improved the understanding of terrorism, its structures and ideologies, and methods to combat it. These publications and original research are the textbooks for an array of cadet courses about non-state actors.

Beginning in the center's initial year, the prospectus of the mandatory International Relations course ensures each cadet received a five-lesson block on terrorism. Beyond terrorism, the CTC expanded the Social Science curriculum with a variety of courses. They included offerings in: Mass Media and American Politics, Homeland Security, Information Warfare, Politics, Democratization, and Government in the Middle East, and Winning the Peace. These courses have facilitated the creation and offering of the Academy's first academic minor in Terrorism Studies.

At the same time that the CTC was established, the Department of Military Science, another department in which there are required classes each year, instituted an academic major. It takes an interdisciplinary approach that combines military science, history, economics, political science, geography, leadership, information technology, and law to understand the nature of warfare and the role of the military as an instrument of national power.[131] It is a mix of historical analysis and contemporary application of military force in

---

[131] "Military Art and Science 2007 Program Guide," United States Military Academy.

support of national military objectives. This department, too, expanded its offerings. There are now courses in convoy conduct and security, counterinsurgency operations, special operations, and low-intensity conflict to meet the specific challenges of an insurgency in Iraq.

With the conclusion of plebe year, a feeling of relief came over Sarah, a reprieve for having completed a demanding academic year with passing grades. Sarah entered the start of her second year and the military training that summer at Camp Buckner with a new mindset toward preparing to become an officer rather than merely surviving the daily challenges of West Point. The changes in the academic and military curriculums brought the war front to the cadets' daily lives. Not only were lessons focused on this next generation of warfare, but the number of soldiers and military professors at the Academy with recent combat experience was increasing.

One of the most evident changes took place in the field training at Camp Bucker the summer prior to Sarah's second year at West Point. While the focus has always been on team and squad level tactics, there was increased emphasis placed on convoy operations, terrain walks, training in the detection of IEDs and establishing forward operating bases. Lieutenant Colonel Dave Jones, a staff officer at West Point, explained.

> Today's West Point Cadets are taught how to react to surprise uprisings, often while accompanied by someone acting as an embedded television reporter. 'We have a road march, and a crowd of people come in the middle of the road. There are vehicles on the side. There's a camera, there's a kid with a bat, there's a pregnant woman.[132]

---

[132] "Iraq Presents Graduating Class at West Point with New Challenges," Michael Wilson. The New York Times. May 25, 2007.

Sarah remembered the laser-like tactical focus of summer training. She said, "We always carried our weapons and were on the lookout for anything suspicious. Every time we conducted a movement, whether on foot or in a vehicle, it was a tactical one. There was always the possibility of an attack." According to Brigadier General Bob Caslen, Commandant of Cadets, "This change is a concerted effort by the Academy to incorporate today's security environments in both Iraq and Afghanistan." For Sarah, the military training, combined with continued swim team practices, helped her demonstrate to herself and others that she was able to perform like any cadet. This gave her a new attitude toward West Point and sense of optimism for the upcoming academic year.

During the second year, Sarah's selection of an academic major reflected the changing geopolitical climate and the role of company grade officers in the on-going Iraqi war. Sarah chose to major in Comparative Politics. Her course of study during the next two and a half years included several of the new classes: Combating Terrorism, Homeland Security, Winning the Peace, National and International Security, and Middle East Politics. Sarah said that classes in the Department of Social Science aim to provoke thought and communication, most classes use the case method and demand student participation in the discussion. Many of her classes focused on the role of the Internet in the current war. She said, "We studied how the Web is being used by Islamic Fundamentalists as a nearly instantaneous and ubiquitous tool for spreading propaganda, recruiting, fundraising, and communicating."

By the end of this year, Sarah became interested in pursuing the Military Intelligence branch after graduation, as it combined her interest in international relations and world politics. It seemed to offer Sarah a good blend of military and intellectual challenge, in that the core mission focuses on gathering, analyzing, and disseminating information about the enemy, terrain, and weather in various areas of operations of interest. Sarah said, "The combination of classes in Comparative Politics, International Relations, and Terrorism will provide a great foundation for working in Military Intelligence. It provides both an academic and realistic picture of the threats we are facing."

As part of her military training the summer before her junior year in 2005, Sarah attended Airborne School in Fort Benning, Georgia. Jump School teaches soldiers how to use parachutes to enter combat. It is really as much about building confidence as it is about parachuting as a military skill. A large part of the three-week course is physical training, with lots of calisthenics and formation runs in combat boots. Despite the Georgia heat and humidity, Sarah thought the physical training at Airborne was easier than that during her initial cadet basic training. Sarah completed all the training and qualifying jumps, earning her Airborne wings. During the training however, Sarah suffered a stress fracture in her leg which would soon pose a significant challenge.

After Airborne school, Sarah returned to West Point for her summer assignment as a cadet platoon sergeant for incoming new cadets. During the two-week leadership training for cadet cadre, she broke the already weakened leg while running. For the next eight weeks, she had a large boot on her leg. Not being able to bear any weight, Sarah walked with the assistance of crutches. Sarah recalled,

> It was trying for me having to depend so much on others to help me do some of the most basic things, such as walking up and down stairs and carrying my own meal trays. It was very frustrating. No one likes to be on medical profile, because everyone thinks you are getting over and trying to avoid your duties. As a cadet leader, this was even more frustrating. I was supposed to be a role model for the new cadets. After the whole experience, I learned that you cannot be afraid to ask for help when you need it, regardless of the situation. In essence, it was a lesson about teamwork, which is what being a platoon leader is about.

The upcoming year was a difficult one for the Corps of Cadets. Shortly after returning to the Academy from assignments around the world, the cadets learned of the deaths of two more soldiers. The first was Command Sergeant Major (retired) Mary Sutherland, who had served in every position from squad leader to Command Sergeant Major. She spent her last seven years of active duty serving as the Command Sergeant Major of the United States Corps of Cadets and the United States Military Academy, the first woman to do so. By the time of her retirement in 2004, she was the senior enlisted soldier in the Army and had earned the distinction of being the longest-serving woman on active duty in Army history. Always visible among the cadets, Sutherland regularly attended sporting events, cheering the Army teams. Sarah remembered Sutherland leading from the front, and leading the Saturday morning Brigade runs of the Corps of Cadets despite a cumbersome knee brace.

The following day came the death announcement of First Lieutenant Laura M. Walker, killed in action at Delak, Afghanistan, on August 18, 2005. Walker had graduated West Point barely two years prior in 2003. She became the first West Point woman graduate to die in combat. Sarah recalled, "This announcement really took everyone by surprise. It was a scary time for many of us—the war kept coming closer and closer as more people we knew were dying and we really couldn't do much about it." Walker was serving in a public affairs capacity when her convoy hit an IED. Sarah later learned after Walker's death, a former Army swim team captain took command of Walker's platoon.

The war continued to invade the training ground. Sarah remembered paying a little more attention to the history surrounding her at West Point. She took more notice of the massive statues of famous generals, such as Eisenhower, Patton, and MacArthur, from wars gone by standing guard over the 4,000 cadets as they walked to and from class and the cadet barracks. The halls of various academic buildings began including memorials and displays of recent graduates killed in the line of duty. She wondered when she would know personally one of the graduates memorialized.

The first day of class for juniors marks their commitment to the Army and the profession of arms. It is on this Affirmation day cadets formally declare their obligation to serve in an active duty military force. Before then cadets were free to resign from the Academy and leave with two full years of college credit. Sarah admitted that she felt awkward about being injured and still on crutches while taking the oath to commit to the Army. She said, "What if my leg did not heal properly? Would I still be commissioned?" Nonetheless, this is what she had always pictured herself doing.

Now a junior with most of the required academic core courses completed, Sarah began taking courses of her own choosing in her academic major. In her Homeland Security Class, the students read and discussed the 9-11 Commission report—all 900 pages. They debated the intelligence and emergency response failures of that fateful day, and what has and has not changed. Sarah said,

> It was incredibly eye opening. One of the most important lessons I took away and will apply as a leader, in any capacity, is that of communication. You have to create and emphasize the importance of communication channels among various agencies, and then you have to double and triple check them. It is easy and academic to say this in hindsight, but that is the point of studying history, as we know, to learn from past mistakes.

In November, news of tragedy, once again, spread quickly throughout the West Point community. Shortly after returning from a four-day Thanksgiving break, Sarah and the Corps of Cadets learned of the combat death of First Lieutenant Dennis W. Zilinski on November 22, 2005. An IED detonated near his vehicle killed Zilinski. He had graduated fewer than two years before in 2004.

Zilinski was the Army Swim team captain Sarah's plebe year. Sarah remembered:

> This was the most difficult one because I knew him personally. Dennis was not the best swimmer on the team, but he was the one who was always there to cheer and motivate us. We returned from break, attended Dennis' funeral, and then we traveled to Navy for a swim meet where we lost miserably. It just sucked. We were all in a state of disbelief. For me, this is when I fully came to understand my choice of attending West Point would mean leading soldiers in combat and possibly getting killed.

Excitement and high energy enveloped the atmosphere around West Point in the early part of 2006. The Army Women's Basketball team completed a dramatic turnaround season, giving the cadets something to celebrate. First year head coach Maggie Dixon had led the team to a 20-11 season, Army's first 20 game winning season, since 1990-1991 and the best basketball season since the legendary Bobby Knight coached at West Point more than 30 years earlier. The team won the Patriot League Championship and earned a berth in college basketball's "Big Dance and March Madness"—the National Collegiate Athletic Association Tournament. It was the first time an Army women's team had earned the right to play at this level. For a few months, women's basketball had everyone's attention and temporarily took their minds off the on-going war.

As ESPN reported, "Maggie Dixon had been a storybook coach of the storybook season, hired from DePaul just days before the start of pre-season practice, winning 20 games, and making her brother and her first siblings ever to make the NCAA Tournaments together as coaches."[133] The team's success gave the entire Academy something to celebrate and enjoy. "It was as if everyone smiled

---

[133] Adrian Wojnarowski, "Dixon's Death cuts short a championship-caliber life." www.espn.go.com, April 17, 2006.

again. It was a really cool time, sharing and celebrating in the success of the women's basketball team. During every home game the stands packed with cadets and fans. It was standing room only," said Sarah.

For the first round of the tournament, Army drew the University of Tennessee Volunteers, coached by the renowned Pat Summit. Although Tennessee blew out the Cadets, 102-54, in that first round game, it did not diminish Army's spirit and the success of the season, which had included a 12-game winning streak. Despite the loss, the teams play and triumphant season lit a wildfire of euphoria that quickly spread throughout the Academy. The flames extinguished less than a month later.

During afternoon military drill and parade practice in early April, a medical transport helicopter flew low over the marching cadets on the parade ground. It landed briefly at the post hospital and then flew back over the grounds. Later that night, the cadets would learn that Coach Maggie Dixon had suffered an arrhythmia heart episode and was in intensive care at the Westchester Medical Center. The helicopter they saw earlier in the day had flown her to Westchester. The following afternoon, Dixon died. She was 28 years old. The announcement to the Corps was devastating, putting most of the cadets, as well as the Academy staff and faculty, into a somber and pensive mood. Just weeks ago, the fairy-tale season of this women's team had been solely responsible for jubilation on campus. Sarah admitted,

> With Maggie's death and the deaths of graduates in Iraq and Afghanistan, the number of people we knew dying was increasing. Plebe and yearling year we did not know those killed. The announcements just got harder to listen to and seemed to be coming more frequently. It helped many of us focus differently. Each time we heard, 'please give your attention to the First Captain,' the prevailing thought was, 'is it going to be someone I know?'

For many, it was a strange juxtaposition of emotions. On the one hand, Sarah and the cadets at the Academy were college students. On the other, they were soldiers training for their future leadership roles as commissioned officers in an Army fighting the Global War on Terror.

During her final cadet summer, Sarah's experiences helped solidify her desire to serve in the Military Intelligence Corps. The first part of the summer, she spent at Fort Bragg, North Carolina with a Military Intelligence unit. Although Bragg was far from her first choice of locations for that summer, the time with these soldiers helped her get a feel for being a platoon leader of a unit scheduled to deploy within the next 18 months. The second half of the summer Sarah spent in Washington, D.C., working as a military analyst in the office of the J5 in the Pentagon. J5 is the Strategic Policy and Plans branch of the Office of the Chief of Staff of the Army. Dan, her father, served a three-year assignment in the latter part of his active duty career in that office. This Directorate is the focal point for assisting the appointed Chairman of the Joint Chiefs of Staff, a four-star general, in the areas of current and future military strategy, planning guidance, and policy, politico-military advice and policies, and military positions on projected and on-going international negotiations.

While working there, Sarah attended a Latin American Conference and learned a great amount about Latin America and Venezuela. She was fortunate to have the opportunity to live at home. "I was busy with something I enjoyed, it was intellectually challenging, and I still was able to hang out with my parents. It was the best of all worlds," she said.

Returning to the Academy for her final year, Sarah was somewhat apprehensive. She had had a great summer, enjoying both her summer assignments and spending some time with her parents. But with less than ten months until graduation and commissioning, the on-going war in Iraq and Afghanistan was on each senior cadet's mind. The war casualty announcements continued and with each, Sarah found herself becoming more introspective. She remarked that she and many of her classmates began to pay attention more closely to the news. Academic classes became more practical and relevant to her future profession.

About three weeks into the academic year, the cadets learned of another graduate killed in Iraq. Second Lieutenant Emily Perez died on September 12, 2006, of injuries sustained at Al Kifl, Iraq, when an IED detonated near her vehicle during combat operations. Just 23 years old, Perez graduated in 2005. She became the 40th West Point graduate killed since September 11, 2001, and the 64th female soldier killed in Iraq or Afghanistan.[134] Sarah recalled Perez, "Everyone knew Emily. She was a small woman with a large voice. She was the brigade command sergeant major her senior year. She was a sprinter on the track team, and she sang in the gospel choir. She did it all with so much energy and passion."

The following week, while in a class, Sarah was reminded of another recently killed graduate. In this particular class, the students were discussing the importance of family support in the casualty notification process. One of the students, Cadet Duncan Walker, raised his hand, and described the notification process when his family learned that his sister, Laura Walker, had been killed. Sarah said, "I was stunned. It took my breath away for a second. Talk about getting an understanding of the process. All of a sudden, I noticed his KIA bracelet."

One of the most provocative classes Sarah took was Winning the Peace, a course created to address aspects of the war not so clearly defined. In large part, it is a proactive ethics discussion. Created in 2004, the semester-long course is an interdisciplinary approach combining sociology, history, religion, and ethics. Designed to help these officers-to-be prepare for the complexities of working in Iraq and Afghanistan, the course helps to create strategically minded soldier-statesmen for the U.S. Army at the company grade level and beyond. Much of the class centered on

---

[134] "West Point Mourns a Font of Energy, Laid to rest by War," Joshua Partlow and Lonnae O'Neal Parker. Washington Post. September 27, 2006.

ethical dilemmas that require the cadets to synthesize all their military experiences, academic classes, and news reports to go beyond the textbook to develop a solution. According to Major Stephanie Ahern, course director and former Army company commander in both Afghanistan and Iraq: "We quickly learned that what may seem like a black and white issue quickly mutes to gray on the battlefield." One of the course's five goals, "to increase awareness and critical thinking about our own perspectives, while more clearly understanding other cultures, how they perceive us, and their own motivations for acting," is illustrated most effectively during a three-day, two-night trip to Jersey City, New Jersey.

Ahern explained, "Located directly across the river from New York City, Jersey City, New Jersey, is a multi-ethnic, multi-religious, and multi-cultural city of 250,000 people, boasting more than 50 spoken languages. With its large Muslim community and continuous influx of diverse immigrants, this city has dealt with many challenges, especially over the past six years."[135] For Sarah, this immersion experience helped her better understand the diverse set of cultural, ethnic, religious, generational, and socio-economic perspectives that she may soon encounter as an Army officer serving on the battlefield. She explained,

> I definitely learned just how much differently women in other cultures are treated. I think all of the cadets were surprised by the different reactions we encountered on the trip. At some places, we were welcomed with open arms and were asked about ourselves and (from some of the kids) how they could be like us. In other places, we were not greeted as warmly, and it was shocking, because it was based on snap judgments of what we looked like, not whom we were or what we were doing there.

---

[135] IBID., p. 47.

Nearly every lesson of this course left an impression on Sarah. The most significant was what she learned from the battlefield. She said:

> One of our assignments was to communicate with three different people we knew serving in a war zone. I chose another woman who had been on the swim team with me, a guy who was a military intelligence officer I knew from several classes, and one who was my sponsor during my summer assignment and who was not a West Point grad.

The assignment was to try to get a sense and feel for what it was like in a war zone. Sarah said, "I asked the simplest of questions, from where you sleep to where you relieve yourself if you are on a mission." It was a form of mentorship, albeit electronically. The exchanges helped to reinforce the complexity and intensity of the classroom information. Major Ahern remarked, "Sarah was one of the most inquisitive students and really struggled to make sense of all the sources of information, from soldiers in combat, to news reports, to speeches from senior military leaders, to those who had ties with the region."

Sarah said her final semester at the Academy passed quickly. Between various academic projects, her cadet job as an assistant brigade operations officer, and all the activities surrounding commissioning, such as uniform fittings and branch and post selection, she had little free time. Although Sarah had not selected Fort Bragg for her summer assignment, she did select it for her first post location.

A myriad of emotions filled graduation week. Sarah recalled being excited, anxious, nervous, thrilled, and nostalgic, all at the same time. She said,

> It was a challenging experience. But I feel well prepared for the future. The next challenge will be

becoming a platoon leader of a group of soldiers who will have a lot of combat experience. All I can do is give it everything I have. This is what I have been preparing for the past four years.

Following graduation exercises, Sarah and her family participated in a commissioning ceremony at a friend's house overlooking the swiftly flowing Hudson River. Colonel (retired) Dan Gerstein administered the oath of office to his daughter, Second Lieutenant Sarah Gerstein. Kathy, Sarah's mom, and Rachel, her sister pinned gold second lieutenants bars on the epaulets of her Army uniform.

Following several weeks of graduation vacation, and a short cruise with friends, Second Lieutenant Gerstein drove across country and reported to Fort Sill, Oklahoma, for the Army's Basic Officer Leadership Course (BOLC).

In 2006, the Army implemented a significant and comprehensive transformation in the Army Officer Education System. The changes were instituted to support the Army's goals of increased readiness and a more joint and expeditionary force. All newly commissioned lieutenants are required to graduate from the three-phased BOLC. The first phase for new officers is their pre-commissioning training, which includes training conducted at the U.S. Military Academy, Reserve Officer Training Corps, and Officer Candidate Schools, the three commissioning sources for Army Officers. Following officer commissioning, the new lieutenants attend BOLC II at their initial entry training point. The second phase is a seven-week, branch-immaterial course in small-unit leadership and tactics.

General Kevin P. Byrnes, the head of the U.S. Army Training and Doctrine Command, explained the rationale for the overhaul of the curriculum.

Leader development—while educating them to think broadly–must prepare them for the complexities on the battlefields they'll see when they join their first units. We're fighting a small-unit war. Staff sergeants, sergeants first class, lieutenants and captains every day are fighting it. They're the ones out on patrol; they're the ones who are in this extremely complex environment where things change from the minute they leave their compound until they return that evening. They may never get to accomplish the objective they had set for the day because things happen en route. We've got to make sure our leaders are prepared for those complexities and changes and have a framework to refer to, a handrail to grab on to, and an understanding of foundational concepts.

The platoon is the focal point of the second phase of BOLC, the size of the unit nearly all second lieutenants, like Sarah, will command. In this phase, newly commissioned lieutenants must face and deal with a myriad of leadership scenarios based on contemporary operating environments. The Army wants to ensure, according to Byrnes that, "All officers will receive common instruction before going off to their branch technical courses. This is a major shift."

With eighty percent of BOLC conducted in a field environment, the officers experience a curriculum that includes physical-fitness training, combatives training, land-navigation training, rifle marksmanship training, weapons training, operations in nuclear, biological and chemical environments, use of night-vision equipment, military operations on urban terrain (MOUT), forward operating base operations, and practical leadership exercises involving various confidence courses with obstacles that challenge the student to overcome personal fears. The goal is to have officers graduate with greater confidence, a greater appreciation for the branches of the combined arms, and a clearer picture of their own personal strengths and weaknesses, officials said.

Sarah said BOLC was similar to the summers of military training she underwent while a cadet at West Point. "While it was not all that physically demanding, it is another opportunity to prepare for the future," she admitted. Lieutenant Gerstein completed the third and final phase of BOLC, the Military Intelligence branch technical course at Fort Huachuca, Arizona. Within six months of arriving at Fort Bragg and taken command of a platoon, Gerstein deployed to Iraq entering the war that four-and-a-half years ago seemed so far into the future.

The Gersteins celebrate Sarah's graduation from West Point, May 2007. Kathy, Rachel, Sarah and Dan. (*Photo courtesy of Kathy Gerstein*)

Second Lieutenants Joe Woods and Sarah Gerstein following graduation from the Basic Officer Leadership Course II. Joe and Sarah, West Point classmates have known each other since their 1st grade year. Joe's father is a 1980 West Point graduate and classmate of both Kathy and Dan Gerstein. (*Photo courtesy of Sarah Gerstein*)

EPILOGUE

America has been engaged in combat in Afghanistan and Iraq longer than in any previous war. By Thanksgiving 2010, U.S. troops will have been in Afghanistan longer than the Soviets were. Of those troops, some 220,000, or 11% of the deployed force, are women; an unprecedented 2% of the casualties are female.

Women have earned decorations for valor in combat, including the Silver Star. They have been killed, wounded and maimed. Women are routinely attached to (a military term of art with powerful legal implications) the same special operations and infantry units from which they are legally barred. Their performance created a database such as never existed before, of men and women serving together as military professionals. Servicewomen routinely do things that only a decade ago we were told were impossible for women to do, and even if the women could somehow perform at that level—the men weren't ready or willing to accept them fully as comrades-in-arms.

While working on this book, time—and the Long Gray Line—marches on. The members of the classes of 2008 and 2009 graduated from West Point and became Second Lieutenants in the U.S. Army. The class of 2008 graduated 988 cadets and included 152 women, and the class of 2009 included 149 women among the 993 cadets. These are the 28th and 29th classes to graduate women from the Military Academy. Of those who entered four years earlier, in both classes, 78% of the women graduated. This is a significant increase when compared to the 52% of entering women who graduated as members of the class of 1980.

Twenty-two members of the class of 2008 had prior combat experience (one of whom is a woman) having served as enlisted soldiers in Iraq or Afghanistan. The class of 2009 had 33 combat veterans of whom 4 are women. Secretary of the Army Pete Geren, the 2008 commencement speaker, told the graduates and their families, "There's always a personal cost in your profession of arms.

Your willingness to bear the cost ennobles you, your calling, and this gathering."[136] West Point graduates continue to serve our nation.

The vast majority of these new officers will lead soldiers in Iraq and Afghanistan within the next 18 months.

West Point is a place of challenges—physical, emotional, intellectual, mental, and spiritual—and changes. Every individual who graduates from the United States Military Academy does so as a changed person. They have changed because they have accepted the call to defend America's freedom. They have changed West Point, by leaving indelible marks on the institution and future members of the Long Gray Line.

In 1946, General Dwight D. Eisenhower, USMA Class of 1915, then Army Chief of Staff, wrote a letter to the then Superintendent of West Point, General Maxwell Taylor, USMA Class of 1922. He stated, "West Point gives its graduates something that far transcends the techniques and knowledge involved in developing, training, and leading an Army. It helps them build character." The changes experienced at West Point have all contributed to building the character Eisenhower referred to more than half a century ago.

Shortly after the graduation of the Class of 2008, Superintendent Lieutenant General Franklin L. Hagenbeck, USMA Class of 1971, announced changes to the words to the Academy's *Alma Mater* and a companion piece, *The Corps*. Every class since 1911 has sung these two songs in versions that refer to the "sons" and "men" of the Academy. The changes, which make the language gender-neutral, themselves are simple and few in number—six words in total, one in the alma mater, and five in *The Corps*. The changes are appropriate, given the current composition of the Corps of Cadets and its alumni body.

Lieutenant General Hagenbeck articulated his decision in a letter to all graduates:

---

[136] www.army.mil/-news/2008/06/02/9573-west-point-commencement-remarks-by-secretary-of-the-army-pete-geren/index.html 31 May 2008.

The realization that these songs explicitly exclude our women graduates–two of whom have given their lives in battle–was the driving force behind the changes, and it's simply the right thing to do.[137]

The Superintendent's decision provoked heated discussion on both sides of the issue. Among the graduates who shared their stories in this book, the reaction was split. Almost half agreed and said the changes were appropriate and timely. Some of them said they should have been made three decades ago. The other half did not support the changes, favoring the preservation of tradition. The latter believe the words belong to history and are part of the very granite of West Point. The controversy over the words demonstrates that West Point is a place that continues to build bridges to the future from a place where the past is always present.

Although the changes are minor, they carry enormous symbolism. They are a validation that women are contributing to the institution, the Army and the Nation. In the long term, most will forget that it was ever an issue, and those who do will look back with a sense of bewilderment, wondering why it was ever considered controversial.

A single chapter about a person provides a mere glimpse into a life. It is not a life's story. Two graduates who died in combat, stories of their service, courage, and sacrifice are missing from this collection, First Lieutenant Laura Walker in Afghanistan in 2005 and Second Lieutenant Emily Perez in Iraq in 2006. Their deaths are too recent and too painful and, therefore, not included. Along with many others, I look forward to their stories being told in the future. One family requested that their daughter's story not be included after reading a draft of her chapter. A second family did not respond to my requests to participate. I respect the positions that both families have taken.

---

[137] Lieutenant General Franklin L. Hagenbeck, letter to graduates and members of the West Point Association of Graduates, 2 June 2009.

The biographies of the women who shared their stories are a mere sample of the total. A recruiting poster for West Point states: "Much of the history we teach was made by people we taught." West Point's women are making history. While women may have changed the face of West Point, they have left untouched the ideals of duty, honor, country, and service to our Nation. The Long Gray Line marches on.

* * *

Since the Global War on Terror began, 77 West Point graduates have died in Afghanistan or Iraq.[138] Most of these fallen alumni were born in the 1980s and held the grade of first lieutenant, a rank achieved within 24 months of graduation. The death rate of graduates is "three times the percentage of graduate deaths in Vietnam, six times higher than what befell former cadets in the Second World War, and thirteen times the proportion of those killed in the First World War," reported Chris Smith of *New York Magazine*.[139]

---

[138] As of April 13, 2010. "In Memoriam," http://www.westpointaog.org/NetCommunity/Page.aspx?pid=734.

[139] "Intro to Warfare—preparing for graduation at West Point, where your first job is the front line." By Chris Smith. June 8, 2007, New York Magazine.

Cadet First Captain Kristen Baker, USMA 1990, leads the United States Corps of Cadets in her final parade, the Class of 1990 Graduation Parade, May 1990. Kristen Baker is the first woman to achieve the cadet rank of First Captain. (*USMA Archives*)

The 970 members of the class of 2009 toss their hats May 23 on the command "Class of 2009—dismissed" after listening to remarks from Superintendent Lt. Gen. Buster Hagenbeck and Defense Secretary Robert Gates and receiving their diplomas. *Photo and caption reprinted from May 28, 2009, Pointer View®. Photo by Eric Bartelt.*

Standing on the steps of Washington Hall in front of the Mess Hall, twenty-four women from the Class of 1980 returned to West Point for the West Point Women's Conference 30 Years Celebration, April 28, 2006. *Front row left to right:* Kathy Silvia, Jan Calhoun Meyers, Carol Barkalow, Anne McDonald, Lil Pfluke, Diane Bracey, Terry Walters, Robin Fennessey, Joan Smith Grey. *Second row left to right:* Brynnen Sheets Hahn, Vicki Martin Lundquist, Carol McGibbon, Mary Rosinski Whitley, Danna Maller, Kathy Wheless Gerstein, Susan Kellett-Forsyth, Donna Alesch White, Debbie Lewis. *Third row left to right:* Christi Stevens, Karen Kelly Stoner, Marene Allison, Nancy Gucwa, Sonya Nikituk, Kathy Gerard Snook. *(Photo courtesy of Diane Bracey)*

30 Years Celebration 2006 West Point Women's Conference 28 April 2006. Standing on the steps of Washington Hall in front of the Mess Hall. *Front row*: Donna (Matturro) McAleer '87, Tracy (Miller) Richardson '87, Tara (Miller) Feir '87. *Second row*: Jacqueline Stennett '90, Cynthia Lindenmeyer '90, Col. Heidi Brown '81. *Third row*: Dawn Halfaker '01, Bridget Altenburg '95, Nancy Hogan '95. (*Photo courtesy of Donna McAleer*)

WHERE THEY ARE TODAY ~ MARCH 2010

Brigadier General Rebecca "Becky" Halstead retired from active duty on June 27, 2008, in a ceremony held at West Point, having relinquished command as the Army's first female Chief of Ordnance the day prior. Retiring due to chronic health challenges, Becky spent the next 18 months regaining her quality of life. She serves as a spokesperson for The Foundation for Chiropractic Progress, and hopes to influence resourcing for the approved, full benefit of chiropractic care for all service members and veterans, especially wounded warriors. Becky serves on the Board of Directors for the West Point Association of Graduates. She credits West Point for her enduring passion for developing leaders of character. She founded her own company, "STEADFAST" Leadership, and specializes in inspirational speaking and developing leader-training programs. Becky is authoring her first book on leadership.

Brigadier General Heidi V. Brown is the Deputy Commanding General for Sustainment I Corps, Fort Lewis, Washington. She returned from Iraq in March 2010, where she served as the Deputy Commanding General for Sustainment, Multinational Corps Iraq. While in Iraq, Brigadier General Brown's primary mission was the development and execution of "The Responsible Drawdown of Forces and Equipment" which became the blueprint for the drawdown of U.S. forces from Iraq while maintaining security and stability operations in partnership with the Iraqi government. The RDOF is the largest reduction of equipment and personnel since WWII. Her responsibilities included Detainee Operations, Base Closure, and overseeing four Brigades (Engineers, Military Police, Signal, and Medical). Brown said, "This was truly one of the most interesting as well as the most important positions I have ever held with the most significant strategic outcome." Heidi is awaiting details on her next assignment.

Colonel Holly Olson, MD is the Director of Medical Education for Tripler Army Medical Center in Hawaii. She is responsible for 13 programs and more than 200 medical residents and continues to see patients, perform surgery, deliver babies, and teach residents. Her role gives her the opportunity to mentor faculty physicians and improve the care for service members and their families by fostering excellence in the various training programs. Brittany, her daughter, is a junior in college, and TJ, her son, is a junior in high school. Both are continuing to challenge and encourage their mother. Holly says, "They remain my greatest joy and remind me daily of what a great father and husband Rob was."

Lissa Young is in the fourth year of her doctoral program at Harvard University studying the History of Science with a focus on how war has shaped the discipline of Social Psychology. Her dissertation focuses on the role of the scholar in service to a nation state that is waging war. She is interested in answering the question: "If a scholar's expressed purpose is the pursuit of truth, then what the implied boundaries of her work, if it is in the service of the State?" Commissioned by the United States Army Research Institute to help soldiers learn to communicate more effectively with host nationals during deployments, Lissa developed curriculum that teaches the art of non-verbal communication and perspective taking. She conducts leader development workshops for the State of Connecticut's Department of Education. Upon completing her PhD, Lissa aspires to return to West Point and teach in the Department of Behavioral Sciences and Leadership. She hopes for judgment based on her merit, and no penalization due to her sexual orientation.

Lillian Pfluke continues to be active in the cancer-treatment community. She mentors cancer patients, especially athletes, to help them through their treatments and does motivational speaking about her experiences. She volunteers several times per week as a guide for blind cyclists and blind skiers. To celebrate the very end of her five years of tamoxifen[140], she and her son Raymond went back to the Alpe d'Huez for another epic climb. They used the ride as training for another crossing of the U.S. by bicycle, this time from Canada to Mexico along the Continental Divide. Her world record still stands. In 2008, Lil founded American War Memorials Overseas, Inc. This non-profit organization documents, promotes, and preserves overseas war memorials and gravesites where the U.S. government has no responsibility. Lillian says, "War Memorials commemorate our shared past, and overseas war memorials honoring Americans are an important symbol of America's international engagement."

Elizabeth Barron continues her work at the National Security Agency (NSA). She moved to Columbia, Maryland to enroll Jacob, now 12 years old, in a school with a newly established Academic Life Skills Program (ALS). Surrounded by children more developed than he, Jacob began the 6th grade in the fall of 2009. The progress he made in his later elementary school years and first year in middle school has been significant and encouraging. Jacob is more aware of his behavioral requirements (such as not screaming out loud or hitting others) and is progressing in his Individual Education Plan goals and Alternative-Maryland State Assessment testing. Many challenges remain ahead. Jacob has only begun to understand that letters make words, that one reads from left to right, or that time exists beyond the right now and the amorphous "later". Diagnosed with seizure disorder, significant spinal disorders, Autism, and having received new braces for his feet, Jacob is brave beyond his years and understanding. Betsy says, "I wonder and watch to try to get a sense of the vector he is on, so I can sandbag or pre-position or whatever, as needed, for what is in his future."

Chaplain Cynthia Lindenmeyer is completing her Doctorate in Ministry from Princeton University Theological Seminary with a focus on the spiritual community and faith of junior officers

---

[140] The gold standard of hormone therapy in breast cancer is tamoxifen.

deployed in Iraq and Afghanistan. Although no longer serving as a chaplain at West Point, Cynthia frequently enjoys officiating weddings of graduates. Sadly, she also conducts funerals for those she came to love dearly during her time at the Academy. Currently stationed at the Army War College with Vince, her husband, Cynthia teaches Spinning and Zumba classes, provides counseling through the Rape and Incest National Network (RAINN) online hotline, teaches Philosophy and Religion with American Military University (AMU), and coaches basketball. In the fall, as her daughter Carly enters fifth grade and her son Luke makes the leap from Kindergarten to first grade, Cynthia will return to full-time ministry leading a United Church of Christ congregation. Before her sabbatical is complete, she hopes to finish a fictional story that helps teach others about the value of diversity and the similarities in Judaism, Christianity, and Islam.

Nancy Hogan is a survivor and owes a lot of her strength to the support of her family and close friends. She is proud of the physical scars she has because of her surgeries and refers to the 36cm scar from her back surgery as her "lifeline." All are reminders that life is short, and not to waste a single day. She believes that everything happens for a reason and has brought her to where she is today. She would not change one thing about her life. Nancy hopes to settle down and have a family of her own someday, but only time will tell if that is meant to happen. In the meantime, she is enjoying being in love with a good man, spending quality time with family and friends, and remains passionate about her work on behalf of veterans. She left Paralyzed Veterans of America (PVA) at the end of 2008 and began work for the U.S. Senate Committee on Veterans' Affairs as one of the majority staff's Health and Benefits Council. Nancy handles issues facing the fastest growing segment of veterans—women. She is a mentor in the West Point Wounded Warrior Mentor Program assisting individual wounded warriors at Walter Reed. Ten years and three months after her accident, Nancy returned to the air to face her fear. Along with a member of the

Golden Knights, she exited an aircraft for a tandem parachute jump at 13,500 feet. This time she landed on her feet and walked off the drop zone saying, "That's the way it's supposed to go."

Kathy Gerstein is still working as a Department of the Army government civilian for the Natick Soldier Research, Engineering, and Development Center (NSRDEC). She is the Science and Technology Liaison to Program Executive Office for Soldier programs at Fort Belvoir, VA. In this role, she is the liaison to the Chief Scientist of the Army, and provides him advice regarding the overall direction and progress of the S&T program for Natick, which does the soldier programs of food, airdrop, and body armor. In 2009, Kathy earned a Masters in Program Management from the Naval Post Graduate School and Dan, her husband, earned his Ph.D in Biodefense. Sarah, her oldest daughter, returned from Iraq in 2008 and deploys to Afghanistan the summer of 2010. Rachel, her youngest daughter, graduated from the University of Mary Washington in Fredericksburg, VA in 2009. She works as a government contractor supporting the Army G-1.

Jackie Stennett is a social entrepreneur, currently serving as the Vice President and board member of AcademyWomen, an organization dedicated to supporting the professional and personal development of all current, former, and future U.S. women military officers. In 2008, she played a key role in launching a Navy-wide mentoring initiative for servicewomen. She serves on the academic advisory board of *LeadAmerica*, a national youth leadership organization dedicated to inspiring and empowering young people to achieve their full potential and to instill in them a sense of purpose, integrity, self-confidence, and personal responsibility. Jackie has not relinquished her vision of building a premier leadership and college-prep academy for underserved youth. She realizes that her first priority must always be to her daughter and has deferred this remarkable dream while attending to the significant task of parenting...for the moment. Until then, Jackie continues to serve her nation with pride in helping to build organizations that serve the common good and the common people. Marjorie Stennett, true to her own creed regarding the value of an education, earned her Bachelor's degree in Business Administration in 1991 at the age of 50, the same year her older daughter graduated from Boston College law school and the year after Jackie's graduation from West Point. Now retired, Marjorie enjoys time spent with her grandchildren...who are constantly reminded by her of the value of a good education.

Bridget Altenburg became the Director of Development for the Academy for Urban School Leadership (AUSL), a Chicago based non-profit in April 2008. As the nation's leading school turnaround operator, AUSL trains teachers in the "West Point" of teacher training programs. They then place teams of teachers in chronically failing Chicago schools as part of a whole school transformation model. AUSL manages 18 schools, including 12 turnaround schools with plans to take over more schools every year. Bridget said, "It's humbling work to be surrounded by people who are passionate about making a difference for children who have been left behind by failing schools. Every day I come to work eager to do my part to make a difference in public education." Bridget continues to fight for the repeal of *"Don't Ask, Don't Tell"*. She and her partner are expecting their first child in August 2010.

Anita Allen graduated from the Mendoza School of Business at the University of Notre Dame in South Bend, Indiana, in 2009. She earned a Masters in Business Administration with a concentration in finance. During her time at school, she was a volunteer coach with the Notre Dame Women's cross country and track teams. She continues to volunteer her time with various youth development organizations and serves on the board of directors for the USA Pentathlon National Governing Body.

Dawn Halfaker continues to build her company in Washington, D.C. Since incorporating Halfaker and Associates in 2006, the company has grown to 135 employees and more than $10 million in revenues. Dawn completed her Masters in Security Studies at Georgetown University in 2009. In addition to running her company, Dawn remains active in veteran's affairs, serving on the board of several service organizations and advisory committees. She is the Vice President of the Wounded Warrior Project Board of Directors, which focuses on raising awareness and enlisting the public's aid for the needs of severely injured service men and women in addition to helping these same service members recover and readjust. The Secretary of Veterans Affairs appointed Dawn to serve on the Committee for Operation Iraqi Freedom/Operation Enduring Freedom soldiers and families that focuses on improving VA policies and care for severely injured combat veterans as well as their families who care for them.

First Lieutenant Sarah Gerstein redeployed from Iraq to Fort Bragg, North Carolina in December 2008, and continued as a platoon leader until the following summer. She is currently an executive officer at the Headquarters Company for a Military Intelligence Battalion and will be moving to S-3 as the Plans Officer just prior to a scheduled deployment to Afghanistan with her unit in the summer of 2010. Sarah is midway through active duty service obligation to the Army and remains undecided about whether she will pursue a career.

AFTERWORD

MOTHERS, DAUGHTERS, AND SOLDIERS

In its simplest definition, motherhood as defined within U.S. culture is both a biological or adoptive relationship to a child and an emotional or sociological responsibility to care adequately for that child. In the U.S., we have added many significant purposes to motherhood, including the expectation that we will raise our children to be well-intentioned, conscientious adults and productive, contributing citizens. A mother nurtures, loves, feeds, clothes, protects, educates, disciplines and guides her child. She works for her family, a calling most often defined by selflessness and love.

By contrast, the military is a vocation whose core business is to deter or fight wars. The U.S. armed forces work directly for the U.S. government and operate in the pursuit of political objectives determined by a democratically elected civilian leadership. In the broadest sense, "the U.S. military is one of several instruments of national policy maintained to help shape the international political environment in support of U.S. interest."[141] The military is charged with training its soldiers to kill and possibly die for the nation when ordered into battle. It is a profession like no other; one that it is distinguished by death and destruction.

A mother's mission directly and thoroughly conflicts with the duty of a soldier called to war. As a daughter, while in the Army, I was blissfully ignorant of this inherent tension and conflict, and my own mother's feelings. Now, as the mother of a daughter, I am acutely aware of the future possibility of a child's desire to enter the military, and its call to service.

During Memorial Day 2009, I learned just how conflicted my own mother, Anna Matturro, must have been supporting my decision to become a soldier. She wrote:

---

[141] Admiral Mike Mullen, "Capstone for Joint Operations," ed. Department of Defense (Washington, DC: United States Joint Forces Command, 2009).

For me, Memorial Day marks a special day and brings back memories that run an array of deep emotions. A few years ago, I had the privilege of being at the bedside of several men who were on end of life comfort care. These men had valiantly fought in World War II. Listening to parts of their stories brought back areas of trauma in my own early life. Each of these individuals, including me, was trying to find their peace with horrific events from a long time ago that affected their entire adult lives. The importance of validating one's personal story can never be underestimated. As a Chaplain, I was not only gifted by their stories but shared mutual healing.

My experience as a refugee, who escaped to Austria from war torn Hungary, and being a displaced person for five years until finally allowed entry into America through New York Harbor and the Statue of Liberty, was an incredible journey. In those intimate moments of mutual sharing, I was given the opportunity to express my heartfelt gratitude for their part in bringing me to safety, a new life, and eventually to United States citizenship. I still feel the poignancy of those moments, the smiles, tears, peace, and gratitude between us. I have a special place in my heart for those I am ever so grateful to. Thank you, this Memorial Day, to Veterans of all wars and to those currently serving throughout the world.[142]

I want my daughter to grow up accepting responsibility for her actions and embracing the ideals that West Point and the military uphold—duty, honor, and country. I hope to raise a child who is mentally and physically acute and tough, independent and

---

[142] Anna Matturro, Chaplain NACC, Health Care Minister at Holy Family Parish, Cape Ann, MA. Weekly Bulletin, May 25, 2009.

adventurous, compassionate and caring, humble and selfless, and a role model. As she matures, I want her to experience a variety of challenges, develop relationship-building skills and collaborate well on teams. I hope that she will become a critical and creative thinker who is able to make decisions without having all the information, and I want her to develop a passion for hard work and the ability to deliver results. I want her to live and love. Achievement of all of these aspirations is highly probable with military training and service.

No matter how noble the profession of arms, the courage and strength of selfless service, and the weight of parental pride, however, it is impossible to quell the fear for a child heading into war or that of the possibility of returning home in a body bag. When your child serves, there is the risk that the remains of a mother's hopes and dreams for their son or daughter, is only a coffin, a headstone, a precisely folded flag, grief and an obliterated heart.

This knowledge and these risks aside, I want my daughter to always make her own decisions. I will deeply respect and support whatever choice she makes regarding military service. She will always remain my daughter, whether a soldier, a mother, or both. I pray, however, she will never have to fight in a war. I wish this for her and me, and for the world in which we live.

Donna and Carlyn McAleer.
(Photo by Michael P. Flaherty)

ACKNOWLEDGEMENTS

West Point has always held meaning and purpose in my life. Not a day passes without a thought of this most special place on the bend of the Hudson River. My bedrock of values developed in its halls. West Point continues to protect American freedoms by producing leaders with character for our Army and great country. West Point engendered life-long friendships for me that were forged in the hot fire of my cadet years and solidified into steel.

Much has been written about the stone buildings of the garrison of West Point, for they represent the core of the history of USMA; often, the structures are referred to as the character of the Academy. While the buildings and other artifacts reveal the history and embody the physicality of West Point, clearly the graduates are its heart and soul. And that is what I wanted to write about—the embodiment of all that West Point "is"—is manifested by those who have walked its halls, endured the crucible and became something unique, a West Point graduate and Army officer.

As I embarked on this writing journey, I quickly collected more stories than I could possibly tell. Six years into the process, I have touched only the surface. This book is a work of non-fiction. I spent hundreds of hours in formal interviews and informal conversations with graduates, faculty, staff, family members and others who served and worked with these women.

My largest debt of gratitude is to each graduate who shared their personal experiences in hopes that others derive relevant lessons or motivation to become better people. Individual chapters spring from interviews with women from 28 graduated classes beginning in 1980–the first class to graduate women–primary source documents and conventional histories. I took copious notes throughout the research phase and relied on various printed and on-line sources. Aside from one person, a non-central figure, in one chapter, no names have been changed. The women featured in the book have all been privy to its content. Any mistakes are mine.

No book of this type is ever written alone by the author. Most books (and this one certainly falls into this category) come to fruition thanks to countless friends, family, mentors, and professionals who believe in the idea, and provide and give freely (literally) endless amounts of support, encouragement, advice and even a few swift kicks in the butt. First and foremost in line for thanks, is my mom, Anna Nagy Matturro. From the original idea for the book through each draft, and every chapter (and that goes on in between), she provided unconditional encouragement. Telling me to "get it done" echoed her same encouraging words throughout my four years at West Point.

The Long Gray Line is in the present, stretches into the future and extends back more than two centuries. It is a stalwart chain, whose members contributed incalculable hours, and expert and priceless advice to the completion of this collection. Ed Ruggero '80 shared his knowledge, experience, and counsel from day two of this endeavor. He became my mentor and friend. Lt. Col. (retired) Jay Olenjencik '61 and Col. (retired) John Calabro '68 edited each page with precision, wisdom, and steadfast guidance. Lt. Gen. (retired) Bill Lennox '71, Superintendent of West Point 2002-2006, supported my concept from the outset. Dan Shea '84 who introduced me to McSorley's Old Ale House and took me there for the first time. Dan's unwavering encouragement and friendship kept me focused on the project's goal. Kevin Stringer '87 reminded me of the importance of telling these graduates' stories and helped tighten each chapter. Dr. Stephen Grove, Historian, United States Military Academy, provided much of the information about the history of women at the Military Academy. Diane Bracey '80 indulged me throughout with frequent conversations and questions over beers, bike rides, ski runs and chairlift rides sharing her experiences and "Old Corps" stories about West Point. She loaned me, for four years, her copy of *Stronger than Custom* by Lance Janda. Michael Pratt '87, in the midst of starting two companies, always had time for a conversation and additional instruction in using technology and social networking to promote this work. Always candid, he kept me thinking strategically and critically, and somehow found the time to create the *Porcelain on Steel* website. Guillermo Rivera '84, while working on his own first book, *The Search for Balboa*, provided sound advice, thoughtful feedback, and many remembrances.

Jeanne and Jack Green '46 introduced me to West Point when I was a sophomore in high school. Jack, a two-time All-American guard and captain of Army's 1945 National Championship football team, inspired me to apply to West Point. Sadly, Jack died of a brain tumor prior to my appointment my senior year in high school. He was 57. Jeanne has remained unwavering in her encouragement and support. Following my West Point graduation, Jeanne gave me the Navy bathrobe Jack received from Navy's football captain following Army's win over Navy in 1945. Dr. Sue Tendy has been a coach and mentor since my own "R-day" on July 1, 1983. Arriving at West Point in 1977 as a professor in the department of Physical Education, Sue is the only faculty member who has seen every woman graduate West Point. During my own cadets days in the mid-1980's, Dr. Tendy was one of six women on West Point's faculty and staff.

Dr. Nate Zinsser, "Doc Z", with whom my relationship began as an aspiring bobsled athlete seeking a competitive edge and a sports psychology coach. He put my mental muscles through a demanding regimen. He taught me that visualization is a skill that responds well to practice and that atrophies with disuse. He remains a coach, mentor and dear friend.

Shirley Sabel, Information Technology Specialist at West Point's Office of Policy, Planning and Analysis, kept me armed with all graduation data. Brad Bond scanned photos for this book. Julie Glusker, my dear friend in Park City, ran with me literally and metaphorically throughout this journey and shared writing and editing expertise and ideas. Barbara Bretz, president of the Park City Library Foundation who provided the opportunity to share with 150 people from my own community, my desire and contribution to the body of knowledge about the importance of strong women role models. Michael P. Flaherty for all of the photo shoots and good cheer. Sara Remke, my high school friend and talented graphic artist, designed the *Porcelain on Steel* logo and original jacket, and always had a laugh to share. Whitney Brazell (www.whitneybrazell.com), the graphic designer whose unique sense for creating a nuanced visual metaphor based on my writings, is a rare talent. In designing the current cover, she nailed it.

In completing this book, I accrued many other debts. I owe gratitude to countless mentors, colleagues, and family members. Joe Matturro, my father, for his unconditional confidence. John Ciarlo '87 heard of my endeavor, read a very early draft, offered candid critique and introduced me to my literary agent, Michele Rubin from Writer's House. Michele's belief in diverse experiences and counsel strengthened the writing in countless ways. Hes Sue Park '87 introduced me to Dennis Lowery and Jim Zumwalt, co-founders of Fortis Publishing. Perhaps inappropriate, but I have ceased to think of Dennis and Jim as my publishers. These two great patriots, despite their distinct Navy and Marine heritages, have become sources of wisdom, counsel, laughter, and dear friendship.

Finally, I am grateful to Ted McAleer '87, my classmate and spouse, for his patience in supporting my "time-off" to pursue this endeavor and to teach skiing, my other passion; to Carlyn Ann, my daughter, for repeatedly asking me about the stories and when I would find a publisher, and Col. (retired) Thayer, my faithful, four-legged companion, who ran many miles with me and sat at my feet while I wrote.

Some people come into our lives and quickly go.
Some people move our souls to dance. They awaken us to new
understanding with the passing whisper of their wisdom.
Some people make the sky more beautiful to gaze upon. They
stay in our lives for awhile, leave footprints on our hearts,
and we are never ever the same.
—Flavia Weedn

THE AESTHETIC OF PORCELAIN ON STEEL

ABOUT THE TITLE & COVER

The title Porcelain on Steel: Women of West Point's Long Gray Line hails from the artistic works of Tara Krause, West Point Class of 1982 and her uniquely crafted sculptures, "Women Soar: Porcelain on Steel", created to honor fallen warrior sisters.

"Lladro meets Brancusi" is Tara's description of the maquettes. Lladro brothers Juan, Jose, and Vicente from Valencia, Spain whose family name became synonymous with porcelain figurines with crystalline finishes and the pastel tonalities, and Constantin Brancusi's breakthrough "Bird In Space" sculpture. Brancusi was a Romanian born sculptor and pioneer of abstraction who concentrated on the movement of the bird rather than on its physical attributes. The bird's wings and feathers are eliminated, the swell of the body is elongated, and the head and beak are compacted to a slanted oval plane. Brancusi's stated intent was "to capture the essence of flight." Some describe "Bird In Space" as sensual and feminine; others describe the sculpture as phallic and symbolic of masculinity.

Tara explained her own artistic process as an interesting dance of seeing how thinly delicate porcelain, wet clay in its most basic form, could be extruded and then draped and shaped over steel so that it would be strong enough to survive the intense heat of the kiln.

Porcelain is a strong, vitreous, translucent ceramic material often used in the making of fine china. Steel is a hard, strong, durable and adaptable alloy of iron and carbon. It is ubiquitously used as a structural material in buildings as well as plowshares and swords. As an adjective, steel is suggestive of such character qualities as hard and unflinching. The two materials, porcelain and steel, honor the beauty and foundational strength of West Point women.

Coming up with a cover that comprised the above elements was almost as challenging as writing the book. How to balance seeming disparate parts and create a cover that represents the complexity of those parts was difficult. The graphic designer, Whitney Brazzell's, unique sense for creating a nuanced visual metaphor based on what I wrote is a rare talent.

The background's rough texture denotes how hard a journey it was for the women profiled in the book. West Point isn't easy. Military service for both genders is not easy. The flag very quietly, waves in the back, but is always present—especially to veterans. It, coupled with that rough background, shows that serving your country is equally hard. Ask any veteran, especially those who served or currently serve in combat.

Pallas Athena depicts the hard determination of women who serve in the military—and the warrior ethos inculcated in all West Point graduates—she is iconic. Her raised arm beckoning to serve the flag and to understand the nature and obligation of such service—and perhaps an invitation to read the book and learn more about some truly remarkable women, who have much in common with you and me (an invitation we hope many people accept).

The smooth curves and whiteness of the title lettering—akin to the smooth, fine china, coolness of porcelain. It rides on top of all that we mentioned above. A strong, stern inside wrapped in a delicate, beautiful exterior. Simple, but complex...as many important principles are.

Like one of the tools that Tara Krause uses in creating her art, West Point too is a kiln of sorts. A four-year leadership crucible of intense heat and pressure, whose mission is to produce leaders of character committed to the values of Duty, Honor, Country, and prepared for careers of professional excellence and service to the Nation as officers in the United States Army.

THE FOLD OF THE BRIGHT-EYED—ATHENA EXPLAINED

Pallas Athena, the beautiful Greek goddess of war and wisdom, combines the martial and the feminine. A provocative mating of seemingly opposite yet related attributes highlights the power and grace explored in the myths of Athena. This juxtaposition of strength and femininity makes Athena the choice for the cover of *Porcelain on Steel*.

Athena's physical beauty mirrored the inner. Her helmet, signifying wisdom and learning, reveals the lines of an elegant yet determined face when pushed back from her brow. Known more for her role as judge, diplomat, and mediator than for actually fighting in battle her decisions were renowned for their fairness and compassion. As a war goddess, her presence on the battlefield meant the contest would be decided by sound strategy, cool courage, and military competence rather than by brute force and unrestrained carnage. She fought with integrity, purpose and justice.

Athena plays a prominent role at West Point. The distinctive unit crest of West Point consists of her helmet and sword. All military faculty and cadets wear a modest Velcro patch on their left shoulder with the Army Combat Uniform. Cadets wear the crest on their class uniforms with varied colored insignia depending on class year. This pose of Athena is derived from a bas-relief statue, standing 18-feet tall, on the old library of West Point. Sculpted by Lee Lawrie, (perhaps the 20th century's most famous architectural sculptor)– Athena was his last commission; he died shortly after its completion in 1963.

West Point women embody the traits and qualities Pallas Athena represents. In their own right, leaders who beget leaders belong to the fold of "the bright-eyed", goddess of wisdom, warfare and martial craft. The trajectories of West Point Women graduates began with strong, insightful and inspiring contributions and coaching in their aim to ensure the successful integration of women...and the integration of successful women. They are the bright-eyed Athenas of today in this mortal world and of the generations to come.

* * *

In December 1975, a team of West Point researchers initiated "Project Athena" to compile an institutional history and database of the admission of women. The longitudinal study became a four-volume source for scholars studying gender integration.

Glossary

AA	Air Assault; an Army qualification to rappel from helicopters that may be earned by cadets.
AAA	Anti-aircraft Artillery
ABN	Airborne; an Army qualification to jump out of moving aircraft and land safely that may be earned by cadets.
ACU	Army Combat Uniform which succeeded the BATTLE DRESS UNIFORM (BDU).
AFC	As for Class
AI	Additional Instruction
AIAD	Additional academic programs of Individual Advanced Development, such as foreign language, public policy, public administration, and international relations. They are usually related to a cadet's major and are offered during the summer leave period.
A.M.I	Morning inspection; Ante Meridiem (AM).
AO	Area of Operation. Slang for "the immediate area".
APFT	Army Physical Fitness Test
Area Bird	A cadet who is obliged to serve punishment by walking back and forth in uniform, under arms, in the Central Area.
Area Tour	An assigned period of punishment in hour long increments.
Army Brat	The son or daughter of a career Army soldier.
Arty	Artillery; a branch specialization in the U.S. Army.
ASAP	(Pronounced as a word, *ae-sap*): As Soon As Possible; at once, immediately.
As you were	The command to disregard the previous statement of the speaker. The literal meaning is "as you were before the last statement or command was issued."
A squad	Cadet varsity intercollegiate team.
Ate up	In disarray or dishevelment.
AUTHOS	Authorization; permission to miss drill or other company training.
AWOL	Absent Without Leave
Balloon goes up	A saying that refers to the moment a war or battle begins. Possibly originated from the barrage balloons used in World Wars I and II to protect cities from air raids. When the balloons went up, it meant a bombing raid was about to begin.
BCT	Basic Cadet Training; cadet boot camp.
BDU	Battle Dress Uniform

Beanhead	Slang for a NEW CADET or PLEBE. Possibly originated from a new cadet's head that, when shaved, resembles a bean.
Beast	Slang for basic cadet training derived from pronouncing the acronym "BCT" as a word.
Beast Barracks	The location for basic training.
Beat the Dean	To pass an academic test.
Big bites	Slang for putting a larger than normal-sized portion of food on the fork when eating.
Big brass rocket	A specific cheer during sporting events led by the Superintendent, Commandant or Dean.
BJ	Bold before June. Fresh or lacking in respect; derived from the time when PLEBE recognition was the day before June graduation.
Black Group	The fastest ability group of the three running groups during Cadet Basic Training.
Blow Off	To dismiss something; to ignore or not to worry about something, as "He blew off the assignment."
Blow Post	To depart post without permission.
Blues	Army dress blue uniform.
Blue Suiter	An Army officer wearing the blue uniform.
Bogus	Uncalled for, audacious.
Bone	To study or strive for achievement.
Boodle	Any kind of sweet treat such as cake, cookies, candy, ice cream, etc.
Boodler's	The cadet snack store.
BPP	Blow Post Privileges; to go AWOL.
Brainiac	The merging of 'brain' and 'maniac' to describe an intelligent person or one who learns quickly.
Brass	The insignia worn by upperclassman to designate their class year at the Academy. FIRST CLASSMEN wear black, SECOND CLASSMEN wear gray, THIRD CLASSMEN wear yellow, and FOURTH CLASSMEN wear none. Brass also refers to high ranking officers.
BTO	Brigade Tactical Officer
Bugle Notes	A pocket-sized handbook containing historical West Point trivia, quotations, historical and general information about West Point and the Army for recitation. Also known as the "PLEBE Bible." The information contained is called "PLEBE KNOWLEDGE".
Bust	To reduce in rank as the result of a misconduct proceeding; to revoke the appointment of a cadet.

Butt	The remains of anything; the remaining portion of any whole as the butt of a month, the butt of a tour, or the butt of a cigarette.
Butter bar	A second lieutenant, often new and inexperienced, so called because the rank is designated by a single gold bar.
C-130	Military aircraft used to transport equipment or soldiers. One of the aircraft soldiers jump from during AIRBORNE school.
Cadet	A subaltern in a training, such as a PLEBE, Midshipman, or Doolie; literally meaning "small head", as the younger son of a headman, chieftain, captain, or nobleman
Cadet in Charge of Quarters (CCQ or CQ)	An upperclass cadet whose duty for the day is to sit at a desk outside the orderly room and answer the telephone, relay messages, and guard the barracks.
Cadidiot	Derogatory term for cadets of West Point or ROTC derived by merging of 'cadet' and 'idiot'.
Camo	Camouflage
Camp Buckner	Field training area near the USMA Military Reservation and named after General Simon Bolivar Buckner, West Point Class of 1908. It is also the eight-week military training camp for all THIRD CLASSMEN.
Cannon cocker	Someone who is in the Field Artillery branch.
Carry on	To resume activity, to go about your business.
CBT	Cadet Basic Training. A summer leadership assignment for upperclass cadets.
CDLT	Cadet Drill Leader Training, a 30-day summer leadership course option for a subaltern (or "third lieutenant") with an active duty Army basic training unit.
CFT	Cadet Field Training, an 8-week summer course at Camp Buckner; also a leadership assignment for upperclass cadets
Charlie Mike	Phonetic alphabet for the initial letters of Continue-the-Mission.
Chow	Mealtime; food served in military facilities.
Civvies	Civilian clothes
Class godson	In the honorary tradition of primogeniture, the first son born to a member of the class after graduation.
Classmen	Divided into FIRSTIE, a first classman or senior; COW, a second classman or junior; YEARLING / YUK, a third classman or sophomore; PLEBE, a fourth classman or freshman; NEW CADET (i.e., during CBT).
CME	Department of Civil and Mechanical Engineering

CO	Commanding Officer typically used to refer to the Company Commander.
Coastie	Any member of the Coast Guard Academy (USCGA)
Cold	Absolutely without error, as in "a cold max"
Combat Medical Badge	A badge awarded to any member of the Army Medical Department, at the rank of Colonel or below, who is assigned or attached to a medical unit (company or smaller size) which provides medical support to a ground combat arms unit during any period in which the unit was engaged in active ground combat.
COMM/COM	The Commandant of Cadets
Commo	Signals communication, especially by radio
Company	A unit of approximately 120-140 soldiers or cadets, consisting of four platoons.
COR	Cadet Observation Report
Corps of Cadets	The student body of West Point.
Corps squader	A varsity or junior varsity National Collegiate Athletics Association (NCAA) athlete.
Corps whore	A civilian female who has dated several different male cadets.
Cow	A member of the second class; a junior [allegedly derived from cadet resemblance to bloated bovines and/or cows coming home]
CPR	Cadet Performance Report
Crab	One who attends the Naval Academy (USNA); a Midshipman
Crossed idiot sticks	Infantry branch insignia
C-store	Cadet store
CTLT	Cadet Troop Leader Training, a 30-day summer leadership course option for a subaltern (or "third lieutenant") with an active duty Army unit.
D	Deficient; below average, as in academics.
The Days	Required knowledge for PLEBES; signifying the duration to the next major event for the upperclass, and "a finite number for the end of eternity" for PLEBES.
Death from above	Catchphrase for the AIRBORNE doctrine of vertical envelopment.
Death from within	Catchphrase for food prepared and served in military facilities.
Deuce-and-a-half	A two-and-a-half ton truck used to transport military supplies or troops.

DFL	Department of Foreign Languages
DI	Drill Instructor
Dick	To look out for oneself at the expense of others; to take advantage of.
Digitals	Camouflage uniform
Dirt	The core geography class taken by THIRD CLASSMEN/YEARLINGS.
Dirt department	Department of Geography
DMI	Department of Military Instruction
Donkey dick	The fuzzy black plume on the full dress hat.
DPE	Department of Physical Education
DPE&A	Department of Physical Education and Athletics
Drag	A young lady whom a male cadet is escorting.
Dress Right	Perfectly ordered; correct
Dress Right, Dress	The command for all soldiers within a formation to align themselves with the soldier on their right.
Drop	The command to get into the front leaning rest position, the push-up position.
Elephant	An ungainly or graceless cadet who cannot dance, especially one compelled to take lessons.
EM	Enlisted Man/Men, assigned as staff
Emerging leader	A cadet who earns a high position of leadership; usually used sarcastically.
Engineer	One who is ranked high academically, a cadet in the upper section in academic work. Corps of Engineers, a branch specialization in the U.S. Army.
E-tool	Entrenching tool. A small folding shovel about two feet long, carried by soldiers. Designed primarily to dig fighting holes it is also used to dig latrines, bunkers, and firing pits.
FA	Field Artillery; a branch specialization in the U.S. Army.
Fall out	The command for dismissing soldiers from a formation; to relax or disperse. Also used to describe someone lagging behind or not completing a run or ruck sack march.
Fashion show	A form of harassment or punishment wherein the cadet dons, in rapid succession as directed for inspection, each piece of ones complete uniforms, fatigue or dress, summer or winter, including field gear.
Fatigue tour	One hour of punishment
FD	Full Dress Uniform
Find	To discharge a cadet for deficiency in studies, conduct or honor.

First Captain	The highest rank cadet who commands the CORPS OF CADETS.
Firstie	A member of the first class; a senior
First Sergeant	The company commander's chief assistant, responsible for unit accountability and administration; the highest-ranking sergeant in a company-sized unit.
500th Night	A celebration on the Saturday closest to five hundred nights before graduation; a banquet and dance during second class (junior) year.
Flirtie	Flirtation Walk; the scenic walk where only cadets and their escorted guests may go.
Floater	A person without a table at a meal who stands under the poop-deck waiting to be seated.
Fourth Classman	A PLEBE or freshman at West Point.
Fried egg	Insignia of West Point, worn on the service hat or parade tar bucket.
Geek	An intelligent person or one who learns quickly, especially regarding technical matters.
Get Over	A person who consistently doesn't pull his or her own weight or tries to get by with a minimum effort.
Ghost	A Fourth Class cadet who hides in his/her room to avoid the upperclass or to shirk duties; also refers to an upperclass cadet who is rarely seen around a cadet company.
GI	Government Issue; property of the U.S. government (not to be used when referring to enlisted personnel).
Goat	A cadet in the lower academic sections; a cadet near the bottom of the class; the lowest ranking cadet on graduation day.
Going black	Shutting down or closing down, by analogy to a computer shutdown.
Gouge	Reliable information
Gray hog	An extremely West Point oriented cadet.
Gray Matter	A brief, weekly e-mail newsletter on West Point, its cadets and graduates.
Gray Wings	Earned when a male cadet sleeps with a female cadet; carnal knowledge of a female cadet.
Green girl	Comforter on cadet bed
Gray Trou	Cadet uniform pants; a pejorative reference to a female cadet.
Greens	Army Class-A uniform worn by staff, commissioned and enlisted.

Green-suiter	An Army officer, NCO, or Enlisted soldier wearing the green Class-A uniform.
Gross	Blundering; disgusting
Held report	Explanation of report
Hell Cats	Military musicians who sound reveille and the parade calls.
Hive	A cadet ranked in the upper 5% of their class academically; a cadet in the upper section in academic work; one who is well up in studies [v: urticaria].
Hooah	An enthusiastic response meaning 'yes' or 'I understand'. 1. A guttural grunt used by people in the military to show motivation or excitement. Slang for anything except "no." Also, the primary method for soldiers to emphatically affirm or agree with a speaker (e.g., Amen! Yes! Great!). 2. Used as an adjective it means motivated, tough, hard-charging.
Hop	Cadet dance; compulsory training in etiquette and socialization
Hotel night	The one night a week when a cadet sleeps in their ones bed sheets. The sheets are 'broken down' due to laundry send-out the following day.
Hours	A punishment served by a cadet by walking with their rifle or saber in Central Area on a weekend.
Hudson High	Sardonic reference to West Point.
Hudson theta	Derived from the location of West Point on the Hudson River, and the Greek letter Theta's use as a symbol of a plane angle in geometry.
IAD	Individual Advanced Development, including MIAD, PIAD, AIAD
IKE	Eisenhower Barracks or Eisenhower Hall
Ikette	A female who frequents Eisenhower Hall for the sole purpose of picking up a helpless male cadet; a woman who's impressed only by the "man in uniform" image.
IOCT	Indoor Obstacle Course Test
IRP	Immediate Response, Please
Jody	Slang for a boy back home who is dating a soldier's girlfriend. A name often used in cadences.
Juice	Electricity; Electrical Engineering
Junior Bird Man	One who attends the Air Force Academy (USAFA); Doolie
Kickin' the Dean's butt	To do well on a test or assignment
Knowledge	Information that all PLEBES must be able to recite to upperclassmen.

Late lights	Cadet room lights on after midnight
Limits	The boundaries on the reservation to which cadets are restricted.
Long Gray Line	A metaphor for the CORPS OF CADETS and West Point graduates, from the inception of West Point into the indefinite future.
M-14	The primary rifle used by Army between World War II and Vietnam. Currently the M-14 is used at West Point for drill and ceremony.
Man in the Red Sash	The first upperclass cadet to whom NEW CADETS must report during CADET BASIC TRAINING; designated by a scarlet sash worn around the waist.
Mac	MacArthur Barracks named in honor of General Douglas MacArthur, West Point Class of 1903.
Max	Maximum; a complete success, as to make a perfect mark in academic recitation, or to do something perfectly
Meals Rejected by Everyone	Restatement of Meals Ready to Eat (MRE), a field ration
Medevac	Medical evacuation to remove wounded soldiers from an area by helicopter, military aircraft or ambulance.
MIAD	Military programs of Individual Advanced Development, such as AIRBORNE, AIR ASSAULT, SAPPER, and SERE.
Middie	One who attends the Naval Academy (USNA); Midshipman
Military Time	Time of day using a 24-hour clock. The day begins one minute after midnight (12:01 AM) written as 0001.
Minutes	The time remaining before a formation or inspection.
Missouri National	A tune supposedly to bring rain; normally sung before parades in hopes of cancellation
Mister Jackson	Given name of the mule that serves as the Army mascot
NCO	Noncommissioned Officer, assigned as staff.
New Cadet	A cadet who is not yet officially recognized as a member of the CORPS OF CADETS (i.e., during CBT).
Non-Com	Informal for noncommissioned officer
OAO	One And Only; significant other; sweetheart, steady, betrothed, or a fiancée.
OC	Officer in Charge; a commissioned officer from the Department of Tactics serving as the Officer of the Day.
OD	Olive Drab; also, Officer of the Day.
Odin	A Norwegian god to whom cadet's appeal for supernatural intervention (e.g., rain before parades, inspector boredom or blindness, invisibility to upperclass, etc.)

OPP	Off Post Privileges; authorized absence.
Old Corps	The way things used to be at West Point (e.g., "When dinosaurs roamed the plain..."; in reality, when the FIRSTIES were PLEBES)
Old Grad	One who has graduated from West Point.
100th Night	A celebration on the Friday and Saturday closest to 100 nights before graduation; the final class event during first (senior) year, including parodies and skits of classes.
P	A professor; academic instructor; the teacher of a course or subject.
PDA	Public Display of Affection; also, a Personal Digital Assistant (e.g., Palm Pilot, Blackberry).
PIAD	Physical programs of Individual Advanced Development, such as scuba and rock climbing
Phonetic alphabet	A standardized system of words spoken in place of each letter of the alphabet. Used during oral communication to clearly distinguish and minimize confusion among letters of the alphabet.
Ping	The quick pace for a PLEBE to walk (180 steps per minute).
Pip	An emblem of emulated rank or a badge of office bestowed upon subalterns in military training, especially ROTC.
Plebe	A cadet of the fourth class; a freshman [v: pleb, plebeian].
Plebe Bible	*BUGLE NOTES*, the handbook of the CORPS OF CADETS.
Platoon	A unit of approximately 30 to 40 soldiers or cadets, consisting of four squads.
PMI	Afternoon inspection; Post Meridiem.
Pointer View	Weekly publication about cadet life and activities.
Police	To clean up, straighten up, or discard.
Poop	Information to be memorized.
Poop-deck	The balcony in the West Point Cadet Mess from which orders are published (ie: read aloud to the CORPS OF CADETS).
Poop-sheet	A page of information.
Poopster	A USMAPS candidate/graduate.
Pop-off	To sound off in a military manner; a directive to sound off in a military manner.
Post	A command to "take your post" or to "assume (or resume) your proper position" as in a formation or on guard duty.
P-rade	Parade
Preppy	A USMAPS candidate/graduate.
Prepster	A United States Military Academy Preparatory School candidate/graduate.

Pro	Proficient, being above passing; also used to refer to attractive dates of cadets as likewise being "above passing".
Promotion	To place a FOURTH CLASSMAN on upperclass status
Prop jockey	Slang for the pilot of a propeller-driven aircraft, either rotary ("chopper") or fixed wing ("slow mover"), also known as "rotor head"; qualification for Aviation, a branch specialization in the U.S. Army [cf: USAF "jet jockey"].
Pro word	A specialized procedure word used to improve communications.
PT	Physical Training
Pull out	To barely complete an assignment on time and meeting only the minimum standards.
Quill	A report for delinquency.
Rabble-rouser	Cadet cheerleader.
Rack	Cadet bed; also, to sleep.
Ranger	Specialized infantry training in scouting and patrolling; an Army qualification that may be earned by cadets.
R-Day	Reception Day; date for reporting and registration at West Point.
RD=FC	Rough Draft equals Final Copy; the art of completing a paper or project in one sitting.
Recognize	To place a FOURTH CLASSMAN on a first-name basis with an upperclass cadet.
Recondo	A specialized infantry training course at West Point in scouting and patrolling.
Regiment	A unit of approximately 1200 cadets or soldiers; consisting of three battalions.
Ring-knocker	A West Point graduate who flaunts such status, and attempts to exploit it [nb: West Point was the first school to use finger-rings as a unified symbol; obtained informally from 1835, then designed by a committee in each class after 1869; after 1917, each class ring must bear the USMA initials, motto, crest, eagle, saber, and other elements, although the stone is individual to each graduate].
RHIP	Rank Hath Its Privileges (and responsibilities)
Rock	An individual who struggles in academics and "sinks" to the bottom of the class; "Rock Math" is the lowest section in PLEBE math.
Rock Squad Remedial Swimming	An additional class for PLEBE non-swimmers.

Roger	Radio brevity code for "I understand." It is used to expedite communication.
Room con	Confinement to quarters, as a punishment for breach of discipline.
ROTC	Reserve Officer's Training Corps; a commissioning program in select colleges and universities.
Rotor head	Helicopter Aviation; a branch specialization in the U.S. Army.
RTO	Regimental Tactical Officer. Also, Radio Telephone Operator, radioman or phone talker.
Sack	Cadet bed; also, to sleep.
Sally port	The arched entrances into the barracks areas; from the gateway in fortifications.
SAMI	Saturday morning inspection; Ante meridiem.
Sapper	Specialized training for combat engineer unit leaders in leadership skills, combat engineer and infantry battle drills, and the specialized engineer and infantry; an Army qualification that may be earned by cadets.
Second classman	Also called a COW; a junior at West Point.
SERE	Survival, Evasion, Resistance, Escape training program, an Army qualification that may be earned by cadets; this 3-week course has been expanded to "Survival, Evasion, Resistance, Escape, Recovery" (SERER) so as to include rescue modalities.
SF	Special Forces; a branch specialization in the U.S. Army.
Sham	To shirk; to avoid work or duty, to evade responsibility; to take the easy way out.
Short	Close to graduation.
Skinny	Information; derived from the intramural tutoring in physics and astronomy that's needed for satisfactory course completion.
Skivvies	Underwear, underclothing.
Slam	To impose a special punishment on someone for a serious offense.
Slug	A special punishment for a serious offense, which may result in a loss of privileges, special duty, walking punishment tours, or confinement to room during off duty hours. Also, a lazy cadet, one who's out of shape, one who's not pulling his load, or one who's not doing his duty.
Slug-stopper	To barely complete an assignment on time and meeting only the minimum standards.

Smack	Soldier Minus Ability, Coordination and Knowledge. Slang for a FOURTH CLASSMAN or NEW CADET. Originating from a time when Fourth Classmen were required to smack against the wall in the position of attention when encountering an upperclassmen in a hallway or stairwell.
Snake	One who has or will cut-in on dance partners at hops; to cut in.
Solids	Engineering Mechanics
SOD	Senior Officer of the Day
SOG	Senior Officer of the Guard
SOP	Standing or Standard Operating Procedure
Sound off	To voice a response powerfully; to shout loud and clear, so as to be heard and understood at a distance. To direct a cadet to reply or recite in a military manner. To count off or count cadence.
Spaz	To make a gross error; an inept or maladroit cadet who repeatedly makes gross errors.
Spec	To memorize verbatim, as "to spec blind".
Spec and dump	To memorize material long enough to pass a test, then forget it.
Spoon up	To put in proper order, to clean up.
Spoony	Neat and tidy in personal appearance.
Squad	A unit of approximately 10 soldiers; the Army's smallest tactical unit.
Squared Away	Fit, ready, reliable; competent and well-prepared.
Squid	One who attends the Naval Academy (USNA); Midshipman.
Star Man	A cadet ranked in the top 5% of the class academically and entitled to wear gold stars on the collar of a cadet uniform.
Storm	When said of things, a disordered condition; when said of people, a nervous haste.
STRAC	Straight, Tough, and Ready Around the Clock; being organized and excellent in appearance.
Straight	Observant of the rules; organized, dutiful.
Striper	A cadet captain or wears several stripes of rank on their uniform.
Subaltern	A subordinate, especially an officer trainee; formerly known as "third lieutenant".
Supe	The Superintendent of the U.S. Military Academy.
TAC	A tactical officer assigned to supervise the four classes in a cadet company.

TAC NCO	A tactical noncommissioned officer assigned to supervise the cadets in a company.
Tanker	Armor; a branch specialization in the U.S. Army.
Tar Bucket	Parade hat
TED	Tactical Eye Device; an intelligent person or one who learns quickly.
TEE	Term End Examination; final exams or finals; formerly known as WRITTEN GENERAL REVIEW (WGR).
Thayer Angle	The angle a saber makes on the hip of a female FIRSTIE while dressed under arms.
Thayer Week	A week with numerous graded events.
Third Classman	Also YEARLING; a sophomore at West Point.
Tie up	To make a gross error.
Tour	One hour's punishment walk on the area; a period of duty, as a fatigue or guard tour.
Trade School	A military service academy (e.g., USMA, USNA, USAFA, USCGA).
Trophy Point	A scenic overlook of the Hudson River Valley located at West Point. Trophy Point gets its name from the numerous displayed pieces of captured artillery spanning from the Revolutionary War to the Spanish-American War.
Trou	Trousers; also, a female cadet.
Turnback	A re-admitted cadet sent to the next lowest class.
Unsat	Unsatisfactory performance; an evaluation or rating for unsatisfactory performance.
Upperclassman	A cadet in his second, third, or fourth year at West Point.
USMA	United States Military Academy; West Point or The Academy. Often pronounced as a word; *yoos-may*.
USMAPS	United States Military Academy Preparatory School; a preliminary course established for enlisted (EM/NCO) candidates to become West Point cadets.
Walrus	Someone who cannot swim.
Went-off	Special attention from an upperclass cadet.
WGR	Written General Review; final exams or finals; redesignated TERM END EXAMINATION (TEE).
Wife	Cadet roommate.
Wig-wagger	Signaler, Signal Corps; a branch specialization in the U.S. Army.
WILCO	Radio brevity code for "(I) will comply". It is used to expedite communication.
Woo-Poo-U	Informal for West Point University; USMA.

Woop	What members of other service academies call a West Point Cadet.
Wopper	Pronunciation of 'WOPR', a WRITTEN ORAL PARTIAL REVIEW.
WOPR	Written Oral Partial Review
The Word	Current information; the latest update.
WPPA	West Point Protective Association; the ostensible gang of thugs that rescues any malefactor or transgressor to preserve the "honor" of The Academy or the LONG GRAY LINE; a secret "old boy's club".
WPPWE	West Point Professional Writing Examination, administered during English course in compositional writing.
WPR	Written Partial Review; major exam or midterm examination.
Writ	A written recitation; an examination.
Yearling	A member of the third class; a sophomore [deriv: horse aged over one year].
You fly, I buy	Catchphrase meaning that "I'll pay for the food, if you'll go get it."
Yuk	A member of the third class; a sophomore; derived as an epithet for the marginal appearance and comportment of cadets who have escaped the rigorous scrutiny of Plebe year, hence the contrivance of a euphemistic acronym: Young Upper-Klassman.
Zoomie	One who attends the Air Force Academy (USAFA); Doolie.
2% Club	Informal league of cadets who have sustained a committed romantic relationship with the same individual throughout their USMA attendance, from R-Day through graduation.
2.0 and go	The practice of meeting the minimum passing grade.

ARMY RANKS [143]

OFFICERS

-Gold Bar-

SECOND LIEUTENANT (2LT)
(Addressed as "Lieutenant")

Typically the entry-level rank for most Commissioned Officers. Leads platoon-size elements consisting of the platoon SGT and two or more squads (16 to 44 Soldiers).

-Silver Bar-

FIRST LIEUTENANT (1LT)
(Addressed as "Lieutenant")

A seasoned lieutenant with 18 to 24 months service. Leads more specialized weapons platoons and indirect fire computation centers. As a senior Lieutenant, they are often selected to be the Executive Officer of a company-sized unit (110 to 140 personnel).

CAPTAIN (CPT)
(Addressed as "Captain")

Commands and controls company-sized units (62 to 190 Soldiers), together with a principal NCO assistant. Instructs skills at service schools and The United States Army combat training centers and is often a Staff Officer at the battalion level.

---

[143] http://www.army.mil/symbols/armyranks.html

-Gold Oak Leaf-

MAJOR (MAJ)
(Addressed as "Major")

Serves as primary Staff Officer for brigade and task force command regarding personnel, logistical and operational missions.

 -Silver Oak Leaf-

LIEUTENANT COLONEL (LTC)
(Addressed as "Lieutenant Colonel" or "Colonel")

Typically commands battalion-sized units (300 to 1,000 Soldiers), with a CSM as principal NCO assistant. May also be selected for brigade and task force Executive Officer.

COLONEL (COL)
(Addressed as "Colonel")

Typically commands brigade-sized units (3,000 to 5,000 Soldiers), with a CSM as principal NCO assistant. Also found as the chief of divisional-level staff agencies.

GENERALS

BRIGADIER GENERAL (BG)
(Addressed as "General")

Serves as Deputy Commander to the commanding general for Army divisions. Assists in overseeing the staff's planning and coordination of a mission.

MAJOR GENERAL (MG)
(Addressed as "General")

Typically commands division-sized units (10,000 to 15,000 Soldiers).

LIEUTENANT GENERAL (LTG)
(Addressed as "General")

Typically commands corps-sized units (20,000 to 45,000 Soldiers).

GENERAL (GEN)
(Addressed as "General")

The senior level of Commissioned Officer typically has over 30 years of experience and service. Commands all operations that fall within their geographical area. The Chief of Staff of the Army is a four-star General.

GENERAL OF THE ARMY (GOA)

This is only used in time of War where the Commanding Officer must be equal or of higher rank than those commanding armies from other nations. The last officers to hold this rank served during and immediately following WWII.

ENLISTED

PRIVATE (PVT/PV2)
(Addressed as "Private")

Lowest rank: a trainee who's starting Basic Combat Training (BCT). Primary role is to carry out orders issued to them to the best of his/her ability. (PVT does not have an insignia)

PRIVATE FIRST CLASS (PFC)
(Addressed as "Private")

PV2s are promoted to this level after one year—or earlier by request of supervisor. Individual can begin BCT at this level with experience or prior military training. Carries out orders issued to them to the best of his/her ability.

SPECIALIST (SPC)
(Addressed as "Specialist")

Can manage other enlisted Soldiers of lower rank. Has served a minimum of two years and attended a specific training class to earn this promotion. People enlisting with a four year college degree can enter BCT as a Specialist.

CORPORAL (CPL)
(Addressed as "Corporal")

The base of the Non-Commissioned Officer (NCO) ranks, CPLs serve as team leader of the smallest Army units. Like SGTs, they are responsible for individual training, personal appearance and cleanliness of Soldiers.

SERGEANT (SGT)
(Addressed as "Sergeant")

Typically commands a squad (9 to 10 Soldiers). Considered to have the greatest impact on Soldiers because SGTs oversee them in their daily tasks. In short, SGTs set an example and the standard for Privates to look up to, and live up to.

STAFF SERGEANT (SSG)
(Addressed as "Sergeant")

Also commands a squad (9 to 10 Soldiers). Often has one or more SGTs under their leadership. Responsible for developing, maintaining and utilizing the full range of his Soldiers' potential.

SERGEANT FIRST CLASS (SFC)
(Addressed as "Sergeant")

Key assistant and advisor to the platoon leader. Generally has 15 to 18 years of Army experience and puts it to use by making quick, accurate decisions in the best interests of the Soldiers and the country.

MASTER SERGEANT (MSG)
(Addressed as "Sergeant")

Principal NCO at the battalion level, and often higher. Not charged with all the leadership responsibilities of a 1SG, but expected to dispatch leadership and other duties with the same professionalism.

FIRST SERGEANT (1SG)
(Addressed as "First Sergeant")

Principal NCO and life-blood of the company: the provider, disciplinarian and wise counselor. Instructs other SGTs, advises the Commander and helps train all enlisted Soldiers. Assists Officers at the company level (62 to 190 Soldiers).

SERGEANT MAJOR (SGM)
(Addressed as "Sergeant Major")

SGMs experience and abilities are equal to that of the CSM, but the sphere of influence regarding leadership is generally limited to those directly under his charge. Assists Officers at the battalion level (300 to 1,000 Soldiers).

COMMAND SERGEANT MAJOR (CSM)
(Addressed as "Command Sergeant Major")

Functioning without supervision, a CSM's counsel is expected to be calm, settled and accurate—with unflagging enthusiasm. Supplies recommendations to the commander and staff, and carries out policies and standards on the performance, training, appearance and conduct of enlisted personnel. Assists Officers at the brigade level (3,000 to 5,000 Soldiers).

SERGEANT MAJOR OF THE ARMY

There's only one Sergeant Major of the Army. This rank is the epitome of what it means to be a Sergeant and oversees all Non-Commissioned Officers. Serves as the senior enlisted advisor and consultant to the Chief of Staff of the Army (a four-star General).

BIBLIOGRAPHY

BOOKS

Atkinson, Rick. *The Long Gray Line*. Boston: Houghton Mifflin Company, 1989.

Barber, Brace E. Ranger School: *No Excuse Leadership*. Mt Pleasant: Patrol Leader Press, 2001.

Barkalow, Carol, with Andrea Raab. *In the Men's House: An Inside Account of Life in the Army by One of West Point's First Female Graduates*. New York: Berkeley Books, 1992.

Brokaw, Tom. *The Greatest Generation*. New York: Random House, 1998. *Bugle Notes 1983-1987*. West Point: US Military Academy, 1983.

Carhart, Tom. *West Point Warriors: Profiles of Duty, Honor, and Country in Battle*. New York: Grand Central Publishing, 2002.

Cowley, Robert and Thomas Guinzburg, eds. *West Point: Two Centuries of Honor and Tradition*. New York: Warner Books, 2002.

Donnithorne, Col. Larry R., Retired. *The West Point Way of Leadership*. New York: Doubleday, 1993.

Endler, James R. *Other Leaders, Other Heroes: West Point's Legacy to America Beyond the Field of Battle*. Westport: Praeger Publishers, 1998.

D'Amico, Francine and Laurie Weinstein. *Gender Camouflage: Women and the US Military*. New York: New York University Press, 1999

Green, Jane. *Powder, Paper and Lace: An Anecdotal Herstory of Women at West Point*. Charlottesville: Priority Press, 1988.

Grant, John, James Lynch and Ronald Bailey. *West Point: The First Two Hundred Years*. Gilford: The Globe Pequot Press, 2002.

Hason, Janet. *More than 85 Broads: Women Making Career Choices, Taking Risks and Defining Success on Their Own Terms*. New York: McGraw-Hill, 2006.

Holm, Major General Jeanne (Ret.) *Women in the Military: An Unfinished Revolution*. Novato: Presidio Press, 1982.

Howitzer, Class of 1979. West Point: US Military Academy, 1979.

Janda, Lance. *Stronger Than Custom: West Point and the Admission of Women*. Westport: Praeger Publishers, 2002.

Lipsky, David. *Absolutely American.* Boston: Houghton Mifflin Company, 2003.

Marella, Len. *In Search of Ethics, Conversations with Men and Women of Character.* Stanford: DC Press, 2001.

Naber, John. *Awaken the Olympian Within: Stories from America's Greatest Olympic Motivators.* Torrence: Griffin Publishing Group, 1999.

Olson, Col. Kim, USAF Retired. *Iraq and Back: Inside the War to Win the Peace.* Annapolis: Naval Institute Press, 2006

Ruggero, Ed. *Duty First: West Point and the Making of American Leaders.* New York: HarperCollins Publishers, 2001.

Samet, Elizabeth D. *soldier's heart: Reading Literature Through Peace and War at West Point.* New York: Farrar, Straus and Giroux, 2007.

Solaro, Erin. *Women in the Line of Fire: What you Should Know About Women in the Military.* Emeryville: Seal Press, 2006.

NEWSPAPERS AND MAGAZINES

Associated Press, "Report: Don't Ask, Don't Tell Cost $363m," *USA Today,* 14 February 2006. www.usatoday.com/news/Washington/2006-02-14-don't-ask-report_x.htm

Associated Press, "The soldiers of the ambushed 507th Maintenance Company finally tell their story," *Houston Chronicle,* 20 July 2003. http://www.chron.com/cs/CDA/printsotry.mpl/special/iraq/2002636

Chaze, William L. "Academy Women: Ready to Take Command," *US News & World Report,* 2 May 1980.

Dolan, Barbara. "West Point: The Coed Class of '80," *Time Magazine,* 19 May 1980.

Doherty, John. "Women at War," *The Times Herald Record,* 8 March 2005.

Eagly, Alice H. and Linda L. Carli. "Women and the Labyrinth of Leadership," *Harvard Business Review,* September 2007, 2-10.

Finch, Erika Ayn. "RB alum recovering from injuries suffered in Iraq," *North County Times,* 22 July 2004.

Feron, James. "Service Academies Hail First Female Graduates," *New York Times*, 29 May 1980, A18.

Giordano, Mary Ann. "61 Pinked the Long Gray Line," *Daily News*, 29 May 1980. 4.

Gibbs, Nancy and Nathan Thornburgh. "The Class of 9/11," *Time Magazine*, 30 May 2005, 28-43.

Halley, Janet. "Despite Reforms, "Don't Ask, Don't Tell"," *Los Angeles Times*, August 22, 1999, Op-Ed, at M5.

Harper, Matthew. "The Iraq Infection," *Forbes Magazine*, 2 August 2005.

Hopkinson, Natalie. "SEED's Harvest: For Monique Matthews and Other Grads, the Charter School Sowed Success," 30 June 2004, *The Washington Post*, C01.

Macur, Juliet. "Two Women Bound by Sports, War and Injuries." *New York Times*, 10 April 2005, national ed.

McLeary, Paul. "Progress at West Point, A new, privately funded institution teaches cadets about a new enemy." *The Weekly Standard*, 18 October 2007.

Moniz, Dave. "Female Amputees Make Clear that All Troops are on Front Lines," *USA Today*, 28 April 2005, national ed., 1A.

Kerber, Ross. "MIT professor faults operation of Patriot missile," *The Boston Globe*, 30 April 2004.

Lavandera, Ed. "That happened to the 507th? Fate of private raises questions about how unit was ambushed," *CNN.com*, 31 March 2003.
http://www.cnn.com/2003/US/Southwest/03/31/sprj.irq.piestewa.

McCormack, Patricia. "NOW says women given few opportunities in today's Army," *Oneida Daily Dispatch*, 14 April 1980.

McEntee, Marni. "Brigadier general in Germany is first female West Point grad to reach rank," *Stars & Stripes*, European ed. 1 September 2004.

Montgomery, Nancy. "Halstead: A woman among generals," *Stars and Stripes*, Mideast ed. 16 April 2006.
http://www.stripes.com/article.asp?section=104&article=35642&archive=true

Montgomery, Nancy. "One-of-a-kind leadership runs support command in Iraq," *Stars and Stripes,* Mideast ed. 16 April 2006.

Partlow, Joshua and Lonnae O'Neal Parker. "West Point Mourns a Font of Energy, Laid to rest by War," *The Washington Post,* 27 September 2006.

Postol, Theodore. "Friendly Fire Shootdown," *The Boston Globe,* 19 September 2004. http://www.commondreams.org/views04/0919-05.htm

Reid, David W. "Soldiers Marching Onward to a Different Drum." *Divinity Magazine,* Volume One, Number One, Spring 2002, 14-16.

Rosenfeld, Rachel. "Female Leader Development in the Military: An Interview Response to Reichard (2006) with COL Heidi Brown," *Leadership Review,* Summer 2006: Kravis Leadership Institute, Claremont McKenna College, Vol. 6. 110-116.

Salter, James. "It's Not the Old Point," *Life Magazine,* Volume 3, Number 5, May 1980, 70-79.

Seelye, Katharine. "West Point pioneers are seniors now," *The Daily Press,* 17 October 1979, 1.

_____. "Will women cadets face combat duty?" *The Daily Press,* 18 October 1979, 1.

_____. "Army may have to improve to keep women" *The Daily Press,* 19 October 1979, 1.

Sittenfeld, Curtis. "Planting the SEED of Education," *Fast Company,* 19 December 2007.

Smith, Chris. "Intro to Warfare—Preparing for graduation at West Point, where your first job is the front line," *New York Magazine,* 8 June, 2007.

Smith, Larry. "Are They Still The Best," *Parade Magazine,* 7 May 2000, 6-9.

Thomas, Evan. "West Point Makes a Comeback," *Time Magazine,* 18 April 2005.

Time Magazine, "What Price for Honor," 7 June 1976. http://www.time.com/time/magazine/article/0,9171,947701,00.html

US News & World Report. "Breaking the long gray line," 5 September 2004.

http://www.usnews.com/usnews/news/articles/040913/13spotlight. htm

Vanasco, Jennifer. "Another Casualty of Don't Ask, Don't Tell," *Chicago Free Press*, 2 August 2006.

Wansley, Joy. "The First Women Graduates of West Point Say with Pride: It Was Tough But We Survived," *People Magazine*, 21 April 1980, 28-31.

Wilson, Michael. "Iraq Presents Graduating Class at West Point with New Challenges," *The New York Times*, 25 May 2007.

Woods, David. "From Army to Athens," *Indianapolis Star*, 27 August 2004.

Zucchino, David. "War More Than Academic Exercise For West Point Class of 2004," *Los Angeles Times*, 21 May 2004

JOURNALS

Lockwood, Penelope. "Someone like me can be successful": Do college students need same-gender role models?" *Psychology of Women Quarterly*, 30, 2006, 36-46.

Snook, Scott. "Be, Know, Do: Forming character the West Point Way," *Compass: A Journal for Leadership*, Spring 2004: Center for Public Leadership, John F. Kennedy School of Government, Harvard University, 16-20.

Young, Lissa. "All That You Can Be: Stereotyping of Self and Others in a Military Context." *The Journal of Personality and Social Psychology*, Volume 75, Number 2, August 1998.

Young, Lissa. "Service and Disservice," *Compass: A Journal for Leadership*, Volume 1, Number 2, Spring 2004, Center for Public Leadership, John F. Kennedy School of Government, Harvard University, 26-27.

SPEECHES

Geren, Pete. "West Point Commencement Remarks," Remarks delivered 28 April 2006. http://www.army.mil/-

news/2008/06/02/9573-west-point-commencement-remarks-by-
secretary-of-the-army-pete-geren/index.html

Grove, Dr. Stephen. "Overview and History of Women at West
Point," Remarks delivered at historical overview panel, USMA
Women's Conference, April 28, 2006.

Scaparrotti, Brigadier General Curtis M. Remarks at Plebe Parent
Weekend, October 16 2004.

FEDERAL DOCUMENTS

Admitting Women to the Service Academies, Public L. no. 94-106
(1975).

Policy concerning homosexuals in the armed forces § 10 U.S.C. § 654
(1993).

Seidenberg v. McSorleys' Old Ale House, Inc., 1970, U.S. District Court,
Southern District of New York.

GOVERNMENT AND MILITARY PUBLICATIONS

Adams, Jerome. *Report on the Admission of Women to the United States
Military Academy (Project Athena III).* West Point: USMA
Department of Behavioral Sciences and Leadership (BS&L), June
1979.

Adams, Jerome. *Report on the Admission of Women to the United States
Military Academy (Project Athena IV).* West Point: USMA
Department of Behavioral Sciences and Leadership (BS&L), June
1980.

Banusiewicz, John D., Armed Forces Information Services "3rd
Support Command Delivers Food for OIF Forces." 28 January 04,
www.defense.gov/news/Jan2004/n01282004_200401281.html.

Boomer, Major Jane E., USAF. *Women Warriors Fighting a Three-Front
War: On the Battlefield, in Congress, and in the Courtroom.* Air
Command and Staff College, Air University, Maxwell Air Force
Base, Alabama. April 2007.

Department of Defense, Department of the Army. "AE Pamphlet 525-100 Military Operations: The US Army in Bosnia and Herzegovina." 7 October 2003.

Department of Defense, Department of the Army. "Army Field Manual 7-20, The Infantry Battalion." 6 April 1992.

Department of Defense, Department of the Army. "Army Regulation 600-13, Army Policy for the Assignment of Female Soldiers." 27 March 1992. http://www.army.mil/USAPA/epubs/pdf/r600_13.pdf

U.S. Department of Health and Human Services. National Institutes of Health. National Heart, Lung and Blood Institute. Diseases and conditions Index. Acute Respiratory Distress Syndrome (ARDS).

U.S. Department of State, Office of the Spokesman, Fact Sheet "Ten Years of Dayton Progress." 21 November 2005.

United States Military Academy (USMA). *Cadet Leadership Development System for Cadet.* USMA Circular 1-101-1. West Point: USMA, February 2005.

United States Military Academy (USMA). *The Howitzer: The Annual of the United States Corps of Cadets,* West Point: USMA 1979, 1980.

United States Military Academy (USMA). *Military Art and Science 2007 Program Guide.* West Point: USMA Department of Military Art and Science (MS), 2007.

Register of Graduates and Former Cadets of the United States Military Academy, West Point, NY, West Point Association of Graduates, 2002.

Register of Graduates and Former Cadets of the United States Military Academy, West Point, NY, West Point Association of Graduates, 2005.

Vitters, Alan G. and Nora Scott Kinzer. *Report of the Admission of Women to the United States Military Academy* (Project Athena I). West Point: USMA Department of Behavioral Sciences and Leadership (BS&L), June 1978.

OTHER

Columbia Pictures Television. "Women at West Point." Scripted dated August 1, 1978.

"Female General Looks Back on Her Climb." Camp Anaconda, Iraq, 13 August 2006.
www.cbsnews.com/stories/2006/08/13/ap/national.html

Hagenbeck, Lieutenant General Franklin L. Letter to graduates and members of the West Point Association of Graduates, 2 June 2009.

Holland, Marty. Eulogy for Rob Olson. 21 February 2001.
http://defender.west-point.org/service/display.mhtml?u=44560&i=1112

"In Memoriam," As of December 31, 2008.
http://www.westpointaog.org/NetCommunity/Page.aspx?pid=734

Padavic, Irene. "Patterns of Labor Force Participation and Sex Segregation" Conference paper presented at the 3rd Annual Invitational Journalism-Work/Family Conference, Boston University and Brandeis University, Community, Families & Work Program, May 20–21, 2004.

Parker, Paige and Alex Pulask, Richard Read, Peter Sleeth, Bryan Denson. "Army details what went wrong on fateful Iraq mission." http://www.signonsandiego.com/news/world/iraq/memorial/507.html

Tuchman, G. (Correspondent). *West Point Marks 20 years as a Co-Ed School.* [Television]. 1 July 1996. Atlanta: CNN.

Young, Lissa. Interview by Amy Mayer. *Weather Notebook Radio Show.* 30 September 2002.
http://www.weathernotebook.org/transcripts/2002/09/30.php

Wojnarowski, Adrain. "Dixon's Death cuts short a championship-caliber life." www.espn.go.com , 17 April 2006.

WEBSITES

http://www.army.mil/symbols/officerdescription.html
http://www.army.mil/symbols/armyranks.html
www.kidsindistress/org
www.elpomar.org
www.feminist.org
www.globalsecurity.org/
www.globalsecurity.org/military/agency/army/1ad.htmcom

www.globalsecurity.org/military/agency/army/3coscom.htm
www.globalsecurity.org/military/ops/joint_endeavor.htm
www.globalsecurity.org/military/ops/river.htm
www.goarmysports.com
www.mcsorleysnewyork.com
www.modern-pentathlon.com
www.pva.org
www.sldn.org/pages/about-dadt
www.totten60.com/usma/IOCT_Tab.htm
www.tourofhope.org/team/2003_toh_team.htm
www.usacac.army.mil/cac2/cgsc/about.asp
www.usma.edu

UNPUBLISHED SOURCES

[Author's note: *Interviews conducted with each of the subjects in this book as well as other graduates are included as primary sources, but are not published.*]

Aviation Systems Capabilities Analyst Rick White, Force Applications Division, Capabilities Developments Directorate, Army Capabilities Integration Center, HQ TRADOC, Fort Monroe, VA 23651.

Data provided by Office of Policy, Planning, and Analysis, Institutional Research & Analysis Branch, USMA.

CPSIA information can be obtained at www.ICGtesting.com
Printed in the USA
LVOW131059210613

339640LV00001B/319/P